'As riveting as the fiction the Wolffs themselves have published, and deeply affecting'   *Newsweek*

'Alexander Wolff is keen, after a generation of silence, to follow the untold stories wherever they might lead'

Claire Messud, *Harpers Magazine*

'Meticulously researched and beautifully written, *Endpapers*, at its heart, is an absorbing family history. But it is so much more than that, a haunting exploration of guilt and responsibility, of roots and new beginnings. Filled with stunning literary details that any biblio-phile will cherish, this is an intimate and complex portrait of a re-markable family that also tells a wider story of Europe and America in the twentieth century. *Endpapers* is a treasure – a brave and mov-ing book'   Ariana Neumann, author of *When Time Stopped*

'An astonishing, compelling, confronting story of a divided family, reaching sharply into the present'

Tim Bonyhady, author of *Good Living Street*

'A powerfully told story of family, honor, love and truth, by a mas-terful writer who sees across the oceans and through the genera-tions. In *Endpapers* we see the Wolff family through war and love, detention camps and immigration hearings, kindness and betrayal, occupying a world equal parts *Casablanca* and Kafka. It is engrossing and entertaining, a book of conscience and remembrance that tells the beautiful truth that so often those who contribute most to the culture and civic life of a place are the outcast and the refugee'

Beto O'Rourke

'Alexander Wolff – a writer of superb grace – traces a complex and compelling family history in this deeply absorbing narrative of high culture under threat, of political and moral violence, and the deep wish for what Wolff refers to as Heimkehr or "homecoming." *End-papers* held me in its spell for days'

Jay Parini, author of *Borges And Me*

ENDPAPERS

A Family Story of Books,
War, Escape and Home

ALEXANDER WOLFF

Grove Press UK

First published in the United States of America in 2021 by Grove Atlantic
This paperback edition first published in Great Britain in 2022 by Grove Press UK,
an imprint of Grove Atlantic

1 3 5 7 9 8 6 4 2

A CIP record for this book is available from the British Library.

Paperback ISBN 978 1 61185 447 3
E-book ISBN 978 1 61185 889 1

Printed and bound by CPI Group (UK) Ltd, Croydon, CR0 4YY

Grove Press UK
Ormond House
26–27 Boswell Street
London
WC1N 3JZ

www.groveatlantic.com

For Frank and Clara,
American, German—
citizens

Every time we reached the page which described the snow falling through the branches of the trees, soon to shroud the entire forest floor, I would look up at her and ask: But if it's all white, how do the squirrels know where they've buried their hoard? . . . How indeed do the squirrels know, what do we know ourselves, how do we remember, and what is it we find in the end?

—W. G. Sebald, *Austerlitz*

CONTENTS

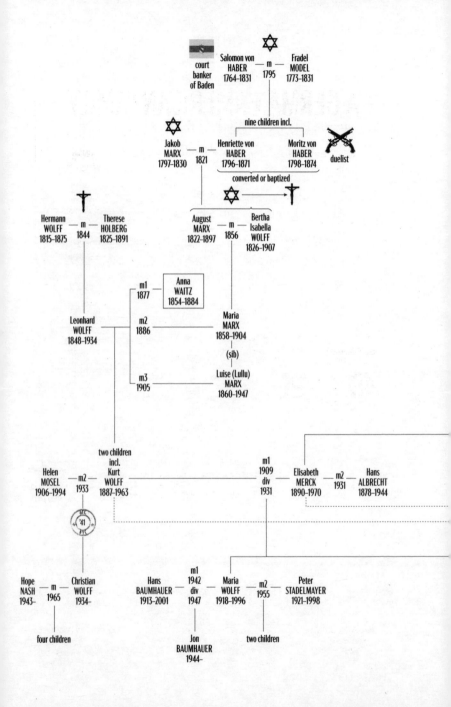

A GERMAN-AMERICAN FAMILY

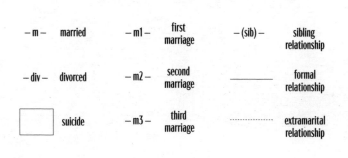

– m – married	– m1 – first marriage	– (sib) – sibling relationship
– div – divorced	– m2 – second marriage	———— formal relationship
☐ suicide	– m3 – third marriage	·········· extramarital relationship

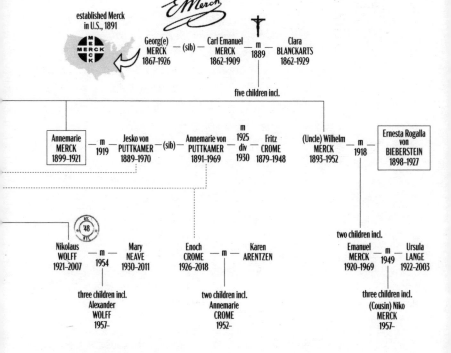

established Merck in U.S., 1891

E. Merck

Georg(e) MERCK 1867–1926 — (sib) — Carl Emanuel MERCK 1862–1909 — m 1889 — Clara BLANCKARTS 1862–1929

five children incl.

Annemarie MERCK 1899–1921 — m 1919 — Jesko von PUTTKAMER 1889–1970 — (sib) — Annemarie von PUTTKAMER 1891–1969 — m 1925 div 1930 — Fritz CROME 1879–1948

(Uncle) Wilhelm MERCK 1893–1952 — m 1918 — Ernesta Rogalla von BIEBERSTEIN 1898–1927

Nikolaus WOLFF 1921–2007 — m 1954 — Mary NEAVE 1930–2011

three children incl.
Alexander WOLFF 1957–

Enoch CROME 1926–2018 — m — Karen ARENTZEN

two children incl.
Annemarie CROME 1952–

two children incl.
Emanuel MERCK 1920–1969 — m 1949 — Ursula LANGE 1922–2003

three children incl.
(Cousin) Niko MERCK 1957–

PROLOGUE

A jab of his elbow, and my father: "It's like the Gestapo!"
For me, a teenager during the seventies in suburban Rochester, New York, access to what my father called "the *Glotzofon*" was strictly limited: a sitcom on weekend evenings, a game on Saturday or Sunday, nothing on school nights, until the great exception, that stretch during 1973 when, weekdays in prime time, public television rebroadcast hearings of the Senate Select Committee on Watergate.

Until that point I had suffered my father's interests. At sixteen, I hardly wanted a place on his turf of chamber music and kit radios and things to be found under the hood of a car. Nor would he edge toward mine, where British art rock and the fortunes of the Knicks ruled. But Washington blood sport engrossed us both. We followed our team and scouted out theirs, memorizing rosters of names with Rs and Ds attached. And we agreed that some cosmic casting director had had a hand in Senator Sam Ervin's jowls and John Dean's wife and a witness named Anthony Ulasewicz, who was Runyonesque relief to American viewers but to my father the kind of cop with a conscience that the Germany of his youth had failed to sufficiently produce.

I would come to understand what drew my father to the TV each evening. Born into the Weimar Republic, not quite twelve when Adolf Hitler came to power, he was now a citizen of another country and savored this second chance to stand up for democracy. Homework could wait. On school nights I found a place on the couch next to him, to share the first thing over which we really connected.

Until one day our weeknight miniseries spilled into the weekend, with what came to be known as the Saturday Night Massacre. First one Justice Department official, then a second, was dismissed for failing to carry out President Nixon's demand to fire the Watergate special prosecutor. Nixon's assault on the rule of law helped lead the House to pass the articles of impeachment that led to his resignation.

For my father this all came more than thirty years too late. But he kindled to the thrill of it—the thrill of watching public servants of this country to which he now belonged refuse on principle to follow orders.

ENDPAPERS

Cover of 1927 *Almanac of Art and Poetry*, published by
Kurt Wolff Verlag, Munich
Woodcut by Frans Masereel from the graphic novel *Le Soleil*,
published by KWV in 1920 as *Die Sonne*

Street scene in Lübeck, August 1936
Photograph by Nikolaus Wolff, age fifteen

INTRODUCTION

In the Footsteps of Kurt and Niko

This is a story that spans the lives of my grandfather and father, two German-born men turned American citizens. It recounts the fortunes of each—the first an exile, the second an emigrant—based on a year I spent in Berlin, taking the measure of blood and history in the midst of rising rightist populism on both sides of the Atlantic.

My grandfather was a book publisher who commanded the German literary landscape before World War I. Kurt Wolff had been born to a mother of Jewish descent, but it was his eye for *das Neue*, the new, that would put him at odds with the times, as Adolf Hitler and his repressive and hateful politics grew more and more popular. A balky peace, hyperinflation, and social turmoil conspired to undermine the Kurt Wolff Verlag, until he was forced to shut down his publishing house in 1930. Three years later Kurt fled Nazi Germany, eventually landing in New York, where in 1941 he founded Pantheon Books. He left behind my father, Nikolaus Wolff, who served in the Wehrmacht—the armed forces of the Third Reich—and wound up in an American POW camp before emigrating to the United States in 1948.

From my birth in 1957 until my father's death fifty years later, the prevailing winds of assimilation kept his eyes trained ahead. I contented myself with a seat in that boat, facing those calm waters. The fresh-start conformism of postwar America did nothing to encourage him to glance backward, and if he didn't look back, I was hardly moved to do so. I joined him in making our way through the world with purpose and hard work. Germans call this therapy by industriousness "taking the *Arbeitskur*."

But a decade after my father's death, having just turned sixty, I found myself being pulled back through the years. I wanted a better sense of the European chapters in the lives of my forefathers and the bloody period in which they unfolded. I was moved more than anything by a nagging sense of oversight—a feeling that I had failed somehow in not investigating my family's past. Germans of my generation grilled their elders about National Socialism, asking parents and grandparents, aunts and uncles, what they had known and what they had done. In Germany the convulsions of the sixties and early seventies came with dope and rock and civil unrest, to be sure, but also with the belief that the *Wirtschaftswunder*, the West German economic boom, had been enabled by a corporate and political establishment studded with ex-Nazis. A younger generation charged its elders with suspending accountability and remembrance and indulging in an *Arbeitskur* writ large. A broadly held willingness to take up and work through questions of guilt, shame, and responsibility, known as *Vergangenheitsaufarbeitung*, or "working off the past," has since become a marker of modern Germany.

A German cousin—my father's godson and his namesake, exactly my age and a fellow journalist—asked me pointedly why we decided to up and move to Berlin. You, I replied, took up the whole "working off the past" thing long ago. As an American, I never did. Cousin Niko understood right away. He had spent his youth brandishing his countercultural sympathies, taking part in the "purification ritual for the sins of the fathers." But surely I could be excused for being late to that work. Our family—the Wolffs of Wilmington, Delaware; Princeton, New Jersey; and Rochester, New York—was hardly German anymore. What historical stocktaking I'd done dealt with American evils, slavery and Jim Crow, sins that implicated my mother's ancestors. Though my father arrived in the United States as a twenty-seven-year-old speaking only basic English, his new country's integrative ways ensured that he was quickly regarded as no less American than the Connecticut-raised WASP he would marry.

So it was, after thirty-six years on the staff of *Sports Illustrated*, that I took a buyout and wired the severance payment to a German bank. My wife, Vanessa, gave notice at the agency where she worked as a visiting nurse. We found a couple to move into our old farmhouse in Vermont and look after our dog and cat, and enrolled our teenage children, Frank and Clara, in an international school on the outskirts of Berlin. We signed a year's lease on an apartment in Kreuzberg, where our neighbors would hail from more than 190 countries and gentrification hadn't entirely sanded down a gritty, Levantine edge. Berlin is infested with co-working spaces, so it was easy to find a desk only a few doors away, in the AHA Factory, whose very name seemed to promise that tenants would push out some kind of revelation every few minutes.

When our plane touched down at Tegel Airport on an August afternoon in 2017, I knew only the vague contours of the European lives of the two men to precede me. Kurt Wolff left Germany for good on the night of February 28, 1933, fleeing Berlin as the ashes of the Reichstag fire still smoldered. Over the next six and a half years, before war broke out, he shuttled between

Switzerland, France, and Italy with a soon-to-expire German passport he was struggling to renew. My grandparents' divorce, finalized in 1931, had left my father and his older sister, Maria, then eleven and fourteen, in Munich with their mother, whose family owned the Merck pharmaceutical empire, and her second husband, Gentiles both.

The Nazis likely objected less to Kurt's mother's Jewish ancestry than to his authors, many of them Jewish, like Franz Kafka, or Expressionist, pacifist, or "degenerate" besides. Works by Karl Kraus, Walter Mehring, Heinrich Mann, Joseph Roth, Carl Sternheim, Georg Trakl, and Franz Werfel all became fuel for book burnings. After the Germans invaded and occupied France, Kurt and his second wife, Helen, with support from the American journalist Varian Fry and his Emergency Rescue Committee, fled Nice with their son, my half uncle Christian, and in March 1941 sailed from Lisbon to New York. By early the following year Kurt and Helen were running Pantheon Books out of their Manhattan apartment.

Kurt would go on to leave the larger public mark, and in some literary circles his name still sparks curiosity. But the great questions that fall to me now come refracted through my father, who did not live a public life. How could Niko Wolff have served in the Wehrmacht despite his Jewish heritage? When his father fled Germany, why didn't my father join him, rather than be left to live through the Nazis' rise and rule? What burdens of guilt or shame did Niko carry into the New World and through the rest of his life? To what interventions, exemptions, or privileges did he owe his survival—and do I owe my existence? Of what should I be ashamed?

Unlike Kurt's, my father's story comes with none of the ennobling accents of the *Gesinnungsemigrant*, the German who went into exile out of conviction. I arrived in Berlin knowing little more than what Niko had told me: that he had been forced to join the Hitler Youth chapter at his Bavarian boarding school; that he had served with the paramilitary Reichsarbeitsdienst, the Reich Labor Service, as a nineteen-year-old; and that he had driven a supply truck in support of a Luftwaffe squadron during the invasion of the Soviet Union. I asked if he had ever killed anyone, and he told me: never knowingly. He spent the three years after the war in Munich literally picking up rubble, a duty required to earn a place as a chemistry student at the Institute of Technology. Kurt helped Niko land the student visa that brought him to the United States for graduate work. Other than for occasional family visits, my father didn't go back.

Kurt was sixty when he became a hyphenated American, and he took that interstitial bit of punctuation, connective and disruptive, as a license to reinvent himself. He did so not once but twice. Within a few years of literally stepping off the boat, he was publishing best sellers in a language he hadn't mastered; two decades later, back in Europe after having been more or less chased into exile again, he found himself resurrected by the same species of ruthless American executive that had just turned him out. He enjoyed several unexpected years of professional satisfaction as a redeemed German-American before his death.

Kurt flaunted his enthusiasms, and he worked relentlessly, and for the most part cheerfully, to dragoon others into seeing things as he did. And while he sometimes struggled to gracefully take no for an answer, that obstinacy was made tolerable by the enthusiasm with which he worked to get colleagues, guests, readers, or companions to acquiesce to some recommendation of his, usually for a book but often for a work of art or music, or a dish or a vintage. During the first two-thirds of a century marked by destruction and dread, Kurt was forever in search of people with the good taste to recognize his good taste. It couldn't have been easy being the son of such a man, particularly if your interests and experiences ran in other directions. My father was picking his way through ruins while his father was safely in Manhattan, prospecting for another universalist essay or sumptuous folio with which to favor the public.

From handed-down stories and a few secondary sources, this is more or less what I knew before leaving for Berlin. Indeed, hovering over the entirety of this account is astonishment at how much I would discover about my family and the corollary to that—how little my father had told me. Fortunately, my grandfather's papers are archived in Germany and the United States and many have been published. *Dear Dr. Kafka: Mr. Franz Werfel has told me so much about your new novella—is it called* The Bug?*— that I would like to acquaint myself with it. Would you send it to me?* From his appointment books, diaries, and notes, I know that Kurt, an amateur cellist, played trios with the Swiss Expressionist painter Paul Klee, a violinist, on a September day in 1919, and that the bill for taking T. S. Eliot to lunch at the Grand Ticino in Greenwich Village during the fifties came to seventy-five cents. Late in his life Niko put together a guide to several decades of his father's diaries, a spreadsheet of Who, When, Where, and *Weiteres* (miscellaneous) that attests to both Kurt's compulsive sociability and why I called my father the Human Flowchart.

Kurt himself vowed never to write anything "along the lines of 'my life and loves.'" To produce a memoir is a fool's errand, he liked to say: "What one can write is not interesting, and what is interesting one cannot write." Beyond an outline of my grandfather's life, I've nonetheless tried to grant the wish of the critic D. J. R. Bruckner, who in a 1992 review of a collection of Kurt's essays and letters called him "a difficult man, it is clear enough from his own words—for all his passion for good writing, his warmth, gentleness and loyalty. Even a reader at a distance can be made uneasy by his clarity, unyielding logic and lofty rules of conduct. But it is all so inspiring. . . . What is so fine is Wolff himself. To be talked to in confidence by such a human being lifts the spirit." May that invocation help justify how much unmediated Kurt Wolff fills the pages that follow.

I brought reams of family letters to Berlin and began to read them knowing that thousands more sit in repositories elsewhere. To get lost in more than a half century of correspondence is to hear a recitation of the epistolary rules my ancestors lived by. It isn't enough to hold on to what the postman delivers; you also make sure to save a copy of whatever you send. What's the point of keeping some sentiment or aperçu to yourself, stashed away in a private journal or diary (or so I hear my grandfather declaiming from across the years), when it can be confided to another person? If the essence of publishing is to share the written word, writing a letter is publication in the most limited edition possible.

Kurt let his enthusiasm run. "In the case of other authors, a small lapse on my part now and then as their business representative means some annoyance," he wrote Heinrich Mann. "In your case, it seems to me today that it would be a crime." And in reply to Hermann Hesse, not one of his authors but a friend: "It's like magic: here I am, living tucked away in a quiet corner of southern France, and suddenly I hear my name called. . . . My heartfelt thanks to you, the magician."

He lavished as much attention on sentences he wrote as on those he published. Even his insults came well packaged; bad writing wasn't "dross" or "crap" but something much worse: it "reduces the value of paper by printing on it." In 1917, as a thirty-year-old, he described his vocation to Rainer Maria Rilke:

*We publishers are alive for only a few short years, if we
have ever been truly alive at all. . . . Thus our task is to
remain alert and youthful, so the mirror does not tarnish
too quickly. I am still young, these are my own years; I take
pleasure in deploying my powers and seeing them grow with
tasks to be done, seeing them redoubled through struggles
and obstacles. I enjoy the give and take, the opportunity
to make a difference, and although I may be mistaken, I
believe the small amount of good I am able to accomplish
makes up for my errors.*

In the writing of letters, Kurt knew exactly what was important, and it was worth keeping this in mind as I rummaged deeper
in the pile. "Who is interested in the recipients of letters?" he
once observed. "People read them because they are interested in
the writer."

Whereupon he gives up the game: "Often authors of letters
are actually writing to themselves."

My father was no Kurt Wolff on the page. But he was a dutiful
correspondent who wrote detailed letters home to his mother,
Elisabeth Merck Wolff Albrecht, who remained in Munich
throughout the war. I consider these surviving letters and the
photographs Niko enclosed—as well as documents like a Nazi
certificate called the *Nachweis der arischen Abstammung*, or certificate of "Aryan" ancestry, which as the grandson and great-
grandson of baptized Jews my father was able to receive—to be
bread crumbs to follow.

Over the years I'd heard that my grandmother altered genealogies for Niko and his sister, using Gentile ancestors to mask
Jewish forebears with the same surname. This subterfuge, the tale
goes, may have been abetted by well-placed acquaintances of her

second husband, an obstetrician whose patients included the wife of Deputy Führer Rudolf Hess, the man to whom Hitler dictated *Mein Kampf*. Today this story is impossible to confirm, but its resonances hang heavily. In 2012, in London to cover the Olympics, I spent a morning with my wife and children at the Cabinet War Rooms from which Churchill directed Britain's response to the Blitz. By the time we sat down for lunch in the café, our nine-year-old daughter had worked out who the good guys and the bad guys were, and where her grandfather lined up. She wanted to know: "Isn't there some way Opa could have been a spy?"

I think I mumbled something about the sacred responsibility of citizenship and how each of us is pledged to make sure government never acts unjustly in our name. But I don't feel I adequately answered Clara that day, and I still wonder whether I'll ever be able to engage her question in the way it deserves. This book is an attempt at the beginning of a proper response.

As a starting point, nowhere seemed more appropriate than Berlin, the modern European city closest in spirit to the Manhattan of the forties where Kurt and Niko both landed. A 1983 comment by the late *Bundesrepublik* president Richard von Weizsäcker captured it for me: "In good and in evil, Berlin is the trustee of German history, which has left its scars here as nowhere else." So here I had come, to run a finger over those scars, to measure the length of each cut and feel the thickness of the tissue.

ONE
BILDUNG AND BOOKS
Kurt, 1887 to 1913

A s Kurt Wolff's grandson, I came swaddled in the certainty that I would play the cello. It was explained at an early age: with a pianist mother and violinist father, little Alex on the cello would make a trio. I broke in on a half-size instrument and graduated in middle school to a three-quarter size, with the expectation that I'd soon be fitted with Kurt's well-varnished heirloom, crafted in the Tyrol in 1779 from maple and a majestic wide-grain spruce.

You don't have to look too far back into the Wolff male lineage to see that this is how things were done. My grandfather grew up in Bonn, where his father taught music at the university and kept up an exhausting schedule as a conductor, string player, and organist as well as a choirmaster. On Sundays, at the Lutheran church on Kaiserplatz, Leonhard Wolff sandwiched organ and choral pieces around the sermons of Pfarrer Bleibtreu—literally, Pastor Stay Faithful. A scholar of Bach and friend of Brahms's, Leonhard was a composer himself, part of his inheritance as the third Wolff in a line of professional musicians from the Rhineland town of Krefeld. When the pianist Clara Schumann passed through to perform in winter concerts staged by his father during the 1850s, young Leonhard had been dispatched to deliver flowers or fruit to her hotel room.

In 1886, twenty months after his first wife, Anna, took her life by throwing herself into the Rhine, Leonhard remarried. His new bride, Maria Marx, was the daughter of two Rhinelanders who could trace their Jewish roots as far back as records were kept. She gave up her job as a teacher at a secondary school for girls to assume stepmother duties to Leonhard and Anna's two children. On a March evening in 1887, Maria gave birth to Kurt while Leonhard conducted Handel's *Messiah* in the old Beethoven Hall. *Unto us a son is given*, the family joke would go.

Christian by baptism, as her own parents were, Maria ran a culturally German if mostly secular home. Her training as a teacher showed up in her parenting, as she shared a love of poetry with her stepchildren and Kurt, as well as with his sister Else, who was born three years later. Kurt began those requisite cello lessons and set out on a path toward a *Gymnasium* education. By the time of her death in 1904, at forty-six, Maria had made a decisive mark on the formation of her now seventeen-year-old son.

Preoccupied and more introverted than his wife, Leonhard liked to go for long walks, and as an adolescent my grandfather often joined him. Kurt would draw his father out about composers, performers, and two paternal forebears. Leonhard's grandfather Johann Nikolaus, a Franconian miller's son born in 1770, the same year as Beethoven, had served as music director in Krefeld. Leonhard's father, Hermann, who succeeded Johann Nikolaus in that post, befriended Clara Schumann as well as her composer husband, Robert. Hermann was such an early champion of Brahms's that in 1870 he left Krefeld in defeat after hostile reaction to a performance of *A German Requiem*, a piece apparently too radical for the town at that time. Leonhard would honor his father's forerunning taste by embracing Brahms with gusto. Before arriving in Bonn he had played chamber music with the master, and successfully foisted *A German Requiem* on the city soon after taking up his post there in 1884.

In the predawn of a spring day in 1896, a few hours before Leonhard was to lead the chorus at Clara Schumann's funeral, Brahms himself showed up at the Wolffs' home on the Bonner-thalweg. "I remember the consternation, excitement, and grief at that unexpected appearance of Brahms at five in the morning at my parents' door," my grandfather, then nine, would recall more than a half century later. "Breakfast was like a Last Supper. My father would not see Brahms again after that funeral." This photograph survives from a gathering the next day. Brahms is the bereft, white-bearded figure in the middle. Thanks to the Human Flowchart's annotations on a tracing-paper overlay, I know my

great-grandparents stand on either side of the man with the hat and dark beard just behind the composer.

The Wolffs fixed themselves among that class of Germans known as the *Bildungsbürgertum*, the haute bourgeoisie who devoted themselves to *Bildung*, lifelong learning and a cultural patrimony of art, music, and books. By age ten, Kurt had come under the spell of the stories of Theodor Fontane, and a love of literature propelled him further toward the *Abitur*, the capstone of a secondary education in the liberal arts. This kind of humanistic self-cultivation was taken for granted in a university town like Bonn. "Should, on occasion, the embarrassing event occur that a son of a faculty member elected not to study but rather pursue a career in business or trade, he'd be lost and abandoned," my grandfather noted. "It was a disgrace to the family, which profoundly regretted it, and the unhappy episode was tactfully never mentioned."

Besieged by "snobs and burghers," as Kurt later put it, young Bonners eager to express themselves turned to music and poetry. Leonhard championed the piano prodigy Elly Ney, daughter of a Bonn city councilman, who lived across the street from the sports hall at Kurt's school. After World War II the city would ban Ney from its stages for her Nazism. But here Kurt, not yet a teenager, skipped phys ed to slip into her salon and ask the sixteen-year-old Elly to play for him. And play she did, as if he were punching up tunes on a jukebox—"whatever I wished, for hours without tiring: Bach, Mozart, Beethoven, Schubert, Chopin . . . Brahms's sonatas in C and F. I owe my knowledge of the major piano works to those hours with Elly. . . . [I] was totally smitten by the highly spirited young lioness."

Kurt turned similarly to literature. As a nineteen-year-old he met Friedrich Gundolf, the literary titan who would go on to teach at the University of Heidelberg. Gundolf was close to the poet Stefan George, who had attracted a circle of acolytes that eventually included the von Stauffenberg brothers, the aristocratic German officers who would lead the unsuccessful Valkyrie plot to kill Hitler. "Refined, handsome, studious, modest, well-bred, possessed of a touching, inquiring, and searching spirit and freshness," Gundolf wrote to George, describing Kurt in advance of bringing him by for an introduction. "[He is] one of those young men so essential to creating an atmosphere and elevating standards."

Soon after that meeting, at the risk of mortifying academic Bonn, Kurt sailed to São Paulo, Brazil, for a six-month training program sponsored by the German banking industry. But he threw himself back into books as soon as he returned. With the 100,000 gold marks he inherited upon his mother's death, a sum that would be worth more than $1 million today, he had begun to buy up first editions and incunabula, books produced during the fifteenth century shortly after the invention of the printing press. He would eventually count some twelve thousand volumes in his collection. But much like his father, a champion of music both old and new, Kurt let his eye wander from literature gathering dust to what was then being written—to those writers challenging the staid assumptions of the Wilhelmine era. Migrating from campus to campus in a fashion common at the time, he studied German literature at universities in Marburg, Munich, Bonn, and, most fatefully, Leipzig, then the seat of the country's book publishing industry. In 1908, at twenty-one, he set aside work on a PhD in literature to take an editorial position there with Insel Verlag. "I loved books, especially beautiful books, and as an adolescent and student collected them even as I knew it to be an unproductive pursuit," he would recall. "But I knew I had to find a profession in books. What was left? You become a publisher."

One of his first projects came out of the family archives. As a teenager, while helping his maternal grandmother, Bertha, clear out a bookshelf in her home one day, he had discovered notes and visiting cards from Adele Schopenhauer, sister of the philosopher, and Ottilie von Goethe, the writer's daughter-in-law. Kurt pressed his grandmother for details. It turned out that Bertha's mother, Jeanetta, had been friendly with both women. Bertha unearthed further correspondence, and in 1909, supplementing those letters with a diary of Adele's he'd found in private hands, Kurt assembled it all into two volumes to be published by Insel.

He turned next to the work of an associate of Johann Wolfgang von Goethe's, the writer Johann Heinrich Merck, an ancestor of the seventeen-year-old woman Kurt had begun courting while posted with the military in Darmstadt and would later marry—my grandmother, Elisabeth Merck. Her family, with its international pharmaceutical business, at first balked at him as a suitor for the opposite reason the professoriat in Bonn might have found him wanting: Kurt struck them as a man too much of letters and not enough of commerce. But book publishing plausibly split the difference, and by the end of 1907 the Mercks had signed off on the marriage, which took place in 1909, shortly after these portraits were taken.

In 1910 Kurt hitched himself as silent partner to the publisher Ernst Rowohlt, who had just launched what would
become one of Germany's most important houses. With his lean
frame and drawing-room manners, now installed with his wife
in a Leipzig apartment with household help, Kurt cut a starkly
different figure from Rowohlt, a bluff and earthy character who
would conduct business in taverns and wine bars around town
and sometimes sleep in the office. By June 1912, having abandoned his doctoral work, Kurt found more time to stick his
nose into the affairs of the publishing house. Thus he was in the
office the day Max Brod, a writer from Prague, turned up with a
protégé named Franz Kafka. Kurt recalled that visit years later:

> In that first moment I received an indelible impression: the
> impresario was presenting the star he had discovered. This
> was true, of course, and if the impression was embarrassing,
> it had to do with Kafka's personality; he was incapable of
> overcoming the awkwardness of the introduction with a
> casual gesture or a joke.
>
> Oh, how he suffered. Taciturn, ill at ease, frail, vul-
> nerable, intimidated like a schoolboy facing his examiners,
> he was sure he could never live up to the claims voiced so
> forcefully by his impresario. Why had he ever gotten him-
> self into this spot; how could he have agreed to be presented
> to a potential buyer like a piece of merchandise! Did he
> really wish to have anyone print his worthless trifles—no,
> no, out of the question! I breathed a sigh of relief when the
> visit was over, and said goodbye to this man with the most
> beautiful eyes and the most touching expression, someone
> who seemed to exist outside the category of age. Kafka was
> not quite thirty, but his appearance, as he went from sick
> to sicker, always left an impression of agelessness on me:

*one could describe him as a youth who had never taken a
step into manhood.*

One remark of Kafka's that day helped account for Kurt's
impression of him as an innocent with wobbly confidence: "I will
always be much more grateful to you for returning my manuscripts than for publishing them."

The relationship with Ernst Rowohlt fell apart a few months
later, after Kurt retained Franz Werfel, the Prague-born novelist,
playwright, and poet, as a reader on lavish terms without clear-
ing the arrangement with his business partner. By February 1913,
using money from both his late mother's prosperous ancestors
and the Merck family of his bride, Kurt had bought out Rowohlt,
eventually christening the new firm Kurt Wolff Verlag and bringing Kafka and Brod with him. He raised more cash needed for
the business by auctioning off parts of his book collection, and in
case anyone missed the symbolism—may the old underwrite the
new!—Kurt adopted a credo he articulated in a letter to the Viennese critic and editor Karl Kraus: "I for my part consider a publisher to be—how shall I put it?—a kind of seismographer, whose
task is to keep an accurate record of earthquakes. I try to take
note of what the times bring forth in the way of expression and,
if it seems worthwhile in any way, place it before the public."

In 1912, at Werfel's urging, Kurt had gone to Vienna to meet
Kraus for the first time. Kurt found himself overcome by the
exhausting intensity of this literary provocateur. Whether dis-
cussing literature or leading him on a tour of the city, Kraus, then
thirty-eight, wanted the full attention of his twenty-five-year-old
visitor. "If he wants to walk you back to your hotel, you mustn't
take it for a polite gesture and refuse," Werfel had warned him.
"Kraus walks people home. He can't bear the thought that they
would meet someone else after being with him. If you want to

disentangle yourself, there's only one excuse that Kraus will accept, though with bad grace. Somewhere between midnight and one o'clock, you may hint at a rendezvous with a woman. It's your only chance."

Kurt's first visit to Kraus's apartment spilled into the early hours of the morning, whereupon his host pulled a book of poems from a shelf and began reciting several favorites. "The poetry itself barely penetrated the fog of my fatigue," Kurt recalled. "I was spellbound not by the familiar verses, but by the singular man who was reading them. Mechanically I began to recite the last few lines of the 'Mondlied' ['Moon Song,' by the poet Matthias Claudius] along with him, but soon found myself speaking alone as Kraus fell silent:

> Spare thy wrath, Lord, we entreat;
> Let our sleep and dreams be sweet,
> And our sick neighbor's too.

"He stared at me in astonishment and asked in a tone of voice that betrayed dismay as well as surprise, 'But how do you know that? Matthias Claudius is completely unknown!'

"'Perhaps in Austria,' I replied, 'but not where I'm from. When I must have been between five and eight and tired of the usual bedtime prayers for children, my mother used to recite the "Mondlied" with me every night.'

"His joy at finding someone to share his enthusiasm was greater than the disappointment over not being the first to introduce me."

The first had been Maria Marx Wolff, the acculturated Rhinelander of Jewish descent. A young rebel in turn-of-the-century Bonn found his voice in music and poetry, and Kurt

inherited his love of the first from his father. Love of literature—the passion with which he would make his way and name and eventually reinvent himself in exile—came from his mother, pictured above.

But the story only begins here. The world into which this fully formed young man was launched would not be kind to *Bildungsbürger* who shunned the grubbiness of politics. For Germans content to lose themselves in books and art and music, history held out consequences—and left clues to what might be in store.

It's impossible to fully understand my family without excavating a strange and historically significant series of events that took place in Karlsruhe, the capital of Baden in Germany's southwest, during the first half of the nineteenth century.

Kurt Wolff's great-great-grandfather Salomon von Haber, pictured overleaf, served three grand dukes of Baden, first as an independent financier and, beginning in 1811, as banker for the grand duchy. By the early nineteenth century, Baden had

developed extensive material needs, and Salomon knew the levers to pull to pay for them. If the state needed tack for cavalry horses or satin for ladies' dresses, "court Jews" called on trusted co-religionists around Europe to move gold or float loans. At the same time, Salomon was active in Karlsruhe's Jewish community, advocating for such reforms as a modernized liturgy and worship in German rather than Hebrew. With Grand Duke Louis I taking his cues from the Habsburgs' Edict of Toleration, my ancestor the *Hofbankier* seemed safe and content in his identity as both a member of the elite and a practicing German Jew.

But in 1819 antisemitic riots broke out among university students in the Bavarian city of Würzburg and soon spread across Germany. Mobs of citizens, many of them members of the educated middle class, chanted *Hep, hep, Jude verreck!* (Death to the Jews!) as they trashed shops and homes and chased Jewish citizens into the countryside. In Baden, even the grand duke's court banker wasn't safe. On the night of August 27, a mob gathered outside the Haber palace, Salomon's home across Markt-platz from Karlsruhe's main synagogue, pelting it with rocks and chanting anti-Jewish slogans. Escorted by a detachment of bodyguards supplied by the grand duke, Salomon fled to safety in the town of Steinach, sixty miles south.

A Jewish-born Berliner named Ludwig Robert, a playwright and recent convert to Christianity who happened to be in Karlsruhe visiting his fiancée, witnessed the riot and its aftermath: troops on horseback patrolling rubble-strewn streets; placards that read DEATH AND DESTRUCTION TO THE JEWS; townspeople not just laughing at the spectacle but grumbling that the commandant had shut down the city's taverns to quell the unrest. This was antisemitism as festival. The emancipation of Jews within the German Confederation, decreed by Prussia seven years earlier, meant little, a disgusted Robert wrote to his sister in Berlin: "How corrupt people really are and how inadequate their sense of law and justice—not to mention their love of humanity—is clear from the fact that there was no indignation expressed at these incidents, not even in the official papers."

It took days to restore order, which came only after the grand duke sent cannons into the streets. In place of incendiary posters, new ones appeared: EMPERORS, KINGS, DUKES, BEGGARS, CATHOLICS, AND JEWS ARE ALL HUMAN AND AS SUCH OUR EQUALS. In a carriage pulled by six horses, Louis I personally escorted Salomon back from Steinach before making a show of solidarity by temporarily moving into the Haber palace.

Louis I so appreciated Haber's work on behalf of the grand duchy that in 1829, a year before his own death and two years before Salomon's, he bestowed on him the title that permitted the family to use the noble "von." The von Habers had done much to earn the honor. They had developed Baden's three largest industrial sites—a sugar factory, a cotton mill, and a machine works that built railway locomotives. After Salomon's death, two of his sons, Louis and Jourdan, took charge of those enterprises, and Louis assumed his father's role as court banker.

Even as these two von Haber sons remained Jewish, their older brother, Model (Moritz) von Haber, pictured here, had long since converted. In 1819, at twenty-two, he married the daughter of a Parisian banker in a Catholic ceremony and over the following two decades lived a life of social prominence in Paris and London. With the help of agents around the continent, Moritz tended to a portfolio of interests, including mining enterprises in France and Portugal. He also handled the financial affairs of both the French king Charles X and Don Carlos, the Bourbon pretender to the Spanish throne.

Sometime in the late 1830s, Moritz had a run-in that touched off what would come to be known throughout Europe as the Haber Affair. The story goes that an English officer named George Hawkins was carrying documents from Spain to England when French authorities with Carlist sympathies detained him. Hawkins suspected Moritz of engineering his arrest and challenged him to a duel. Insisting that the Englishman lacked any standing to do so, Moritz sloughed Hawkins off.

Around the same time, after two decades of consorting with nobility around Europe, Moritz returned to Karlsruhe with the swagger of a man of the world. Thanks to the marriages of his brothers Louis and Jourdan, the prodigal son now had connections to the Rothschild banking family, and he took to describing himself as "a man of private means." Moritz became a regular at the court of Sophie, the Swedish-born grand duchess of Baden, who shared his worldly outlook and high-spirited nature. Soon gossips had Moritz trysting with the grand duchess at Schloss Favorite, the royal hunting lodge south of the city, and eventually pegged him as father of her youngest daughter, Princess Cäcilie. Officers and courtiers around the ducal palace—to say nothing of Sophie's husband, Leopold, Louis I's son and the new grand duke—disapproved of this interloper and the loose talk he was touching off.

At one point Moritz's old nemesis George Hawkins turned up in Karlsruhe looking for him. Hawkins died before he could get satisfaction in their dispute, but in 1843, Julius Göler von Ravensburg, a Badenese army officer who had sided with Hawkins, decided to take up the late English officer's cause. He called Moritz *ein Hundsfott*—a scoundrel. Moritz refused to take the bait and challenge Ravensburg to a duel, and there matters might have ended. But soon the social season in the spa town of Baden-Baden was in full swing, and it seems that Moritz had been dropped from the guest list for one of the fancy balls on the calendar. When he pressed social arbiters for an explanation, Moritz was told that he wasn't "a man of honor" because he had let a slur go unanswered—at which point Moritz concluded he had no choice but to take Ravensburg on.

In Europe during the first half of the nineteenth century, a man of rank or social standing who had been wronged didn't seek redress through the police or the courts. He insisted instead on an engagement with deadly weapons under prescribed rules. If you had been insulted and didn't demand a duel, you forfeited your right to associate with people of good repute. For Jews, matters were more complicated; it wasn't unusual for a German Jewish university student with pistoling skills, slighted by some anti-semitic remark, to challenge the offender—but this only touched off a movement among non-Jewish fraternities at German universities to declare Jews categorically "unworthy of satisfaction." In 1843, such was the disposition, at first, of Moritz's challenge to Ravensburg: a court of honor declared Moritz too disreputable to be party to a duel—he wasn't, as the Germans would say, *satisfaktionsfähig*. And that appeared to be that.

But the protocol of dueling held that each principal nominate a "second," someone to hammer out logistics and act as a go-between. As his second, Moritz had selected a Russian officer named Mikhail von Werefkin. Ravensburg's chosen second, a Spanish-born official of the Baden court, Georg von Sarachaga-Uria, didn't simply reiterate to Werefkin his patron's refusal to duel—he also joined Ravensburg to assault the Russian on a Karlsruhe street.

As a result of that incident, Werefkin and Ravensburg hastily agreed to duel each other at a riflery range in the Forchheimer forest south of the city. There, on September 2, Werefkin mortally wounded Ravensburg with his first shot. But as he lay on the ground, Ravensburg was able to squeeze off a shot of his own, killing Werefkin.

The death of both duelists set Baden on edge. Three days later, in the aftermath of Ravensburg's funeral, a procession of mourners made its way along Langestrasse, Karlsruhe's main east-west thoroughfare. As the funeral train reached the Haber palace, pictured here, and dusk settled over the city, a rumor spread that Moritz himself was watching from an upper window.

At that, the ranks of the mourners dissolved. Students and soldiers led a mob of 150 people that stormed and ransacked the same home Moritz's father had been chased from during the *Hep, Hep* riots two dozen years before. "Down with the Jews!" the crowd shouted, and "Tonight we'll finish the *Hep, Hep* over there!" Rioters set upon two Jewish-owned businesses nearby, throwing the owners through their shop windows. David Meola, director of the Jewish and Holocaust Studies Program at the University of South Alabama and an expert on the history of the Haber Affair, told me that the attack lasted hours, with soldiers egging on townspeople, who yelled things like "drown them in blood!" The rioting caused tens of thousands of florins in damage, the equivalent of at least several million dollars today. This time the incumbent grand duke supplied no protection. During those intervening years, the status of even Karlsruhe's most prominent Jews had grown ever more tenuous.

In fact, as the riot raged, Moritz was no longer in the family home. A half hour earlier police had remanded him to Rastatt, south of the city. There he was quickly convicted of inciting the Ravensburg-Werefkin duel and sentenced to fourteen days in prison. As soon as he served his sentence, the authorities deported him to Hesse.

Over the following weeks Sarachaga-Uria vowed to avenge the death of his comrade. He challenged Moritz in an open letter, using language so inflammatory that it made clear he had no misgivings about dueling someone he would call in print *ein geborener Israelit*, a Jew by blood. Moritz accepted, and on December 14—this time well north of Karlsruhe, near the Hessian village of Roggenheim—my ancestor killed Sarachaga-Uria with his second shot. Afterward Moritz was detained, charged with illegal dueling, and convicted by a Hessian military court, which sentenced him to six months in prison, four of them suspended for good behavior and community service. Upon his release Moritz filed and won libel suits against a Karlsruhe newspaper and a Frankfurt-based journalist, donating the settlement monies to charity.

As it unspooled over those months, the Haber Affair caused a sensation around the continent. Moritz had his sympathizers, especially in the Rhenish press. Many Germans knew of the family's public spiritedness and Moritz's own charitable giving, including a large donation to recovery efforts in Hamburg after the city's fire of 1842. But much of the coverage pandered to the basest instincts of an inflamed population. To most Badeners, the events of late 1843 came down to a simple accounting: on one side, three dead Christians; on the other, one uppity and still-at-liberty Jew.

*   *   *

At the time of the Haber Affair, Baden's Jews stood on the cusp of emancipation. The legislature of the grand duchy had taken up the issue for a dozen consecutive sessions, and only a few months earlier the parliament of the nearby Prussian Rhineland had voted to grant Jews full civil rights. As Baden celebrated the twenty-fifth anniversary of its constitution, the Jewish-born writer Heinrich Heine was hailing full freedom as "the call of the times." Yet even though Jews in 1843 made up no more than 1.5 percent of the grand duchy's population, and perhaps 5 or 6 percent within Karlsruhe's city limits, Badenese Christians feared Jewish emancipation.

At trial, Moritz's liberal, Christian lawyer had enumerated the many ways his client had been done wrong. His home had been invaded, his property destroyed, his freedom taken away. Yet because of press censorship, the public could take only some of this into account. Then, upon his release, Moritz was summarily expelled from Baden. All these injustices were visited upon a citizen of the grand duchy—one whose family had been ennobled by the grand duke's father—just days after Baden celebrated its status as a *Rechtsstaat*, a government of laws.

In the years afterward, framing of the Haber Affair took on an increasingly antisemitic cast. The publisher of a manifesto that Sarachaga-Uria had written before the second duel, distributed after the Spanish officer's death, chose to pair the text with an engraving of Sarachaga-Uria alongside Ravensburg and Werefkin over the caption *Duell-Opfern* (Duel Sacrifices). Popular accounts called Ravensburg a *Landeskind*, a "child of the nation" who had given his life for the fatherland.

That story line would persist into the next century with the publication in 1926 of the historical novella *King Haber*. The book doesn't bother to change the name of its main character, "the banker, Moritz Haber, or to give him his recent title, Baron von Haber." In it Moritz cuckolds the grand duke, fathers a child with the grand duchess, and meets his comeuppance after a procession of mourners leaving the funeral of a "Baron Raven" spot him on the balcony of his own home and pelt him with rocks. Someone in the crowd finally fires the shot that kills him. The story has such defamatory resonances that in 1947 one of Salomon's descendants, Willy Model, tried to claw back some of our common ancestor's reputation with an affidavit sorting out what was hearsay from what was known to have happened.

The Haber Affair foreshadowed atrocities to come. The timing of the publication of *King Haber*—on the cusp of the Nazis' seizure of power—helped stoke the antisemitism that Hitler and his propaganda minister, Joseph Goebbels, would step in to exploit. And the episode conformed with *Jud Süss*, the 1940 film based on an eighteenth-century Jewish court banker who became a recurring figure in Nazi propaganda.

In the anti-Moritz manifesto written before his death in the second duel, Sarachaga-Uria declared that "religion and honor" would prevent Moritz from ever being "true and straight." Whatever the outcome of the duel, the Badenese officer further proclaimed, it would be "a judgment of God between good and evil, right and wrong."

After winning his duel with Sarachaga-Uria, Moritz couldn't resist a triumphant riposte. In January 1844, having served out his sentence in Hesse, he bought space in newspapers around the German states. "So!" read one of his *Erklärungen*, or declarations. "The highest driver of all human fate has judged according to his wisdom between good and evil, right and wrong."

David Meola puts it this way in a scholarly article about the Haber Affair: "As victor of the duel, Haber can be seen as having been judged—by God—to be both *good* and *right*. Moreover, in the public sphere, Haber would also have the last word, defeating his opponent again posthumously using his adversary's own words and beliefs."

For Uncle Moritz, it must have made for the most satisfying touché.

I have few clues to how my ancestors processed the life and trials of Moritz von Haber through the years. Kurt's grandfather August, the eldest son of Moritz's sister Henriette von Haber, would go on to handle some of his uncle's business affairs, so it's hard to imagine my grandfather not having heard of his notorious forebear. But my father never mentioned Moritz. I learned of him and this entire saga only after arriving in Berlin, from pursuing a throwaway line in a genealogical essay by my aunt Holly, Kurt's daughter-in-law. She refers to "an internationally known rake, duelist, and adventurer" and suggests that, in his great-great-uncle's cosmopolitan instincts, generous spirit, nose for commerce, and eye for women, Kurt may have found both inspiration and template.

Kurt and Moritz shared one more thing. Both believed they enjoyed all the rights of a citizen of a constitutional state, only to discover that they didn't.

The journeys of my exile grandfather and emigrant father stand as a rebuke to the anti-immigrant mood in much of the United States, the country that once took them in. Today the German chancellor, not the American president, is welcoming asylum seekers, denouncing neo-Nazism, and banging the drum for global integration and liberal democracy. The contrast appears even more stark when viewed from Berlin, perhaps the most radically welcoming city on earth—not just over the previous few years, as Angela Merkel threw Germany open to more than a million refugees, mostly from Syria, but also through much of the city's history, dating back to when the Duke of Prussia invited fifty Viennese Jewish families to settle there after the Thirty Years' War.

Not all Germans are offering an embrace. Merkel has failed to win over followers of the anti-immigrant Alternative für Deutschland party, the AfD, which is especially popular in the villages and countryside of the old East Germany encircling the city. But in Berlin proper, particularly where we've landed, in Kreuzberg, a defiant cosmopolitanism obtains. We see it in graffiti like NAZIS RAUS (Nazis out) and find it in clubs like SO36, which hosts a monthly dance night for gay Muslims. It's heralded by a banner reading ISLAMOPHOBIA DAMAGES THE SOUL, hung from the facade of the church around the corner, where we're as likely to hear world music as Lutheran liturgy. It comes with the lingering spirit of the activists who once organized squats in abandoned buildings, and shortly before the fall of the Wall declared the Free Republic of Kreuzberg, issuing "visas" and building "customs posts" of papier-mâché. And it validates what the exiled journalist Sebastian Haffner wrote from the safety of England on the eve of World War II: "Berlin was, let us say it with Prussian precision, the very essence of an international metropolis. It had, so to speak, roots in the air. It extracted its life force not from the native soil of the surrounding country . . . but from all the great cities of the world."

The six-hour time difference between Washington, DC, and Berlin ensures that a sleep-cycle's worth of backed-up US news alerts greets us each morning. Three days after our arrival comes news that ethnonationalists have engineered a white supremacist rally in Charlottesville, Virginia. Donald Trump fails to condemn the neo-Nazis who assembled, one of whom struck and killed a protestor, Heather Heyer, with his car. The president goes on to describe the day's actors as including "very fine people, on both sides."

These events have a pointed local parallel. Germans will soon go to the polls, to weigh in on Merkel's 2015 decision to welcome refugees in defiance of the AfD, which has been dog-whistling the doctrine of "blood and soil" at the heart of National Socialism. For most of my life I've been aware of the stakes of a choice like this for Germany. And here it lies before me, at the same time America seems to stand at a similar crossroads.

TWO
DONE WITH THE WAR
Kurt, 1913 to 1924

M y grandfather had barely reached his midtwenties, but his adult life was off to the headiest kind of start. In 1913 Kurt brought out the work of his two in-house readers, Franz Werfel and the Expressionist poet and playwright Walter Hasenclever. He foreshadowed a long devotion to the visual arts by publishing the writings of the Austrian painter Oskar Kokoschka. And he launched the Expressionist literary magazine *Der jüngste Tag* (The Judgment Day), with which he pledged to showcase writing that, "while drawing strength from roots in the present, shows promise of lasting life." Several years later the edition seen here would feature the novella Kurt had asked after in that note to Kafka, which my grandfather referred to as "The Bug" and we know today as *The Metamorphosis*.

In 1913 the Bengali poet Rabindranath Tagore became the first non-European to win the Nobel Prize for Literature, and the Kurt Wolff Verlag eventually sold more than a million hardcover copies of a collection of his work, turning it into an under-the-Christmas-tree staple throughout Germany. In a January 1914 diary entry, Robert Musil, an Austrian writer in Kurt's stable, described the man presiding over it all: "Tall. Slim. Clad in

English gray. Elegant. Light-haired. Clean-shaven. Boyish face. Blue-gray eyes, which can grow hard."

Kurt's firm seemed to be making its way without having to compromise. "The house often functioned more as a patron of the arts than according to commercial calculations," remembered Willy Haas, who joined Werfel and Hasenclever as a Kurt Wolff Verlag reader in 1914. Kurt had no interest in a kind of publishing where "you simply supply the products for which there is a demand," he would write, the kind where you need only "know what activates the tear glands, the sex glands, or any other glands, what makes the sportsman's heart beat faster, what makes the flesh crawl in horror, etc." My grandfather held fast to another view, a luxury he could afford, but that would later make his

row tougher to hoe: "I only want to publish books I won't be ashamed of on my deathbed. Books by dead authors in whom we believe. Books by living authors we don't need to lie to. All my life, two elements have seemed to me to be the worst and basically inevitable burden of being a publisher: lying to authors and feigning knowledge that one doesn't have. . . . We might err, that is inevitable, but the premise for each and every book should always be unconditional conviction, the absolute belief in the authentic word and worth of what you champion."

In 1914 Kurt finally landed Karl Kraus as an author. The Viennese Mencken was so prickly about whom he shared a publisher with that he and Kurt agreed on the only solution: to set up a subsidiary devoted solely to his work. Kurt also took over publication of the pacifist and anti-nationalist journal *Die weissen Blätter* (The White Pages), which would have to be printed in Switzerland after war broke out to dodge the censors. Even from his provincial haunts in Prague, Kafka noticed that Kurt was riding high, and said as much in a letter to his fiancée, Felice Bauer: "He is a very beautiful man, about twenty-five, whom God has given a beautiful wife, several million marks, a pleasure in publishing, and little aptitude for the publishing business."

Even after allowing that no publisher is commercially minded enough to satisfy the typical author, Kafka was on to something. "In the beginning was the word, not the number," Kurt would say, many years later, in a riff on the Gospel of John. *Der jüngste Tag* nonetheless helped the Kurt Wolff Verlag carve out a niche as purveyor of cutting-edge writing, and that was worth something. Though my grandfather had been raised to revere the classics, he knew enough to step back and let that rule of twentieth-century marketing—if it's new, it's better—carry the day. For a while this worked. And it was an exhilarating time to be in the book business: during Kurt's first year out on his own, no country produced more books than Germany, some thirty-one thousand new titles in 1913 alone.

With the outbreak of war in August 1914, both the Kurt Wolff Verlag and German publishing at large were changed forever. Eleven of the thirteen members of the firm's staff were called up, including *Leutnant* Wolff, who was sent with an artillery regiment to the Western Front. "I flatter myself in thinking that I have some understanding of artillery service," he wrote in an early entry in the diary he kept throughout his tour of duty, "and above all I love my weapon very much."

Within a few weeks Kurt felt the full force of the carnage delivered by this "war that will end war." His unit was dispatched to a forest south of the Belgian village of Neufchâteau to assess casualties after the 1914 Battle of the Ardennes. "The dead lie in monstrous numbers within a very small space," he wrote. "One notices that every inch of earth was bitterly fought over and gets a sense of how dreadful a fight for a forest can be."

Scattered among hundreds of corpses, Kurt's unit discovered eighteen survivors, fifteen Frenchmen and three Germans,

> *who had passed days and nights since the battle without dressing or water or food amidst the horrific stench of decaying bodies, through the heat of the days and the damp cold of the nights. . . . It goes without saying that only in very rare, exceptional cases could some living thing, weakened by the heavy exertions and deprivations of the past days and weeks, without any food and especially with fevers from their untreated wounds, cling to life as long as these eighteen did. Most of these wounded, to the extent that they were able to utter a few words or communicate in any way, explained that they had had no sustenance. In every case their wounds were so severe that they had been*

unable to move at all. Only one, a German, in despair at
slowly dying of starvation yet nursing hopes of being found
if he could only hang on a little longer, had resorted to a
desperate measure: he took the only thing left of his meager
rations, a cube of condensed pea soup, dissolved it in his
own urine, and drank it.

Kurt had arranged to have Hasenclever assigned to his unit,
so in the midst of the war, even as they were deployed in France,
eastern European Galicia, and the Balkans, the two imagined the
directions German literature might take after hostilities ended.
Riding the Orient Express back from Macedonia on leave, Kurt
would stop off in Vienna to visit Kraus, a loud and consistent
critic of the conflict—one of the few among German-language
intellectuals of the time.

It's hard to fathom the enthusiasm with which Germany
greeted the outbreak of war. In an act of mass self-delusion, Germans across the political spectrum believed this common call to
sacrifice would help Wilhelmine society bridge its many differences. Almost no one foresaw the duration of the stalemate or the
scale of the slaughter. Shortly after its end, one of Kurt's authors,
Joseph Roth, declared the war a "great annihilative nothingness."

The Kurt Wolff Verlag would be the only major house in
Germany to refuse to publish pro-war literature. But like most
of his countrymen, Kurt at the outset seemed open to victory
by arms and tried to suppress his doubts. In December 1914 he
wrote from Ghent:

I drive into the darkness and light my pipe. I think about
my conversations with the military authorities, of the report
of my female spy this morning, of the war and how we will
win a victory over France. And suddenly all those with

whom I so often, so bitterly, argued over these past months seem to be right: We must continue on over the rubble of these countries, and there must be misery and distress among our enemies and in enemy territory, and they must feel this bitter, unrelenting war, feel it until the hunger for peace is so great that the cry for the war's end becomes so loud and penetrating, and so unanimously does the wailing rise, from Liège to Reims, from Namur to Lille, from Brussels to Calais, and also in the east, that it mingles with the groans of the exhausted in the trenches at the front, all of it swelling into a hurricane, into a raging, incessant sound that will ring in their ears in Bordeaux, Le Havre, and Petersburg, until they give up.

The young officer, pictured here, seemed to be writing for an audience beyond my grandmother, who had moved in with her mother in Darmstadt and to whom he sent his dispatches. In November 1914 he noted that a British torpedo had roared

up the beach at Ostend, Flanders, ripping a hole in the dining room of the Majestic Palace, a hotel then billeting German officers, killing two as they ate their breakfast. The attack held two lessons, concluded Kurt, who noted that the Majestic Palace was built by British investors: "The British simply assume that German officers take their breakfast at only the finest hotels; and the blood of German officers seems to be of more value to them than British capital."

But as the war progressed, his diary began to betray disillusionment. The first hint came that same month while he was still in Belgium. "I do not know if the weather has made me melancholy," he wrote. "But all at once I found myself in the bleakest, darkest mood as I reflected on this country and its history. What great potential lies in the fertile soil here, what riches were accumulated from trade by sea and over land, from fishing, from the breeding of horses, cattle, flowers, lacemaking, and much else—and over and over again, this land and its people have suffered from war. And now this war has impoverished everything once more, a war that the Germans have delivered to their country."

In December he wrote that he had been reading *War and Peace*:

> I don't want to go off on a literary digression here, but only quote a passage I've read many times, and which, it seems to me, should serve as an epigraph for the hundreds of books that now appear, or will appear, touching off millions of reviews. . . . : "Rostov knew from experience, from Austerlitz and the campaign of 1807, that men always lie when describing military exploits, as he himself had done in recounting them; furthermore, he had experience enough to know that what happens in war is entirely different from how we imagine it or relate it to others. . . . But he didn't

express his thoughts, for in such matters he had also gained
experience. He knew that this tale redounded to the glory
of our arms, and so one had to pretend not to doubt it."

And then: "I must relate a story here, to free myself of it, of
what unfolded on January 17, 1915. It is one story of many. Such
things and occurrences are slowly but surely destroying my nerves.
They (taken together) seem almost to have a more lasting effect on
me than thoughts of many of the other horrors that war brings."

The incident he recounted took place in a military court-
room presided over by a German judge. A Belgian district
administrator reported that a stable boy had witnessed a soldier
in a *feldgrau* (field-gray) uniform, with regimental number 207
stitched on his epaulettes, steal a farmer's horse.

"Sir, I must warn you against using the word 'steal' when
referring to a member of the German army," the military judge
said.

"In Germany this may be called something else," the Belgian
bureaucrat replied evenly. "Here in Belgium we call it 'stealing.'"

At that, the judge ordered the district administrator jailed,
and Kurt privately renders his judgment:

When I think of isolated incidents like these, and what
thousands of decent Belgians living among such barbarians
will think and say, and swallow and swallow, and hold on
to, hold on to . . . I find it hard to take. . . . I nurse feelings
of shame while walking down the street the next day . . . [at]
all those who accept these things as standard operating pro-
cedure, who cheerfully, blithely, confidently, with a sense of
relativism and the heady feelings of the conqueror, stride
steadily and proudly along, thinking that everything is just
as it is, as it can be, as it must be, as it should be.

Out on the town seven weeks later to celebrate his twenty-eighth birthday, Kurt and three comrades capered about the alleys and squares of Ghent. Eventually they came upon the Gravensteen, the castle of the counts of Flanders, where they woke the guards to be let in.

> *We climbed up on the ramparts and looked down on the beautiful, sleeping city, whose sons are yonder on the Yser, with no connection to, no news of, their fathers, who have been left behind, bitter and full of grief. . . . But at least this beautiful, imposing city with its proud cathedrals still stands. . . . Here it smells not of war, fire, destruction, and putrefaction but of home and stone, water and fish, healthy, alive, with the promise of spring.*
>
> *What will spring bring—? The end of the Battle of the Nations, the great Peace of the Nations? It's strange that this age of great deeds has also become a time of eternal question marks. . . . Why, when, how much longer, for what?*

World War I has been called a conflict "that sloshed back and forth like waves in a basin: the trigger lay in the East, the escalation in the West, but the greatest destruction ultimately occurred, again, in the East." In April 1915, Kurt found his unit redeployed to Galicia, where this picture was taken, for a spring offensive against Russian forces.

From Gorlice, southeast of Krakow, he devoted a telegraphic entry to what he called "a day in the war":

> *Dust, columns of troops, supply trains, Russian prisoners, dust, shouting: Polish, Russian, Austrian, German, Hungarian, Czech, dust, columns marching, columns at rest, mobile messes, dust, vehicles in motion, wheelbarrows,*

artillery columns, broken-down vehicles, abandoned bivouac sites, fresh graves with and without crosses, the entrails of slaughtered cattle. . . .

Overturned wagons, dead horses, dust, the smells of August, supply columns, road work, dead Russians, the casings of two mortar shells, a live white cat on the windowsill of a shot-up house. Galicians burying dead Austrians, Germans, and Russians, a mountain of empty tin cans flashing in the sun. . . .

Dust, fatigue, evening, prisoners, many thousands of them in a long procession, stench, cars, infantry columns, dust, prisoners, infantry columns, dust, prisoners, infantry columns, dust—dusk, fatigue, darkness. Shots in the distance. A few lights. The soft sounds of German, Russian, Polish. . . . Dust, stench, prisoners, infantry columns, cooler, darker, campfires.

Nightfall. And through the dust and haze, the stars . . .

He asked forgiveness for his fragmentary reportage. "But what should I do?" he wrote. "It is too much. One cannot form out of chaos sentences with a subject and a predicate, cannot (should not) transform the madness into meaning."

By summer, almost two years in, ennui had enveloped him. In June he wrote from Galicia.

How long the war has gone on. You have no idea how long. For a couple of hours you sleep in a car; the next night, you sleep in the villa of some Galician con man who has fled, with the newspaper on the nightstand left by the Russian officer who was here a week ago, and with dead bedbugs plastered to the wall. In the morning, at sunrise, still half-asleep, you mount your trusty horse, always there for you despite shrapnel wounds in its haunches and the scant oats to be had. You ride into the world with unbrushed teeth — you're out of drinking water and don't want to put cholera-swill in your mouth — off to nowhere in particular, gazing sleepily more within yourself than at the world around you; and when, stirred by the dazzling sun or a sudden jolt of your horse, you do look around, aware, you're in a completely alien world, which might be strangely beautiful but through which you never intended to travel or ride. . . . For ten months now you've been looking into a kaleidoscope, and the very real and brutal facts it reveals seem more and more unreal, more vivid, and more improbable than the reality of what was once your everyday, civilian existence. And yet everyday life back home has also slipped away, like some feast day long since gone. What is, you want no part of; what was, no longer exists. . . . Who can blame me for being done with the war, even if the war isn't done with me?

In September 1916, Ernst Ludwig, the Grand Duke of Hesse-Darmstadt, declared the war indeed done with Kurt, intervening to spring him from military service. A man of literary interests and a poet and playwright himself, the grand duke wanted his own work published, and Kurt was happy to oblige if that were the price to return him to Leipzig. Marketing director Georg Heinrich Meyer had run the firm in Kurt's absence and regularly traveled to the Western Front to go over business while Kurt served in Belgium. My grandfather's redeployment east had left Meyer on his own. But Meyer's knack for selling books held up even in wartime; upon Kurt's return, the firm's backlist featured more than four hundred titles, among them Gustav Meyrink's *The Golem*, a notable best seller. "I extend my warmest greetings now that you are near us once again," Kafka wrote Kurt in October 1916. "Though these days there is little difference between being near and being far."

After the peace of 1918, Kurt brought out several books from an inventory that war fever had precluded from publication. Foremost was Heinrich Mann's novel *Der Untertan* (literally, "The Underling"), held back for its anti-war and anti-monarchy themes. Kurt read the manuscript while serving on the Western Front and wrote Meyer right away: "I am entranced. After the war it is to appear immediately, marketed courageously, with timpani and trumpets. . . . Especially at a time the field-gray publicists will be swamping us with their deluge, *Der Untertan* should and must be published." Although the kaiser, Wilhelm II, had abdicated and fled, the book appeared in a Germany riven by political intrigue and factional violence. The publication of *Der Untertan* earned Mann death threats—and the Kurt Wolff Verlag sales of one hundred thousand copies in six weeks.

A year later Kurt published Kafka's short story "In the Penal Colony." He had balked at doing so during the war, writing the author that he feared its gruesome subject would be too "painful" for readers. In fact, Kurt knew that this book too would have run afoul of the censors. "Your criticism of the painful element accords completely with my opinion, but then I feel the same way about almost everything I have written so far," Kafka had replied. "Have you noticed how few things are free of this painful element in one form or another?"

Kurt had surely noticed. At the same time, the flight of the kaiser and the promise of democracy seemed to foretell the kind of Germany in which the Kurt Wolff Verlag would flourish. In its 1918 catalog the house foreswore "prejudices of a literary, political, national nature" and vowed instead simply to "consider the question of whether a book is good." But post-traumatic social conditions and an economy shackled by reparations imperiled the book business. Bureaucrats with authoritarian sympathies remained in place. The first democracy in Germany's history, established in the cultural capital of Weimar, lacked the hardheadedness to enforce the lofty values in its constitution. Communists and reactionaries clashed violently with one another from their respective camps, and the idealism and confidence that had marked German literary culture before 1914 became collateral damage. Karl Kraus put it succinctly: "[The Germans] will have forgotten that they lost the war, forgotten that they started it, forgotten that they waged it. For this reason, it will not end."

The Wolffs now had an infant daughter, my aunt Maria, and in October 1919 Kurt moved the firm from Leipzig to Munich.

With supply chains disrupted and habitable apartments for its employees scarce, he nonetheless set up shop in a neo-Baroque villa on Luisenstrasse. It quickly became a house of culture, accommodating Kurt's still-substantial library and hosting regular readings, concerts, and exhibits. But my grandfather soon fell into a funk. "More than ever, Kurt Wolff is a slave to the Kurt Wolff Verlag," he wrote Hasenclever in November 1920. Nine months later it was Werfel's turn to hear out one of my grandfather's lamentations—that their generation had groomed "no young creative successors."

Kurt began to choose titles that were more bourgeois and less adventurous. He shut down *Der jüngste Tag* and threw his house open to European writers, not just German ones. All good as it went, but crotchets and peeves sometimes rushed in where sure-handed seismography once prevailed. In 1920, when a "Professor James Joyce" offered him the German rights to a novel that was probably *A Portrait of the Artist as a Young Man*, Kurt wondered who "this idiotic 'professor' who has written me from Trieste in bad German" could be. Forty years later my grandfather confessed, "If the Kurt Wolff Verlag had published an early book by Joyce, it would certainly also have acquired *Ulysses*, the most important work to be written in English in our century."

In Munich he turned more often to the arts, to painters of Der Blaue Reiter (the Blue Rider), such as Paul Klee and Wassily Kandinsky, whom he had begun to patronize before the war. During his exile to come, Kurt would pawn some of their works to support himself and his family.

Carrying a payroll of one hundred, the firm in 1923 began steadily shedding staff. "The times are bad," Kurt wrote his mother-in-law, Clara Merck, that June, "and the publishing business accords with the times." Kurt started to hedge his bets. Instead of the new, he published more of the tried-and-true, including authors from countries with which Germany had just been at war—Émile Zola and Guy de Maupassant, Maxim Gorky and Anton Chekhov, even Sinclair Lewis. Hoping to become less dependent on the fragile German economy, he founded a house in Florence, Pantheon Casa Editrice, the first pan-European firm to specialize in art books. He brought out volumes with text in five languages, cutting deals with foreign publishers to share costs. But the uncertainty of the times left even wealthy continental book buyers reluctant to spring for lavish editions, and rising nationalism began to subvert the cosmopolitan assumptions at the heart of these copublishing arrangements. The firm's prewar reputation as safe harbor for avant-garde playwrights, poets, and authors of fiction vanished as these kinds of writers seemed to disappear too. As the worst of the hyperinflation set in, Kurt paid his staff daily, so that, he wrote, "they could spend it the same day for purchases that would be unaffordable the day after."

My father was born into this gathering chaos, in July 1921. When Niko was two, my grandfather made an entry in his diary that is almost unimaginable today: "A KW novel now priced at 5 million marks."

The Berlin skyline is almost too jumbled to qualify as one. It's as if city planners took instructions from Karl Scheffler's 1910 observation that fate "condemns Berlin forever to become and never to be." Yet a protean cityscape is somehow appropriate for a place that, during the lifetimes of my grandfather and father, has been by turns imperial, impoverished, heedlessly carefree, fascist, ruined, occupied, and divided, until its ultimate reunification and position at the center of the European project.

The renovated Reichstag is an exception to all this visual unruliness. To tour the building and its dome, you ascend the ramp that spirals up underneath the distinctive glass dome, then gaze down at the seats of the MPs in the chamber below. Symbolism is at play here twice over: government should be sheathed in transparency, and there's no better way to remind a parliament of its proper place than to have constituents literally look down on it from above.

Germans can be relentless in their remembrance. During the Reichstag's restoration, project managers chose to preserve Cyrillic graffiti left by some triumphant Soviet soldier that reads I FUCK HITLER IN THE ASS. Visible to the south is the Memorial to the Murdered Jews of Europe; it's no accident that the site, known informally as "the Holocaust memorial," goes by such a precise and explicit official name or that it occupies a spot so central that no visitor to Berlin is likely to miss it. This historical humility informs much of current German political life, keeps memory alive, and drives the far-right Alternative für Deustchland crazy. If, as the AfD legislator Björn Höcke has grumbled, Germans are "the only people in the world who plant a monument of shame in the heart of the capital," it's because they're discerning enough to recognize that they need to, especially as long as politicians like Höcke have a following.

One of the authors Kurt and Helen published in New York, Günter Grass, served as the moral compass of postwar West Germany, even as he felt uncomfortable in the role. "You cannot delegate your conscience to writers or anyone else," Grass said in 2000. "I don't speak out because I am a writer. My profession is a writer, but I speak out because I am a citizen. I think the Weimar Republic collapsed and the Nazis took over in 1933 because there were not enough citizens. That's the lesson I have learned. Citizens cannot leave politics just to politicians."

In late 1944, as a seventeen-year-old responding to a draft notice, Grass joined the Waffen-SS. He never admitted having done so until the end of a career in which he hectored Germans to engage with their past. In that, he was surely wrong. But Grass is right about the lesson worth carrying forward: there were not enough citizens.

The AHA Factory occupies much of an upper floor in an old *Mietskaserne*, one of countless five-story "rental barracks" built to accommodate workers who flocked to Berlin during the Industrial Revolution. Around me turn the cogs of the creative economy. Moritz, a jazz guitarist and arts impresario, swans into our shared office aglow from his success fishing over the weekend. Aidan, an Irishman married to a German of Turkish descent, is performing motion analysis for dancers. Ed, a computer programmer from Holland, is busy coding an app for parents of preschoolers, while Francesco, a filmmaker from Italy, creates videos for corporate clients and humble AHA Factory cohabitants alike. Each contributes to Berlin's status as home to more start-ups than any other city in Europe. The cost of living is still cheap enough for the starving artist, and any day can deliver an energizing encounter with someone in flight from convention or repression. All of which leaves you with the thrill of being on the crest of a wave.

But this wave comes with an undertow that can yank you from the present when you least expect it. Each morning our kids go off to school on an S-Bahn headed for the Wannsee, where in January 1942 the Nazis signed off on the Final Solution; in the afternoon they return on a train bound for Oranienburg, from which the Schutzstaffel (SS) oversaw it. We buy meat and produce in the market hall in which Carl Herz, the Jewish mayor of Kreuzberg, after being chased from city hall and dragged through the streets by Brownshirts of the Sturmabteilung (SA), was beaten on a spring day in 1933. Walking around our *Kiez*, as Berliners call a neighborhood, we come across some of the more than five thousand *Stolpersteine*, or stumbling stones—brass cobblestone memorials nested in the sidewalks of the city, each commemorating a Berliner victimized by the Nazis and set outside the last home he or she freely chose. Dates of detention and murder come inscribed beneath each name in recitative simplicity. The power of the *Stolpersteine* lies in their subtle obtrusiveness. Whereas you must consciously make a destination of immured, monochromatic gravestones in a cemetery, stumbling stones glint up at you throughout the open city, nuggets in the creek bed. To read an inscription you bend at the waist in a kind of bow of respect. As memorials go, *Stolpersteine* derive an animating power from being a work in progress, as tens of thousands of Berliners are yet to be memorialized.

It's a sobering fact, the historian Timothy Snyder points out, that "cultures of memory are organized by round numbers, intervals of ten; but somehow the remembrance of the dead is easier when the numbers are not round, when the final digit is not a zero." That's precisely why each stone in our neighborhood calls out as it does, testifying to the meaning of one particular spot in the life of one particular person, insisting on its place in our daily routine. Cross the street to the ice-cream stand, weighing whether to enjoy one scoop or two, but only after you remember Wilhelm Böttcher, the widower with a wooden leg who, rather than finger other gay Berliners, killed himself in September 1936 in the Alexanderplatz jail two weeks after police took him into custody. Fill out a transfer slip at the bank on the corner, and you do so steps from where, a month apart in early 1943, the Jewish cousins Ruth Gerstel and Erwin Rones were detained and deported, *Schicksal ???*, fate unknown, their stone tells us. Approach the threshold of the nearest chain store to buy sundries, and you're reminded that a tailor and postal worker named Martin Jaffé, who performed six years of forced labor at a chemical plant in nearby Tempelhof, lived here in a third-floor apartment before being arrested at work in February 1943—whereupon the Nazis, having decided to bring in captured Slavs from the east to replace Jews like Jaffé,

sent him first to the ghetto at Theresienstadt and then to his death.

Just around the corner from where we live, the stumbling stone nearest to us, ERNA WOLFF, deported on December 14, 1942, murdered in Auschwitz. No relation, as far as I know. And I really don't know.

My writ as a journalist often ran beyond sports, to how the games we play and watch spill into the world at large. So it's hard not to see two events scheduled for the same day—the Berlin Marathon and the German election—as an invitation to find a spot along the marathon route a block from our apartment and riddle out what both mean.

The procession begins with outriding cop cars, follows with the African favorites, and soon delivers the pack, its riot of color at odds with a slate-gray sky. This being Kreuzberg, no one gets a bigger cheer than the competitors the Nazis would have eliminated: the handcyclists and a man with one arm. To watch anyone run is to realize how much this enterprise of the legs depends on swinging whatever arms you have.

Despite the breadth of candidates and parties on the ballot, most Germans regard today's election as a binary choice. On one side stands Merkel, with her decision to welcome those million-plus refugees. Taking seriously the Christianity in the pedigree of her party, the Christian Democratic Union, she invoked the biblical injunction to welcome the stranger. Her mantra of *Wir schaffen das*—"We'll manage it"—was an appeal to German practicality and willingness to tackle challenges. "I grew up behind a wall," Merkel liked to say, "and have no desire to repeat the experience." Her refugee policy was a spectacularly risky political choice, but it was the brave one, the righteous one, and, once asylum seekers had massed at the border, given German history, really the only one.

On the other side there's the Alternative for Germany. The AfD began as an anti-European protest movement and gained strength after Merkel led the European Union's bailout of Greece. Soon the party became a catch basin for anyone with a gripe about immigrants, Islam, or the ostensibly uncontroversial matter of whether National Socialism should be held up as a national shame. Some party members no longer even bother to cloak their Nazi sympathies. A regional AfD official, Alexander Gauland, said, "If the French are rightly proud of their Emperor, and the Britons of Nelson and Churchill, we have the right to be proud of the achievements of German soldiers in two world wars." Another, a judge from Saxony named Jens Maier, once called racially mixed people "unbearable" and said that Anders Breivik, the Norwegian terrorist and anti-Islam extremist, "became a mass murderer out of pure desperation."

It's a vocational tic of mine to be attuned to sports references: Of course, Gauland said, he cheered for Jérôme Boateng, the defender on the German national soccer team whose father comes from Ghana. But to have Boateng as a neighbor, Gauland went on to say—that would be another matter altogether.

The AfD winds up capturing 13 percent of the vote, enough to qualify for representation in the Bundestag, the federal assembly, for the first time. But Merkel easily wins reelection as chancellor. Opinion polls suggest that Germany has built a firewall against extremism. Some 80 percent of the population identifies with the political center, almost 30 percent more than the French do. Historian Konrad Jarausch credits the Federal Republic's extraordinary political stability to an aging generation of peaceprizing, centrist, small-*d* democrats, many of whom have faced up to what happened during the Nazi era and their own ancestors' complicity in it. That a country so late to democracy, and until the mid-twentieth-century so apparently indifferent to it, is now its beau ideal, surely qualifies as "an irony of history." The trauma of Nazism—and for those in the east, the ensuing oppression by the Stasi, the secret police of the German Democratic Republic—will do that to a people. Which leads me to conclude hopefully that, even with one impaired political limb, Germany can count on its others to keep moving forward.

THREE

TECHNICAL BOY AND THE DEPOSED SOVEREIGN

Niko, 1921 to 1939
Kurt, 1924 to 1933

A child's life in the Wolff home on Munich's Königinstrasse came circumscribed and regimented. The upstairs nursery lay beyond a padded leather door with brass buttons and smelled of buffed linoleum and tar soap. Here Niko and his older sister, Maria, were confined, for this was the domain of the family nanny. Only occasionally did the children cross paths with some visiting literary figure, such as Rabindranath Tagore, who came by for lunch just before my father was born. "With his long grayish-white beard and great dignity he presented a most impressive figure," Kurt would recall forty years later. "So that it seemed a completely natural error when my three-year-old daughter assumed God was paying us a visit, and settled contentedly in the lap of the Lord."

Except for the Sunday midday meal, the Wolff siblings ate apart from their parents and always a custom menu. Lunch might be *Tafelspitz*, boiled beef and spinach, which Niko would hamster in his cheeks until naptime gave him a chance to spit it out. Melanie Zieher, the nanny everyone called Bulle (Cop), was expected to enforce the rules: no water with meals, for it filled up

the stomach before a child could be properly nourished; and strict adherence to Fletcherism, which calls for chewing food until it liquifies. With little salt in their diet, Maria and Niko sometimes took to licking the walls.

Though she never married, Bulle once had to give up a baby for adoption. So she channeled unfulfilled maternal instincts into proxies, championing the children in their battles with Kurt and Elisabeth, sometimes slipping her charges food on the sly. "Bulle and Maria and I were in one camp," Niko once told me. "My mother was in another. My father, we never saw." Bulle, pictured here with her campmates, treated my father's stuffed bear Zoschl—a gift from the Italian consul in Munich, a friend of my grandparents', when Niko was three—as another child in her care.

On a family trip during the mid-twenties, Kurt's Buick broke down in the Bergell Valley of Switzerland's Engadine, on a steep and narrow unpaved road up to the village of Soglio. Niko got out and beat the car angrily with his fists. Kurt the technophobe sat there in his characteristic way, white gloves unsoiled, confident a handy Samaritan would turn up. Someone always did.

My father was curious about how things worked in a way his father wasn't. Listening to the family gramophone, Niko strained to find the tiny instrumentalists inside. "Be still!" a photographer might say before pressing the bulb attached to his camera. "Watch for the birdie!" No birdie ever appeared, and logical little Niko came to regard photographers as loathsome con men. But suffering minor betrayals like these failed to subvert an otherwise cheerful constitution. Niko had few of the anarchic instincts of his sister. Wearing a Sunday dress for a walk through the English Garden, ten-year-old Maria once responded to the oohing and cooing of two elegant ladies by throwing herself into a mud puddle, rolling around, and popping up to scream, *Schweine Dame!* (Pig Lady!) A gap would soon open up between Kurt and Elisabeth, leading to divorce, and you could see the fracture in just such a moment, when Maria's mother cringed and her father beamed at this behavioral equivalent of Expressionism. Scrawnier than his sister, unable to win Kurt's favor the way she could, Niko was cursed with more than just being the beta male of the family—he was the beta sibling. Maria would invite her little brother to play a game of "Kurt Wolff Verlag," insisting that she be Kurt Wolff; my father could join her only if he agreed to be Frau Hertlein and take dictation. Niko would object, but with the advantage of three years and more than a head in size, Maria got her way.

Yet a flip side to all this redounded to my father's benefit. He didn't yearn for the attention of remote or absent parents, not as palpably as his sister, who would sneak into her mother's dressing room, shut herself in the wardrobe, and press silk against her face to luxuriate in its texture and scent. Niko grew up obliging and relatively angst-free, with a knack for self-amusement that others in the family came to envy. To be a budding *homo faber* among aesthetes—the son of a man who wouldn't deign to pick up a hammer and chisel unless he needed to open a case of wine— left plenty of running room to define oneself. So Niko took apart

clocks to see how they worked and, satisfied, put them back
together. One time he dismantled and reassembled his mother's
sewing machine and got it to work with a part to spare. "You will
win the Nobel Prize someday," Maria announced, "and support
me in my old age!" In time Niko would come around to books
and painting and music, but for the moment none could compete
with gadgets and cars and planes. When Bulle had enough of taking him to the Deutsches Museum to ogle the locomotives and
flying machines, the family hired others to do it.

My grandparents spent the spring of 1925 in the Villa Canta-
galli, a rental in the Florentine suburb of Fiesole, where the Italian artist Felice Casorati painted these portraits. Those months
would constitute the last extended idyll of Niko and Maria's
childhood as an intact family. Somewhere over the Tuscan hills,
beyond that garden wall by which Elisabeth sits, a storm is about
to break.

The following year Kurt auctioned off another tranche of
his first editions and incunabula. The sale grossed more than
375,000 Reichsmarks, roughly $1.26 million today, a nut he

would rely on for nearly twenty years, until he finally earned a steady income again. For all of Kurt's delight in life's pleasures, the hyperinflation—"to see wealth just melt away before your eyes," as my uncle Christian puts it—had taught him caution with money. Yet the worldwide economic collapse of 1929 would soon leave his firm financially spent. And sandwiched around the crash came two unravelings of the most intimate kind.

"I want to share something wonderful with you," Elisabeth wrote her widowed mother, Clara Merck, just after Christmas 1928. "This summer we'll be welcoming a long-anticipated visitor, a sibling for Maria and Niko. I look unspeakably forward to this child, whom we've wanted for years, even if we have some serious concerns, about which we'll want to speak to you face-to-face."

Those concerns might have been business ones, given that Kurt had by now largely halted his publishing activities. They might have been anxieties over Elisabeth's ability to bring another child to term, for she had just turned thirty-eight and, after giving birth to my father seven years earlier, been hospitalized with a renal pelvis inflammation. What she's probably not alluding to, but was real nonetheless, is the wobbly state of their union.

Soon after his wedding, Kurt had begun a faithful correspondence with his mother-in-law. The two exchanged scores of letters over the next two decades, and Kurt came to rely on Clara's advice. At the end of February 1929, Kurt wrote her about her daughter's pregnancy. "Elisabeth hasn't felt herself over the past weeks," he reported. "Since Monday she's been flat on her back with a fever and frightful case of the flu." A week later: "Things aren't developing according to our hopes, and Elisabeth's illness is proceeding downright unfavorably." And two weeks after that: "She's had a case of bleeding, which given her condition is of particular concern. As a precaution the obstetrician sent her to the hospital."

The ordeal ended two days later, on March 21. "Today I must share my latest letter, full of horrible news," Kurt wrote Clara. "Early today, more than forty hours of labor resulted in a stillbirth. (It would have been a baby boy, Dr. Albrecht told me.)"

I never knew I'd lost an uncle. But then my father never told me, and I'd never asked.

My grandmother wound up spending two more months in the hospital recovering from sepsis.

Years later Kurt would describe a feeling of imprisonment early in his marriage, crystallized one evening when he came home from the office to find Elisabeth waiting at the door. For her part, my grandmother told Maria much later, "I was too young. I didn't understand him."

It's unclear exactly when Kurt began to conduct affairs with other women, and there seems to be a question about what kind of philanderer he was—one who liked to maintain a brace of girl-friends, or one in it for the thrill of the hunt and then ready to move on. Support for the first theory comes from a cousin who tells of how Kurt would regularly assemble mistresses for coffee in the lobby of a Munich hotel and lead the conversation, inquiring after each in a roundelay of solicitude. (These *Kaffeeklatsch* signaled that, lest there be any misunderstanding, each woman was on an equal footing, and it was not a full-time domestic one.) Support for the second theory comes from another cousin, who says Kurt's nocturnal activities on lengthy railroad journeys earned him the nickname Night Train.

He may have embodied both types. And in his own mind Kurt seems to have been less a predator than an ingratiator. "If another person's good qualities far outshine one's own, there is no recourse but love," goes one of his favorite quotes from

Goethe. It's the creed of the impresario, of someone who wants to lift others up. Yet those words might also be read as lending polyamory a sheen of inevitability. Maria once told me that Kurt, late in his life, confessed to her that he would have been a better publisher if not for all the women, for they took up so much time. "It was never the making love," she said. "It was the seduction. And he hated to be alone."

His affairs led to one out-of-wedlock child—and only one, as far as I know. On July 7, 1926—five years to the day after my father was born—Annemarie von Puttkamer, a translator for the firm and a sister of an old World War I friend of Kurt's named Jesko von Puttkamer, gave birth to a son she named Enoch. No one was more excited for Annemarie, pictured here, than my grandmother. She made a baby gift of a layette set, unaware that her gesture was dedicated to the child of her husband's mistress. But the truth would become clear soon enough.

Sometime in the late spring of 1929, soon after Elisabeth had recovered, Kurt told his wife that he didn't want to remain "in a marriage." During Clara Merck's visit to Munich that June, the couple shared news of their impending split, and my great-grandmother

took it especially hard. On the morning of June 15, Kurt drove his mother-in-law to Munich's main station and settled her into a train compartment for her trip back to Darmstadt. Before the train pulled out of the station, Mutti Merck died of a massive stroke.

To cease to remain "in a marriage" didn't necessarily require a divorce, and over the near term the four still functioned as a nominal family, even vacationing together in the Engadine as late as Christmas 1930. Meanwhile, Elisabeth had won the heart of Dr. Albrecht, the obstetrician who had nursed her back to health following the stillbirth. Kurt's diary records the jumble their lives had become before the split. February 5: *E* [Elisabeth], *Albrecht, AvP* [Annemarie von Puttkamer] . . . *E with Albrecht*. March 13: *Evening with Albrecht*. May 3: *AvP brings Enoch*.

On the morning of May 16, 1930, Elisabeth wrote in her diary, "Kurt breakfasts with me for the last time. At eight he drives off." She called it "this worst of days." A Darmstadt physician and psychoanalyst who had once treated Elisabeth for a case of nerves spent the afternoon with her in Munich's botanical garden, sharing passages about reconciliation.

After Hans Albrecht made clear his wish to marry her, Elisabeth initiated the divorce, which was granted early the following year. To dissolve a marriage, one party was obliged to assume guilt and stipulate with whom the marriage vows had been broken. Kurt did so, but to protect the reputations of his socially prominent mistresses, a working-class woman took the fall with him. It's unclear whether she had actually been one of his girlfriends or was simply cajoled or paid to testify in court. But the divorce decree states that Kurt confessed to engaging in an "unethical relationship with the baker's wife Ida Pollinger . . . since the spring of 1930 by exchanging kisses and caresses."

Niko and Maria might have suffered more from the split if it had been rancorous or if their parents had been a bigger part of

their lives. Instead, they both seem to have pledged to make the best of their new circumstances. "Niko is a very secretive person," his sister would tell me shortly before her death in 1996. "He never talks about things. He's absolutely marvelous because he *feels* everything. We really were enriched by new people in our lives instead of thinking we had a broken home. We thought it was normal. As a child I wanted to get married twice and have a nice extended family."

My grandmother formalized her relationship with Dr. Albrecht, seen here with a day's harvest, in March 1931, and Niko and Maria joined them in a comfortable home in Munich's Nymphenburg district. No one was surprised by the match: family members recalled Dr. Albrecht being a nervous wreck while delivering my father, so smitten was he by the woman who a decade later would become his wife.

Niko and Maria quickly warmed to their new stepfather. He played the violin and viola, painted watercolors, and had the informal manner of rural Bavaria. An amateur magician who belonged to Der Magische Zirkel, a magicians' guild, he would go into private homes and perform tricks. With his stepchildren he shared stories from the delivery room, tales welcomed even more for how they discomfited their mother—including one about the frantic nurse who would meet him at the curb outside the hospital in the middle of the night and cry, *Herr Doktor! Ihr Muttermund ist ein Fünf-Mark-Stück gross!* (Her cervix is dilated to the size of a five-mark piece!)

As if to guard against all this uninhibited medical talk, Elisabeth threw herself into Christian Science, assigning her children passages by Mary Baker Eddy and dragging them to services at the Tonhalle. Yet Maria continued to act out, and in 1931 she was expelled from boarding school. Her mother and father were so absorbed in their own lives that neither bothered to fetch her from Munich's main station, and as a thirteen-year-old she was left to schlep her suitcases home by herself.

Meanwhile, as an expectant little *Bildungsbürger*, Niko began to work toward his *Abitur* at Munich's Maximilians-Gymnasium. Student and school made for a poor match. Niko turned in homework only on cold or rainy days when, riding the tram instead of walking, he could do assignments en route.

By now Germany had begun its march toward fascism. In March 1933 came the Enabling Act, an amendment to the Weimar constitution passed after the Reichstag fire that granted Hitler broad lawmaking power without any parliamentary restraints. In August 1934 my father and his mother were vacationing in Switzerland when word reached them that German president Paul von Hindenburg was dead, and Hitler had declared himself *Führer*. A year later the Nazis pushed through the Nuremberg Laws at their annual party rally in that city. At a stroke, 450,000 German Jews were reduced from citizens to "state subjects." But another 50,000 Germans—those descended from Jews who had undergone conversions—posed a dilemma. The Nazis regarded Jewishness as a racial construct, so they were unimpressed by baptisms, like those of Kurt's maternal grandparents, unless an act of Christian affirmation had taken place no further back than one's great-grandparents. Nonetheless, if you were what the Nazis called a "*Mischling*," or a German of mixed background—whether a "first-degree *Mischling*," with one parent of Jewish descent, like Kurt, or a "second-degree *Mischling*," like Niko—you could for the moment retain your citizenship, even if the Nazis didn't regard you as belonging fully to the German race and nation.

That same year, after he repeated the equivalent of sixth grade, Niko and the Max-Gymnasium had become exasperated with each other. "The student failed to bring to bear even a modicum of diligence and was wholly indifferent to every subject," reads his report card from the end of the 1934–35 school year. "Despite having repeated the grade, he met the standard by the barest of margins."

All parties were relieved when Niko, now fourteen, left the following fall for Landheim Schondorf, a boarding school on Bavaria's Ammersee. There he flourished. Latin and math came leavened with instruction in sailing and photography and the chance to design and build theater sets. He entered a contest to come up with a logo for a publishing house called Bruckmann, and his entry—an intertwined bridge (*Brücke*) and man (*Mann*)—won first prize. "He got on well at Schondorf, intellectually and physically," Maria once told me. "And out of the shadow of his sister. With no malicious intent, I terrorized him."

By 1939, Niko's mother would take the Schondorf directory and mark swastikas next to the names of a handful of students with prominent Nazi parents. Those notations survive today, indicating the children of Elk Eber, the painter who glorified National Socialist themes; Hermann Boehm, the admiral from Kiel; and Ernst Boepple, the *SS-Oberführer* who would be hanged in Krakow in 1950 for his role in implementing the Holocaust in occupied Poland. But at the time Niko enrolled, Schondorf was still a relative refuge from the *Gleichschaltung*, the Nazification of so much of German life. The school had a headmaster devoted to *Bildung* and could count a number of "*Mischlinge*" in its student body.

Nonetheless, after dinner on Wednesday evenings my father would pull on a brown uniform and swastika armband and, under the leadership of an older student, go off to the weekly meeting, known as *Heimabend*, with the school's Hitler Youth troop. "They indoctrinated us with crap, with distorted history, half-truths about World War I, that Germany had been overrun and stabbed in the back," he once told me. "Antisemitic stuff and innuendo. You had to pretend to like it or you'd get your parents or the school in trouble."

Niko recalled several students of more fully Jewish descent than he who weren't allowed to take part: "We envied them, of course."

However he conducted his personal life, my grandfather hewed to a strict code as he wound down his business. On June 23, 1930, he wrote to Werfel:

> *I cannot, I will not keep the Kurt Wolff Verlag going. . . .*
> *The firm has exhausted me, both physically and materially;*
> *for the past six years I have been slowly bleeding to death.*
> *When the inflation ended and the mark became stable*
> *again, I was left with no cash assets . . . but I did have an*

immense stockpile of books, most of them printed on paper of poor quality. At first sales continued to be good, and this misled me to believe, like so many others, that I had a large operation requiring a large staff. And obviously I also felt that the employees who had stood by me during the hard times of inflation should be kept on as long as possible. . . . There was no cash; the vast majority of the books we had in stock were not selling well, since the public's taste had changed so thoroughly. . . . I refuse to declare bankruptcy, even though these days that is not considered a dishonorable step, nor am I inclined to do what so many of my colleagues have done and become a front man for the manipulations of my creditors, printers, and bookbinders. What money I had of my own is gone. . . . I will sell off enough to get us out of debt (that, actually, is the case already, since we never failed to pay what we owed and do not intend to do so now).

"Why did I stop?" Kurt later asked in a note to himself. "There was nothing new in sight. No sign of anything new." He had made a living off, or a kind of life out of, the new or exotic: Expressionism, Tagore, Fletcherism. Some of the books he published sold briskly right away. But after five years, half of his eight-hundred-copy printing of Kafka's first standalone book remained warehoused, and many other writers—Musil, Roth, Robert Walser—took years to find a following. Kurt published them just the same, as if each were a bond scheduled to mature ten, twenty, fifty years on, time-lapse vindications of his judgment. "That so many of his authors are now part of [the] canon," the *Times Literary Supplement* wrote in 1970, "gave Kurt Wolff the right to claim that he had balanced out any mistakes into which enthusiasm might have led him."

My grandfather doesn't specify what accounted for the public's changing taste. But the Nazis would soon implement the *Gleichschaltung*, and many of the events that fueled their rise, including the crash of 1929, also jeopardized the book business at large and Kurt's firm in particular. Together these circumstances left my grandfather, as another German publisher put it years later, "like a deposed sovereign after a revolution."

He and his old wingman from Leipzig commiserated in an exchange of letters. In March 1930, Werfel urged Kurt to hold fast to what they had once shared. "The Kurt Wolff Verlag was the literary instrument of the last poetic movement to exist in Germany," he wrote. "Regardless of how highly or lowly esteemed its names are today, one thing is clear, that these were poetic-minded people, the last poets to be sacrificed to the war.— The world we see today is so altered that only a look backward from some point in the future could do justice to this movement to which we both belonged."

Even as he let employees go over the course of the decade, in 1925 Kurt hired the person who would change the course of his life and, ultimately, make a significant impact on the publishing business in America.

Helen Mosel, my step-grandmother, was born in 1906 in Vranjska Banja, a spa town in southern Serbia. Her mother, Josephine Fischhof, was a Viennese-born journalist; her father, Ludwig (Louis) Mosel, an engineer from the Rhineland, had been sent to the Ottoman Empire to work on the electrification of Turkey. Afraid that Helen and her three younger siblings would be exposed to cholera in public schools, her parents hired private tutors. Helen was reading by age four. Born with one leg shorter than the other, she walked with a slight limp, but that only encouraged her immersion in books and the languages to be unlocked in their pages.

Soon after the outbreak of the Balkan Wars of 1912 and '13, Helen's parents split up. Louis eventually abandoned the family entirely, and Helen would vow not to bring his name up again. Josephine moved with the children first to Vienna, then to Berlin, and in 1918, with World War I ongoing and food scarce, to the Bavarian countryside. Amidst this vagabonding childhood and the instability of her parents' marriage, books helped provide Helen with the ballast to turn herself into a precocious young woman.

In 1920 her mother enrolled Helen as a day student, and one of the first females, at Schondorf, the same Bavarian boarding school Niko would attend. By fifteen she had mastered English and French and read through many of the classics, so the school pushed her several grades ahead. At seventeen she benefited from the patronage of a few wealthy families near Frankfurt, who learned of her through a school connection and hired her as a nanny and governess. One employer—the mother of a schoolmate—also knew Kurt and helped arrange a three-month position as an unpaid trainee with his firm. Helen went on to work as his secretary; as an editor for Pegasus Press, the Paris-based art-book house that had absorbed what was left of Pantheon Casa Editrice; and then, after that firm also ran into financial trouble, as a translator for a UNESCO-like bureau at the League of Nations in Geneva.

By the fall of 1928, Helen's name appears more and more often in Kurt's diary, in entries datelined Grenoble, Menton, Nice, Paris. For much of that year and the next, the two traveled together through France, as well as England, Spain, Switzerland, and North Africa. In letters to her family she makes clear that a love affair has begun, albeit one encumbered by uncertainty. Kurt continued to avail himself of a range of women, most of higher social standing and from more comfortable circumstances than those of his penniless, twenty-two-year-old protégée. Helen had to content herself with "scraps of time," she wrote her brother Georg in March 1930 — "torn, secret, every word heartfelt, but always knowing the car could stop at the corner a couple of minutes from now and it will all be over."

As she realized how much Kurt was beginning to rely on her emotionally, Helen more firmly reconciled herself to his liaisons with other women. "It's better to spend one week a year with someone like [Kurt], and the rest alone, than to compromise and not be alone for the whole year," she wrote Georg the following September. "One doesn't need to own one's loved one; one has to love that person properly, so as to know each other, to be indestructibly connected by the power of emotion — then there's no distance, no jealousy, no begrudging." By the summer of 1931, Helen — pictured here during the early thirties in the south of France — had become the closest Kurt then had to a permanent partner.

During their travels around Europe, Kurt and Helen had avoided Germany, which was "already gloomy and sickening," Kurt wrote Walter Hasenclever in November 1931. "You can detect it within the first five minutes . . . [a] doomsday mood that has become a common mass psychosis." Otherwise, Kurt wrote Werfel, "I rest, swim, go for walks. In the fall when fully rested, I may think about what to do next."

But what to do next was already weighing on him. Through the late twenties, eating and drinking too much, Kurt had put on almost thirty pounds. In letters he was now bemoaning his "agitation" and "debilitating fatigue." To be so far from the arena was "paralytically exhausting . . . infinitely more difficult than any clearly defined active task." In March 1931, he relayed to a friend, "how much I yearn for a reasonable job, commensurate with my capabilities and skills."

So when Kurt and Helen found their way to Berlin in early January 1933, it was specifically to pursue an opportunity for him with the foreign ministry's Cultural Policy Department, a forerunner of the modern-day Goethe Institute. Moving into a pension on the Kurfürstendamm, they spent what would turn out to be their last weeks in Germany until after the war. Kurt made several visits to the dentist. He and Helen checked out apartments. They socialized with friends who shared their fear that the Nazis would gin up some pretext to abolish any check on their seizure of power. Roth, the former Kurt Wolff Verlag author, was then taking note of what he called the "periodical forest" sprouting in the kiosks of Potsdamer Platz: "The saplings are called the *Völkischer Ratgeber*, the *Kampfbund*, the *Deutscher Ring*, the

Deutsches Tagblatt, and all are marked with the inevitable swastikas cut deeply these days into every bark."

If Kurt's Jewish ancestry wasn't enough to attract the Nazis' attention, his patronage of "degenerate" art and literature ensured his status as their enemy. So with Hitler's installation as chancellor on January 30, the cultural post with the foreign ministry became a nonstarter. Defeated, Kurt soon relocated with Helen from their Ku'damm pension to an artsy neighborhood in Friedenau, into the furnished apartment Hasenclever had just abandoned when he chose to light out for France. The plate by the doorbell was graced with the name of another prior tenant, a Sigrid Engström, whose "Aryan" appellation seemed to promise protection from incursions by SA thugs. "We are now in the midst of fascism," Helen wrote her brother on February 17, the day they moved in. "Have you heard Hitler on the radio? It's enough to make you cry. . . . I look forward to my arrest for impolitic statements about 'the *Führer*,' because one of these days I won't be able to keep my mouth shut."

Nine days later Helen wrote her brother again, declaring that National Socialism promised a "lapse into barbarism," under which she could scarcely imagine "room to live for a halfway decent person." She added a diagnosis: "The original problem of the German people is that what is real is not enough for them. They don't adapt to what is given; life leaves them bored, thus they throw it away. . . . Those for whom normalcy is insufficient always create chaos and destruction."

The Reichstag burned the following night, and Helen and Kurt listened as Nazi parliamentarian Hermann Göring ranted over the radio. "These are madmen," Kurt barked. "Pack!"

They left two days later, alighting in Paris, before continuing on to London, where on March 27 they married. In the meantime, from his home in Switzerland, Hermann Hesse sent Kurt a letter that must have come with a homing device to find him at some address. "The news is sad and strange," Hesse wrote. "I lay [the newspapers] aside and try to remain unaffected by it all. There is no front one could join; everywhere one would have to espouse a creed of cannons and terror. But there is always the 'Kingdom of God' or the *'universitas literarum'* or the 'invisible church,' whose doors remain open to us."

In front of the opera house on Berlin's Bebelplatz that May, egged on by Brownshirts and with Goebbels's blessing, students would make a bonfire of books, many of them from the catalog of the Kurt Wolff Verlag.

How had Kurt known to flee? How would anyone know when to take such an irrevocable step, so shot full of capitulation and foreclosure? "Deciding whether to get out today or whether you've still got until tomorrow," Bertolt Brecht would write, "requires the sort of intelligence with which you could have created an immortal masterpiece a few decades ago." Whatever it was—self-preservationist genius or some primal survival instinct—Kurt, now with Helen, would call on that intuition again and again.

My father had no sense yet of having been left behind. Over school vacations he and Maria would now travel to one Mediterranean idyll or another to visit their father and his new wife, whom they both took to right away. For Niko, boarding school came with the hallmarks of a civilized Germany, those Hitler Youth meetings notwithstanding. At Schondorf a teenage boy could still cultivate learning and arts and crafts, oblivious to the gathering doom.

"The ideal subject of totalitarian rule," wrote Hannah Arendt, a friend of Kurt and Helen's, "is not the convinced Nazi or the convinced Communist, but people for whom the distinction between fact and fiction (i.e., the reality of experience), and the distinction between true and false (i.e., the standards of thought), no longer exists."

What Arendt pays less attention to in her 1951 book *The Origins of Totalitarianism* is the complicity of the deceived in their own deception. Today citizens of Germany and the United States presumably have agency to inspect and sort the fruits of a free press. But under the Nazis many Germans were content to let propaganda distract and mislead them. With the help of Sebastian Haffner, the journalist who spent much of his exile trying to explain the Nazi phenomenon, it's worth exploring why.

My father's first years of sentient childhood fell during the Stresemann era, Germany's interval of calm between 1924 and 1929, which historians have named after the country's sure-handed foreign minister. But a generation of German men born just after 1900 were maladapted to this normalcy. They had grown up treating dispatches from the front as if they were sports scores, and then—after Versailles, during the Weimar-era hyperinflation—watched their mothers and young wives fill laundry baskets with cash simply to go to market. Through the decade beginning in 1914, this cohort had been trained, Haffner explains, to have

> the entire content of their lives delivered gratis, so to speak, by the public sphere, all the raw material for their deeper emotions, for love and hate, for joy and sorrow, but also all their sensations and thrills—accompanied though they might be by poverty, hunger, death, chaos, and peril. Now that these deliveries suddenly ceased, people were

left helpless, impoverished, robbed, and disappointed.
They had never learned to live from within themselves,
how to make an ordinary private life great, beautiful,
and worthwhile, how to enjoy it and make it interesting.
So they regarded the end of the political tension and the
return of private liberty not as a gift, but as a deprivation.

This would not be the case for my father and his *Bildungs-*
bürger family. But most Germans in the half generation Niko
looked up at felt wrong-footed by the postwar era, and that experience scarred and radicalized many of them. Haffner again:

Only a certain cultured class—not particularly small, but
a minority of course—used to find, and still finds, similar
sustenance and pleasure in books and music, in indepen-
dent thought and the creation of a personal "philoso-
phy." ... Outside this cultured class, the great danger of life
in Germany has always been emptiness and boredom. ...
 The menace of monotony hangs, as it has always hung,
over the great plains of northern and eastern Germany,
with their colorless towns and their all too industrious,
efficient, and conscientious businesses and organizations.
With it comes a horror vacui *and the yearning for "salva-*
tion": through alcohol, through superstition or, best of all,
through a vast, overpowering, cheap mass intoxication.

You can apply these words to some of the same parts of Germany today. There, descendants of the people Haffner referred to
find their lives subsumed once more by a menacing monotony.
Fear, hate, or some other base motivation rushes in to fill the
vacui in their lives, and they turn on the thin scattering of immigrants among them.

Haffner believed he knew what accounted for this. "In animals [it] is called 'breeding,'" he wrote. "This is a solid inner kernel that cannot be shaken by external pressures and forces, something noble and steely, a reserve of pride, principle and dignity to be drawn on in the hour of trial. It is missing in the Germans. As a nation they are soft, unreliable, and without backbone."

Albert Einstein also remarked on the "inborn servility" of the German people, and more than three decades before the Nazis' rise to power described his countrymen as being under the spell of *Autoritätsdusel*, a foolish faith in authority that he considered "the worst enemy of truth."

On this, Einstein and Arendt—German exiles turned Americans, one a physicist who sounded an early warning, the other a philosopher who performed a postmortem—agreed. In the end and above all, what matters is truth.

After Günter Demnig, the Berlin artisan who engraves and lays virtually every brass *Stolperstein* himself, learned that his father flew bombing missions during the war, Demnig refused to speak to him for five years.

It never occurred to me to force so pointed a reckoning with my own father. But I find myself hunting for evidence that, given a choice, my ancestors made one I can be proud of. At the same time I'm skeptical of any story that casts some relative in a virtuous light, for each raises the question: Has it survived the years only because it's flattered by the perspective of history?

Maria once told me of her first inkling that something horrific was going on. One day in the late thirties, Hans Albrecht's brother-in-law, then the director of a Munich hospital, came by Hans and Elisabeth's home in an agitated mood. Two SS officers had just brought in a couple of ailing men and insisted on remaining in the operating room for the requisite procedures. He believed the patients were inmates at Dachau, and that the SS was afraid of what they might say under anesthesia.

Maria shared a second story, a kind of bookend to the first. During the fall of 1944 she was driving her mother to the Tegernsee, south of Munich, on a day so warm and clear that they left the top down on the car. Hearing an air-raid siren near Sauerlach, they stopped to take cover in the shade of trees by the roadside. "Suddenly we spotted three men with shaved heads creeping around in the brush," Maria told me. "We called out 'Don't be afraid' in English and French. They told us they had escaped from Dachau."

Hustling the fugitives into their car, they drove off, praying they wouldn't be pulled over. They headed for the nearby home of the widow of a Munich doctor, a woman named Uschi, whom they knew and trusted, because her anti-Nazi sympathies had surfaced during a visit several months earlier, shortly after the abortive attempt on Hitler's life. Uschi fed the escapees and let them bathe before sending them off toward the Swiss border in civilian clothes and with a map.

Or so goes this story passed down to me. "True heroism in such times takes place not only on the battlefields," Helen had written Maria from New York in early 1940, "but works in those souls who still try to live as if there were some eternity, and an accountability to that eternity."

With those words Helen had put Maria on a kind of notice. And my aunt and grandmother seem to have indeed performed an act of bravery and decency that day in the Bavarian countryside. But if I allow myself to feel good that several ancestors bucked the Nazis, how am I to feel upon learning of those who didn't?

When Günter Demnig fields a request for a *Stolperstein*, it's more likely to come from the descendants of perpetrators than the families of victims. This seems to me to be a just and salutary thing. Whether a memorial takes the form of a lone stumbling stone in the sidewalk or a more expansive *Gedenkstätte*, a place of reflection, these impositions of the past unsettle the contemporary conscience. We are raised to regard shame as something to avoid or bury—to not speak about. But shame can be a great animating, activating force if we let it. "Detached from the question of guilt, [shame] seizes anyone who lets themselves be seized," the German scholar, activist, and philanthropist Jan Philipp Reemtsma has written. "To waken and practice consciousness and shame—that is the reason for these monuments."

As I try to construct a frame in which to fit discoveries that lie in wait for me, it's worth considering a few guidelines for what looking back at a Nazi past isn't and is about—or at least ought to be about. For those of us in successor generations, it isn't a matter of collective guilt so much as collective responsibility. And the point of *Vergangenheitsaufarbeitung* isn't just to remember but also to confront and engage and respond. As the political philosopher Susan Neiman puts it in her book *Learning from the Germans: Race and the Memory of Evil*, "You cannot choose your inheritance any more than you can choose your parents. You can only choose your relationship to them."

If only Americans were as scrupulous and imaginative in the excavation of our past. To take up our most shameful historical chapters wouldn't be to perform penance, exactly, for penance, voluntary and self-imposed, usually follows from some sort of personal implication. Germans who today underwrite *Stolpersteine* that memorialize people they never knew are engaging in atonement, an act of repair—but that doesn't fully capture what I have in mind either. To alight on what feels right, it's worth turning over the topsoil around the German word *Erbsünde*, which means both original sin and inherited sin, double duty that highlights the binding of one generation to another. Perhaps there we could find the basis for an American *Erinnerungskultur* (remembrance culture) that puts a current-day frame around a Confederate monument and regards the Stars and Bars as a homegrown swastika.

Since 1993 a museum of and memorial to the Holocaust has stood steps from the Mall in Washington, DC. It's telling that, until the dedication of the Martin Luther King Jr. Memorial in 2011, the US capital had nothing resembling a prominent and standalone *Gedenkstätte* related to slavery and racial violence.

FOUR
MEDITERRANEAN REFUGE
Kurt and Niko, 1931 to 1938

Beginning in 1931, Niko and Maria spent four summers in the south of France, where their father lined up a succession of rentals. It would be their only extended time with Kurt during this span. As the train carrying the Wolff children clattered its way from Munich, cold and order gave way to the sunshine and languor that has long fueled the German yearning for the south. They would use their small fingers to manipulate the signage on the toilet doors, switching VACANT to ENGAGED and delighting in the lines that formed at the ends of the cars. During station stops Niko might get off to run the platform, boarding again only after the train began to move, mortifying their chaperone, their mother's Jewish friend Elisabeth Krämer.

At first their destination wasn't the grandest part of the French Riviera but the more modest Petit Littoral, that coastal stretch anchored by the still-undiscovered fishing port of Saint-Tropez, where Frau Krämer, at right in the photograph, has joined Niko, Helen, and Maria for a swim. The uprooted German Jewish litterateur Sybille Bedford captured the cultural landscape of this patch of meridional France at that time: "The conjunction of the perennial austere beauty of climate and nature—scouring *mistral*, the unfudging sun—with the sweetness and sharpness and quickness, the rippling intelligence, the accommodating

tolerance of the French *manière de vivre* gave one a large sense of living rationally, sensually, *well*. As no other place in Europe, no other place in the world, France between the wars made one this present of the illusion of freedom."

After their mother's fussy domestic standards, Niko and Maria found relief in homes with no running water or electricity, like Le Cabanon, a bungalow set in a vineyard, and the seaside Villa Schlumberger, to which Kurt and Helen brought oil lamps, a hand-cranked gramophone, and a tube radio with a rechargeable lead acid battery. Of the two siblings, one could pull rank as Kurt's favorite. "My father thought Niko illiterate," Maria once told me. "With me he could talk about books and art." And he would take Maria, nearly five foot ten by age

twelve, to the Saint-Tropez Fisherman's Ball, where he ran inter-
ference for her with the men who asked, *Permettez, monsieur?*

My father and his sister, shown here with Kurt in Saint-
Tropez in 1931, spent days free of care, picking figs and paw-
ing through the bonbon bins at the Patisserie Senequier. Outside
the nearby villa La Treille Muscate, they checked the lantern
that glowed green if its occupant, the writer Colette, was receiving visitors and red if she wasn't. Mail would mistakenly arrive
for a German aristocrat named Baron von Wolff, who lived in
a nearby nudist colony, and my grandfather could be counted
on to announce, in a put-upon tone, *Ich muss die Post wieder
den Nudisten zustellen* (I've got to deliver the mail to the nudists

again). For siblings from the steadily Nazifying north, to shuttle across the cleft of a broken home had its compensations.

During their last summer in Saint-Tropez, Niko announced to his astonished father that he had figured out how to drive. Every bit the man of letters, Kurt asked his son to prove it in writing. So Niko, only just twelve, put together an illustrated *Gebrauchsanweisung* (instruction booklet) so thorough that his impressed father might have been tempted to publish it. Behind the wheel of a 1929 Buick four-door convertible, with a spare tire surmounting each running board, Kurt gave his son a place on his lap, and the two set out on the back roads of Provence—until a *gendarme* waved them over.

Niko slid sheepishly on to the shotgun seat.

"He has a hard time seeing over the windshield," Kurt told the policeman preemptively.

"I hope he's not driving."

"Oh, no."

"May I see your driver's license?"

Kurt produced his license. But he also flashed his Friends of the Saint-Tropez Police membership card, and the *gendarme* let them go.

Idyllic though it was, their sojourn in Saint-Tropez did nothing to alter Kurt and Helen's status as *Gesinnungsemigranten*, emigrants of conviction. By the fall of 1933 they had moved east along the coast to La Chiquita, a house in the hills above Nice. There they took in boarders to help cover the rent. My father's half brother Christian was born the following March.

During these years on the lam Kurt auctioned off more books and sold paintings. He stashed liquid assets in banks in Switzerland and England, a hedge that would pay off after the Nazis imposed restrictions on foreign exchange. Whether buying gold or joining organizations like the Friends of the Saint-Tropez

Police, Kurt stayed tuned to a kind of defensive wavelength while keeping an anxious eye on the news.

By the end of 1934, with Italy's fascist government still reasonably independent of Hitler, Kurt and Helen were plotting one more move, to the village of Lastra a Signa outside Florence. In December Kurt wrote Hesse from Nice:

> We cannot remain here, much as we love the house and the countryside. Living here required the presence of paying guests, and although we had a steady stream of them, in the form of German friends, until the fall, the new German currency regulations have prevented them from coming [and spending Reichsmarks] since October. And so we decided to mobilize all our reserves and take advantage of the opportunity to acquire a lovely small property in Tuscany: a house with some good land that will supply us with wine, oil, grain, fruit and vegetables, as well as chickens, eggs, milk, etc. There we hope—Mr. Mussolini and the demons of politics willing—to be able to stay.

Kurt makes himself out to be some back-to-the-lander. In fact, the villa Il Moro, to which they moved in March 1935, included an adjacent *casa colonica* housing a farm family that pulled enough from the property to feed everyone. If an emergency came up, villagers knew they could call on the German in the big house for the use of his car; in return, locals looked out for Kurt and Helen during an unsettled time. Meanwhile Kurt continued to engage in his dalliances. In Italy the Wolffs could take on paying guests again, and Kurt declared to his wife one day that they had on their hands "*ein florierendes Geschäft*," a flourishing business. Helen came right back at him: "Rather more like *ein deflorierendes Geschäft*"—a deflowering business.

Exile did nothing to diminish Kurt's self-image as a grand seigneur who loved to foist high culture on those around him. Willy Haas, one of the original readers from the Kurt Wolff Verlag's Leipzig days, recalled a trip in 1937 to another Wolff rental, this one on that most felicitous of exile landing spots, Elba. Upon meeting Haas at the final train station on the Italian mainland, Kurt demanded to know what his old colleague had seen while passing through Florence.

"I know Florence pretty well," Haas replied.

"Do you know the Castagno frescoes in the Sant'Apollonia?"

"No."

"Then go back to Florence immediately. I'll be here this evening waiting for you."

Haas backtracked and maintained later that he didn't regret it.

As their father and stepmother settled into Italian country life, Niko and Maria learned to look forward to school breaks

Nachweis
der arischen Abstammung
(R. B. Bl. 1933 Seite 88 und 140)

Name	Wolff
Vornamen	Nikolaus Emanuel Karl Emil
Wohnort und Wohnung	München 23 Südliches Schlossrondell
Geburtsort und -Tag	München, 7. Juli 1921
Konfession (auch frühere)	evangelisch
Eltern:	
Name des Vaters	Wolff
Vornamen	Kurt August Paul
Stand und Beruf	Landwirt
Wohnort und Wohnung	Lastra a Signa (Florenz) Italien
Geburtsort und -Tag	Bonn a/ Rhein, 3. März 1887
Sterbeort und -Tag	
Konfession (auch frühere)	evangelisch

and trips to Il Moro, including the visit during which the photograph of my teenage father on the previous page was taken. In the meantime Kurt kept a literary hand in. He prepared the translation of a French text for a Munich publisher, using a pseudonym to keep himself and his client out of trouble. During two weeks in 1935 he hosted the conductor Bruno Walter and his wife, Elsa, as well as Alma Mahler Werfel and her husband, with whom he weighed plans to start an *Exilverlag*. But it became more and more unnerving to live in one fascist country while holding the passport of another, renewable only at the whim of some Nazi.

After the enactment of the Nuremberg Laws in 1935, Kurt and Niko weighed how to secure the *Nachweis der arischen Abstammung*—the certificate of "Aryan" ancestry the regime required of anyone who wanted to remain a German citizen.

Niko's *Nachweis,* pictured opposite and filled out in his father's hand, carries the mark of success. The purple eagle-and-swastika stamp of a Nazi *Amt* on the reverse looks as if it has been affixed yesterday. Kurt indicates his own profession as *Landwirt*, or farmer—no publisher of Jewish authors or patron of "degenerate" artists he. The religion of Niko's paternal grandmother, Kurt's mother, Maria, is listed as *evangelisch*, Protestant, which she claimed by birth to two baptized Christians as well as baptism in her own right. (The parenthetical *auch frühere*, "also earlier," could be an invitation to indicate Maria Marx's Jewish background, but Kurt has pointedly ignored it.) The form, notarized in Munich by a Justizrat Hippler, confirms "that the information contained in the evidence above accords with the content of the corresponding documents submitted to me in original form."

My grandfather's application, just as neatly filled out, survives too. But it was never certified, because it was never submitted. A flurry of letters and forms, mostly from 1937, document Kurt's initial efforts to renew his passport, which was set to expire in November 1938. He signs one letter "*mit deutschem Gruß*," with German greetings, the closest thing to a *Heil Hitler* his dignity would apparently allow. In the end, he and Helen chose to apply for, and secured, French travel documents called *titres de voyage*—"because," Kurt wrote Hasenclever in August 1938, "we both simply don't want the German passport anymore." But he surely knew too that applying to the Nazis for renewal was not a battle to be won, not by someone controversial enough to be suspect for reasons beyond any Jewish ancestry. Several years later, before she would settle with her new husband in Freiburg, Maria was let go from a job at a Munich bookshop. The reason, the proprietor told her, was that her father was *ein Kulturbolschewik*.

At my father's boarding school, *"Mischlinge"* at least had an ally in headmaster Ernst Reisinger. Through 1938, Reisinger used the *mit deutschem Gruß* dodge in official communications, including several invitations to Parents' Day that I unearth. Only in 1939 did he begin to employ *Heil Hitler!* My father remembered Reisinger making tactical compromises to retain influence with the authorities, including a high-ranking local Nazi official, the husband of the school's piano instructor. The Schondorf headmaster did so, Niko told me, to protect "first-degree *Mischlinge*" like Ursula Lange, a student one grade ahead of my father who would marry his first cousin Emanuel Merck after the war.

How one "identifies" is a personal prerogative, a choice we regard today as reserved for every individual. But this photograph, taken at Schondorf during the late thirties, reminds me that, in Germany under Nazi rule, *to identify* was a verb deployed

not in the active sense but the passive. Then and there, you *were identified*. To do the identifying, party bureaucrats could access centuries of civil and ecclesiastical records and trot out crude charts and calipers to back up any judgment they cared to make. Niko stands in the middle at the back here, his dark and curly hair bobbing in a sea of towheads. Did classmates and teachers fully accept him? Or, *Nachweis* notwithstanding, did they regard him as having a secret to keep? To see him as so striking an outsider invites me to consider his and Kurt's and my own Jewish roots. And to do that leads back to the imperiled status of the German Jew long before the Holocaust. The tighter he embraced his Germanness, the more acutely he was made to feel his Jewishness.

I pay a visit to the Jewish Museum Berlin, a labyrinth of canted corridors and disorienting spaces that architect Daniel Libeskind designed to look from above like a shattered Star of David. The permanent exhibition, with its broad focus on the history of German Jewry, fills in the backstory. At the beginning of the nineteenth century, Germany could count only a few hundred thousand Jews, most of them poor and uneducated. Yet some had become prosperous, like the ancestors of Kurt's mother, Maria Marx, and these arrivistes tended to live in cities, where they could integrate themselves into the cultural life to be found there. Excluded from university professorships and denied commissions in the military or civil service, ambitious German Jewish men instead practiced law or medicine, or became merchants, engineers, or entrepreneurs. And to improve prospects for themselves and their children, many adult Jews converted to Christianity. Most of these converts didn't pray to a Catholic or Protestant god so much as the Enlightenment polestars of reason and humankind, and thus made the library, museum, and concert hall their houses of worship. Many well-to-do Germans of Jewish ancestry could recite by heart passages from Goethe, who had endorsed the malleability of faith and the supremacy of *Bildung* with his declaration, "He who possesses art and science has religion; he who does not possess them needs religion."

My ancestors were among the roughly twenty-two thousand German Jews who chose to convert during the nineteenth century. My great-great-grandfather August Karl Ludwig Marx was baptized in 1837, as a fifteen-year-old, although he would go on to donate much of his wealth, accumulated as a civil engineer and mining and railroad baron, to Jewish charities. August married another convert, his first cousin Bertha Isabella, the daughter of a doctor and art and book collector, who with his wife had cultivated friendships with the families of Goethe and Arthur Schopenhauer—the evidence of which Kurt had stumbled upon as a teenager while visiting his grandmother. Bertha's own parents were first cousins too, descended from several generations of prominent Jewish Rhinelanders. In addition to serving as a health administrator for the city of Bonn, Bertha's father owned part of the railroad line that ran between the city and Koblenz.

The phrase "baptized Jew" is among the most striking things I encounter while walking the halls of the Jewish Museum. By modern and secular lights, a Jew who chooses to convert would no longer be considered Jewish. As it happens, rabbinical law and Nazi ideology both hold that a child born to a Jewish mother is a Jew, regardless of any subsequent event. And the persistence of the epithet "baptized Jew" in nineteenth-century Germany shows how conversion from Judaism hardly made it socially so. The writer Heinrich Heine, who grew up in the Rhineland as Harry Heine, once vowed never to convert, yet in 1825 did so in hopes of purchasing what he called "the admission ticket into

European culture." He came to bitterly regret having "crawled to the cross," for it left him "hated by Christian and Jew alike." Heine embodied a paradox that the German Jew came to know well. To be "the arriviste who never arrived" left him "mocked by the elites, vilified by the rabble," writes the German-born historian Fritz Stern, himself the son of "baptized Jews" who escaped to the United States before the war. "Lamentable efforts at being accepted made him the object of backstage malice. . . . [And] his putative power made him the ideal target for the rising anti-Semitism of the 1870s."

For all the complications this duality posed in the private realm, its effect on public life would be dazzling. Germans of Jewish descent accounted for an outsize portion of the culture for which the nation would earn renown. By the middle of the twentieth century they had achieved distinction in the sciences (Albert Einstein, Paul Ehrlich, Fritz Haber, Richard Willstätter, Nobel Prize winners all); music (Felix Mendelssohn-Bartholdy, Arnold Schoenberg, Kurt Weill); philosophy (Hannah Arendt, Theodor Lessing, Moses Mendelssohn—the composer's grandfather); and literature (from the Kurt Wolff catalog alone, Else Lasker-Schüler, Walter Mehring, Carl Sternheim, and Arnold Zweig, as well as writers with roots in Vienna or Prague like Kafka, Kraus, Roth, and Werfel). Yet, amidst the nativism, militarism, and Christianity-infused nationalism that would carry Germany off into three successive wars of aggression, German Jewish accomplishments touched off resentment. Antisemitism draws strength from stigmatization of the alien "other"; in nineteenth-century Germany, it also fed off a desire to punish Jews for their prosperity and acculturation, regardless of what they might have contributed or overcome.

Kurt's ancestors on his mother's side, men like Salomon and Moritz von Haber, traced precisely this kind of bootstrapping but perilous path. The first to settle in Germany were rabbis from Bohemia, Galicia, and Italy. One, who became the chief rabbi of Trier, was also a forebear of the social theorist and *Communist Manifesto* author Karl Marx. During the eighteenth century another Jewish ancestor, a Jesuit-educated doctor named Moses Wolff (unrelated to Kurt's Protestant, paternal Wolff forebears), served as personal physician to Clemens August and Maximilian Friedrich, two of the Rhineland electors who chose the Holy Roman emperor. Ancestors like Moses Wolff sat on local Jewish boards and councils. At the same time, their prosperity and collections of paintings and books signaled how invested they were in German society and culture.

Yet even the most distinguished German Jews of the eighteenth and nineteenth centuries lived precarious lives, as the trials of Salomon and Moritz bear out. And now here was Kurt, on the run, as vulnerable as any von Haber.

FIVE
SURRENDER ON DEMAND
Kurt, 1938 to 1941

B y mid-1938, "Mr. Mussolini and the demons of politics" had their own plans. Italy was now too dangerous for a *Kultur-bolschewik* of Jewish descent. After a visit from Hitler that spring, Mussolini ramped up actions against German exiles and Jews. On a tip, Kurt, Helen, and Christian left Lastra a Signa for France with twenty-four hours' notice, carrying nothing more than two suitcases. To judge by Kurt's diary, the relocation came amidst an ambient melancholy: *Newspaper depressing.... Rain, sad, many letters; afternoon: packing and cemetery.... Departure for Nice.* "We cannot and do not want to return to Italy," Kurt later wrote a German friend who was safely in the United States. "On top of that, I'm without a passport at the moment (I applied for renewal six months ago, but have as yet received no answer), and to live in Italy without one is impossible, as you'll be returned to your country of origin."

In Nice the Wolffs took an apartment on the rue Maréchal Joffre. Joining them there was Luise Marx, Kurt's aunt and step-mother, who shared the Jewish lineage of her late sister Maria Marx Wolff. Luise, whom my father knew as Oma Lullu, had married Leonhard Wolff shortly after Maria's death in 1904 and had been living a widow's life in Bonn since Leonhard died in 1934.

The onset of fall did nothing to buoy Kurt's mood. *Worried about war*, reports his diary for September 9. September 10 and 11: *Worries about war*. September 12–18: *Danger of war*. On September 29, in French, he noted what he may have thought was a brief brightening: "*Les 4 à Munich—accord.*" But Kurt needed only to look at his expiring passport, shown here, to be reminded that he had now cast his lot with another country.

Over the next several months his diary records an anxious and peripatetic existence punctuated by a tragedy. A November visit to the American consulate, where he had hoped to pick up visas, was unavailing. On Kristallnacht, Elisabeth Krämer, Niko and Maria's railway chaperone of a few years earlier, commited suicide with her husband back in Munich. Upon learning that the Gestapo was coming to arrest them, she had swallowed a cyanide capsule; her husband, Emil, legal counsel for Aufhäuser Bank, did so too, but because of an upset stomach the pill failed to stay

down—so, writhing with cramps, he jumped out an upper window of their apartment.

My grandmother showed up the next day to find Gestapo agents on the scene and the Krämers' home already emptied of its contents. "I heard my friends are dead," she told them. They took down her name.

By the spring of 1939, Kurt had moved with Helen and Christian to Paris, to an apartment across from Notre-Dame and overlooking the Seine. Helen found work there with a British publisher, but Kurt could land little more than the occasional freelance assignment. One piece, a December 1939 review of Thomas Mann's *Lotte in Weimar* for a Paris-based German-exile newspaper, reads like therapy, an exercise in working through his own circumstances:

> Habent sua fata libelli [Books have their destiny]: *Written on the shores of Lake Zurich and in southern France, in the cabin of an ocean liner and in an American college town, excerpted in a Swiss magazine, printed in Holland, graced with cover art by an illustrator from Prague, published (by Bermann-Fischer) in Stockholm—can the story of a book possibly be any more "far-flung," any more grotesque a reflection of the diaspora of German intellectual life in our time? Yet no work by Thomas Mann is less distended than this, none more collected, more dense, more imposing, and we bow in awe before the moral achievement of this writer, who in times like these has created a work that so supremely captures the era. For* Lotte in Weimar *is a book of the highest relevance, a book that stands as a radiant and persuasive monument to the German genius, a book to tell the world of the stakes that Europe fights for today.*

And then, as noted in Kurt's diary on September 1, 1939: *0545h Hitler Angriff gegen Polen*. With the German invasion of Poland, everything changed. Despite the Wolffs' anti-fascist credentials and Nice-born son, the French government now regarded Kurt and Helen as enemy aliens. On September 16 police interned Kurt at the Stade de Colombes. Only the intervention of Wladimir d'Ormesson, the brother of a friend who had served as France's chargé d'affaires in Munich, secured his release three weeks later. During Kurt's internment, Helen decided to send my uncle Christian, then five, as far from the Nazi threat as possible. Not willing to risk leaving Paris herself, she called on a neighbor, a Madame Bouty, to escort him west on a train to a convent school in La Rochelle, where France runs into the sea.

By now the so-called *Sitzkrieg* (known in English as the "phony war") had begun, with France and Britain bracing for the inevitable German attack. Through the French playwright and former diplomat Jean Giraudoux, Kurt and Helen had found work with the Ministry of Information, preparing propaganda leaflets to be dropped over those parts of Germany within range of French aircraft. "The only thing we lack is the freedom to travel, which could reunite us with our friends, in particular with you," Kurt wrote his daughter in Munich at the end of April 1940. "But after all, in such times you can't have everything—and it's of course our wish and hope that freedom will return to us and doesn't take too long to do so."

Days later the phony war went real, and the Wehrmacht easily circumvented the Maginot Line. "*Einfall Belgien, Holland*," reads Kurt's diary for May 10—invasion of Belgium and Holland. As Germans who had taken part in the hostile leafleting of German territory, Kurt and Helen knew the stakes if they were to be caught. Under the threat of *Sippenhaft*, a medieval Germanic custom that the Third Reich would invoke to hold all blood relatives responsible for the crimes of any individual, their actions also jeopardized Niko and Maria, as well as Helen's sister Liesl and her family, back in Germany. From two friends, professors of German at French universities, Kurt and Helen exacted a promise: if the Nazis make it to Paris and we're still here, come shoot us so we can't fall into their hands.

Around this time Kurt bought two gold bars and stashed them with one of those professors, Albert Fuchs, a French citizen who taught at the University of Strasbourg.

With the German breakthrough at Sedan on May 15, French authorities interned Kurt again and soon detained Helen too—he first at the Stade de Buffalo in Paris, then at camps in Chambaran and Le Cheylard in the southeast; she at the Vélodrome d'Hiver in the capital before transfer to the Gurs internment camp in the southwest. But these second detentions turned out to be strokes of fortune, for they ensured that both were clear of Paris when the Wehrmacht took the city on June 14.

Only ten days after Helen arrived in Gurs, France formally capitulated, signing an armistice with the Germans that left her free to go. But this was a mixed blessing, for the deal obliged the new, collaborationist Vichy government to "surrender on demand" anyone the Nazis wanted. In the meantime Christian remained at the convent in La Rochelle, and the last Helen knew, her husband was still interned at Le Cheylard. What to do?

Acting on a tip from a fellow Gurs internee, the German painter Anne-Marie Uhde, Helen set out on foot in the vague direction of what would turn out to be a phantasmagoric kind of sanctuary. An anti-Nazi angel, a Habsburg countess, was said to be sheltering the hunted and homeless somewhere in the foothills of the Pyrenees. Feeling her way east along roads paralleling the mountains, Helen hitched a ride with a French military vehicle. When it ran out of gas, she boarded a bus for a village called

Saint-Lary. From there she hiked several kilometers more and, after walking up a narrow, winding road, stopped in her tracks. In front of a medieval château, hewn of yellowing stone and hung with ivy, stood a striking woman, perhaps fifty years old and at least six feet tall, conversing with a knot of French officers.

Several years later Helen would record her first encounter with the Countess Bertha Colloredo-Mansfeld, née Kolowrat-Krakowsky: "When she saw me, she came over with the swift, vigorous step of an Amazon, glanced me up and down, gave me a quick smile and said, 'Thank God, you have an intelligent face. I will enjoy talking to you. But what you need now is a meal, a bath, and a bed.'"

Helen was led into the château and found herself gazing out at a garden from beneath the Gothic arch of a window.

Against a solid wall of intertwined, century-old cypresses stood a multitude of many-colored shrubs and flowers in full bloom. The whole place, inside and out, was such a miracle of beauty and color that it lifted me completely out of the misery of defeat and flight. I blessed the person who was at the core of that miracle and, instead of going to bed, followed the Countess around all afternoon. This was my first and probably unique chance to observe an obsolete remnant of the past: a true, un-degenerate aristocrat in full function.

The Countess adopted me as naturally as if I were a stray cat. In fact, I could make myself useful as a kind of lady-in-waiting, and had a full-time job warding off the numerous French officers in search of romance. One of them commented sentimentally on the color of her dress, chosen, as he suggested, to set off in its ultimate perfection the color of her eyes. She crushed him for the time being with the answer: "That was exactly what I had in mind this morning, after reading the conditions of the armistice."

She spoke Polish with the Pole who cared for the horses, Italian with her farmers, Czech with her maid, and Russian with her foreman. When she heard that I had lost on the road what clothes I had been able to take along on the flight, she took me to the diminutive village adjacent to the castle grounds. Here she housed a Spanish seamstress, come to this place in some inexplicable manner during the civil war in Spain. After four years she was still there, sewing for the whole community, from the Countess' costumes to the workmen's overalls. Mercedes was told in Spanish to make me a complete outfit in the shortest possible time.

The Countess Colloredo-Mansfeld had been raised by an heiress to a cigarette fortune and a Habsburg count who had survived the last fatal duel of the Austro-Hungarian Empire. As a girl, course-correcting a classical education with her own strong will, she had read *Uncle Tom's Cabin* and become inflamed with a spirit of racial justice. In fact, she had taken possession of this château for having acted on those beliefs in the most socially transgressive possible way.

During the early twenties, the countess had become muse to Roland Hayes, the African American tenor then touring the concert halls of Europe, pictured overleaf alongside his patroness. As each got to know the other, she shared with Hayes her broad knowledge of literature and the arts; he in turn credited her with unlocking a sensibility he hadn't realized he had. During long stretches apart they exchanged letters, and in one the countess, who had come to idealize the harmonious blending of the races, wrote, "we must have a child together" — as she would later

put it—"to bring a new light to humanity." In 1925 she informed her husband, Count Hieronymus Colloredo-Mansfeld, that she was carrying Hayes's baby. After processing his anger, the count bought and renovated this château, gifted it to her, and supported her with a regular allowance, to keep his now estranged wife and the daughter she would bear as far from the light of scandal as possible.

That affair did more than certify the countess's anti-Nazi bona fides. It positioned her in those hills outside Toulouse to shelter many strays besides my fugitive step-grandmother: an Austrian whose legs and teeth had been shattered during two years in a concentration camp; a mother from Brittany with a four-year-old in tow; a Romanian soothsayer who kept his divining rod in a Cuban cigar box; and countless Russian refugees, most of them veterans of the Spanish Civil War who had fled over the Pyrenees. One, a former Soviet general's orderly, ended up marrying Maya, the daughter of Bertha Colloredo-Mansfeld and Roland Hayes.

"If I ever figure things out beforehand, nothing would work out," the countess told Helen of her management style. "My head would interfere with my heart. How could I feed and clothe all these people on a budget?"

Now with a temporary address, Helen sent word to a family friend in Switzerland. Kurt, also free now, thanks to the deal struck between the Nazis and the Vichy French, reached out to him too. The friend, the pacifist classical scholar Baron Kurd von Hardt, forwarded to Kurt the location of the château and let Helen know he had done so. Thus, as Helen would recall, "I sat waiting for him, like a damsel in a castle, looking down the only road. And one day I saw him coming up that road."

"I could have stayed there forever," Helen said later. But as much as my grandfather could learn to love château life, he had a healthy understanding of larger circumstances. Knowing the dark heart of the Vichy regime, and fearing the Nazis would soon occupy all of France, he insisted that they quickly find a way out. As Helen would later say, "We had to go someplace we would want to leave . . . near an American consulate." By the second week of August they were back at the apartment in Nice, reunited with Kurt's aunt and stepmother, Lullu.

They still had to spring Christian from La Rochelle, which had since come under German occupation. Here they connected with Tina Vinès, a Parisian friend who worked at the Louvre. Because her duties included evacuating the museum's treasures from the capital—she might stash a painting in this château or a vase in that cloister—Vinès carried papers that allowed her free passage between the Nazi-occupied and the Vichy zones. She agreed to fetch Christian from the convent and deliver him to Nice. The two wound up spending a night in a château in the Loire valley, where Christian slept in a bed he recalls being told had once belonged to Talleyrand. The next day the two simply walked into unoccupied France, smuggling Christian's belongings in the handcart of a farmer on his way to market. Shortly after ten p.m. on September 6, they appeared at the apartment on the rue Maréchal Joffre.

The clause in the armistice that mandated "surrender on demand" struck fear in Kurt and Helen and every refugee in France. It also led to the formation in New York of the Emergency Rescue Committee (ERC), which quickly sent to the unoccupied zone an idealistic thirty-one-year-old Harvard-educated journalist named Varian Fry. Working out of a succession of quarters in Marseille—a hotel room, a second-floor office, a tumbledown villa on the outskirts of the city—Fry helped save as many as two thousand people, most of them artists, writers, thinkers, and other cultural enemies of the Nazis. Sometimes Fry, shown here on a station platform in the French border town of Cerbère, bought visas on the black market. Sometimes he had them forged. Always he battled recalcitrant bureaucracies, including the State Department of his own country and its ingrained antisemitism—although an American vice-consul in Marseille, a former theology student named Hiram (Harry) Bingham IV, would defy orders from Washington and issue life-saving documents off the books. "Like the first bird note of a gloomy morning a rumor ran through the cafés of the *vieux port* and Canebière," wrote Hans Natonek, a Czech journalist Fry would save. "It was said that an American had arrived with the funds and the will to help. It was another distraction in a city in which black-market operators sold hysterical men berths on ships which did not exist to ports which, in any case, would have denied them entry. But the rumor persisted and grew. It was said that this American had a list. . . . The word 'list' electrified us."

The ERC's stateside allies included academics, philanthropists, various labor and anti-fascist organizations, and First Lady Eleanor Roosevelt, as well as escapees who, after making it to the United States, refused to forget those left behind. Fry found himself in and out of trouble as the French tried to mollify their Nazi overlords, and he would be expelled for good after only thirteen months. But by then the ERC had helped such figures as Hannah Arendt, Marc Chagall, Marcel Duchamp, and Max Ernst escape from Vichy France. On September 13, 1940, a Friday the thirteenth, Fry personally escorted Kurt's old authors Franz Werfel and Heinrich Mann—as well as Franz's wife, Alma, and Heinrich's wife, Nelly, and nephew Golo, the son of Thomas Mann—to a rendezvous with a guide at the trailhead of a path leading over the Pyrenees. That evening Fry met them all for dinner in Spain, where he handed over their luggage, which he had taken undisturbed over the border by train.

Fry and his network would soon extend help to Kurt and Helen directly.

Refugees trying to get out of France might have been trapped in one of Kafka's stories. They needed a "safe conduct" pass to cross territory under Vichy control. They needed a French exit visa, which the collaborationists weren't granting to Jews or anyone likely to be sought by the Gestapo. They needed transit visas for every sovereign way station between origin and ultimate destination. And of course there was the holy grail, the US entrance visa. To secure any one document seemed contingent on first having all others in hand.

From Nice on August 27, my grandfather wrote to Fry, then freshly arrived in Marseille—"a romantic, dirty, hard-edged city," as Fry's biographer Andy Marino describes it, "the Casablanca of the northern shore." Kurt asked after the simplest way forward: an "emergency visitor's visa" from the US State Department. Helen seems not to have given his English a polishing, but as a result the letter crackles with urgency:

> My publishing house has been during long years the most active center of democratic German literature, as my American colleagues will be able to confirm, f.i. Mr. A. Knopf, New York, who has edited many of my publications in USA. Of the long list of my authors I mention: Heinrich Mann – Franz Werfel – Gustav Meyrink – René Schickele – Karl Kraus – Romain Rolland etc. I have also published a series of American authors, amongst others Sinclair Lewis. Eighty percent of my production was burnt by the Nazis and my publishing house put on a black list. It is not only on account of my former activity as publisher, that I feel

*myself menaced, but for other reasons which I prefer not
to mention by letter.*

Among the unmentionable reasons Kurt feels endangered is
his work for the French Ministry of Information, which would
seal his fate if he were to fall into the hands of the Gestapo. His
rave review of *Lotte in Weimar*, published in that journal for
German exiles, wouldn't have escaped the Nazis' notice either.

Kurt had no way of knowing, but he and Helen were on the
Emergency Rescue Committee's list of Europeans to help, which
Fry had taped to a leg beneath his trousers before boarding a Pan
Am Clipper for France earlier that month. Two weeks after writing his letter, Kurt received a telegram from the ERC in Manhattan, asking for information about Helen and Christian. A week
after that, two requisite affidavits turned up at the ERC's office on
East Forty-Second Street. One, of sponsorship, came from Thea
Dispeker, the heiress to a Jewish banking family in Munich and an
old flame of Kurt's. She had been a music educator in Berlin and,
since fleeing to New York in 1938, had been working as an agent
for classical musicians. In Berlin in February 1933, Kurt had given
her a simple gold bracelet as a parting gift, with as much practical
as sentimental intent: he told her to pawn it if she had to.

The other affidavit, of support, came from Dispeker's friend
Robert Weinberg, a New York architect and urban planner who
had vouched for so many refugees that he feared his endorsements had begun to arouse suspicion. To the ERC, Dispeker
made sure to mention Kurt and Helen's work for the French,
which placed them, as she put it, "in imminent danger." On September 20, ERC executive secretary Mildred Adams wrote the
President's Advisory Committee on Political Refugees to urge
action on their case.

For the remainder of the fall, holed up on the rue Maréchal Joffre, Kurt heard nothing. From time to time he wrote Fry to recommend other candidates for the ERC's support, using each letter as a chance to nudge along his own application. In the meantime he sent word to Professor Fuchs, who traveled to Nice to deliver the two gold bars, which Kurt exchanged for enough cash to underwrite an Atlantic crossing for three. In November he attended a funeral service for Walter Hasenclever, who five months earlier had killed himself in Les Milles, a Vichy internment camp near Aix-en-Provence, with an overdose of Veronal.

Between Christmas and New Year's, after enervating weeks of waiting, the US visas finally came through. There followed on January 10 the "safe conduct" passes to get them to the Spanish border, and finally, most critically, on February 6, the French exit visas. Shortly after Christian's birth in Nice in 1934, Kurt and Helen had had the good sense to appear with their son at the *hôtel de ville* to have him registered as a French citizen. Their son's status had likely helped them secure French identity documents in 1938; years later his mother theorized that only a seven-year-old French-born boy could induce the Vichy bureaucracy to take mercy on all three of them. "The idea was that a French child needs his parents, and we declared our loyalty to France through him," Helen said. "So, in a sense, our son may have saved our lives."

Several times over these weeks the word *nervös* appears in Kurt's diary. Shortly before their departure, he wired Fry what was left in his French bank account—50,000 francs, a little more than $1,000. The ERC wasn't accustomed to its desperate clients fronting the cost of their passage. Fry responded with thanks, "particularly at a time when we must dedicate our support to so many others in need."

The Wolffs left Nice early on February 9 to allow for a lay-over in Marseille, where Fry saw them off at the station for their onward trip to Toulouse. The next day they reached the border at Canfranc. As soon as the train crossed into Spain, they began to see roofless buildings and charred fields, the aftermath of the civil war. First a late-winter storm, then several days' delay before they could find seats between Madrid and Lisbon, turned their railroad journey into a weeklong ordeal.

From Madrid, Helen sent a postcard, depicting a Diego Velázquez painting in the Prado, to "Señorita Maria Wolff" back in Munich. The card turned up bearing the censor's stamps of two fascist regimes, with the mark of the Spanish authorities defacing Velázquez's rendering of the body of the crucified Christ. Vague though the text on the back was, the card and postmark made clear to Maria that her father and stepmother had reached neutral Spain. Next stop Lisbon.

Of all the advantages to cascade my way—white, male, goy, firstborn, only son, birthright American, upper-middle-class upbringing, Ivy League legatee—few served me better than the grace from which so many good things followed: that, seventeen years before my birth, my grandfather found a place on Varian Fry's list.

Every ship leaving Europe then was an ark, Erich Maria Remarque wrote in his novel *The Night in Lisbon*, with the Americas a remote, beckoning Ararat.

> *The flood waters were rising higher by the day. . . . The coast of Portugal had become the last hope of the fugitives to whom justice, freedom, and tolerance meant more than home and livelihood. This was the gate to America. If you couldn't reach it, you were lost, condemned to bleed*

> *away in a jungle of consulates, police stations, and gov-*
> *ernment offices, where visas were refused and work and*
> *residence permits unattainable, a jungle of internment*
> *camps, bureaucratic red tape, loneliness, homesickness,*
> *and withering, universal indifference.*

Sometimes that jungle concealed a snare. It might take the form of fedora-wearing agents of the Gestapo, known to kidnap their marks off the streets of the Portuguese capital. Or it might be a more prosaic glitch: Kurt and Helen discovered that their ship's cabin—the one for which Kurt had wired those 50,000 francs—hadn't been booked. Further, the immigrant aid group working with the ERC counted only $625 in Kurt's name on account, far less than the cost of passage for three. A contracted ship wasn't due to sail for several months, and by then their visas would be invalid. Only with a flurry of cables to friends was Kurt able to borrow the necessary $1,000 more. He somehow found berths on a Portuguese ship called the *Serpa Pinto*. *Tickets geholt bei Carlos*, reads his diary for March 13—"fetched tickets from Carlos." For a cabin he had coughed up an extortionate $1,594, or more than $28,000 in latter-day dollars.

The *Serpa Pinto* left Lisbon on March 15, 1941, with 637 other passengers, well over capacity. Christian suffered from whooping cough, so his parents ordered him to keep his mouth shut, hurried him up the gangplank, and kept him in their cabin until the ship was well out to sea. For the duration of the trip the crew lit up the funnel and masts to signal neutrality and warn off U-boats menacing the North Atlantic.

Allowing for a three-day stopover in Bermuda, the cross-ing took two weeks. The *Serpa Pinto* docked at Stapleton, Staten Island, on March 31. *Disembarked 10 o'clock*, Kurt noted in his diary. *Glorious weather.*

Decades later one of Helen's authors, Umberto Eco, would liken the Wolffs' flight to "a novel, with a *Casablanca*-like ending." But a screenwriter simply writes things and so they will be. Here their fates had hung on the interventions of a host of earthly angels: Wladimir d'Ormesson, the French diplomat. The Parisian neighbor and child escort No. 1, Madame Bouty. Jean Giraudoux, playwright and government minister. Helen's fellow internee at Gurs, Anne-Marie Uhde. Countess Colloredo-Mansfeld. Baron Kurd von Hardt. The Louvre employee and child escort No. 2, Tina Vinès. Professor Albert Fuchs. Varian Fry. Thea Dispeker—a woman who would eventually play an existential role in my own life—as well as her friend Robert Weinberg, who didn't know Kurt and Helen from Adam or Eve. "Carlos."

Some of these people already counted the Wolffs as friends. Most did not. It took a daisy chain of kindnesses and gallantries, some performed in blind faith and many at great risk, to land them in New York.

Among the figures Varian Fry saved was the German writer Anna Seghers, who in 1941 fled through Lisbon with her husband and their two children. Soon after arriving in Mexico, Seghers wrote *Transit*, a novel inspired by her weeks in Marseille as an émigré-in-waiting. Her story, spun around a love triangle and a case of mistaken identity, is a tragic portrait of the *apatrides* and the French port into which they have been herded. When not condemned to the waiting rooms of the city's consulates, refugees pass time in its cafés and pizzerias, watching "people being disgorged by the revolving door," Seghers writes, "as if it were a mill that was grinding them, body and soul, dozens of times daily."

The Berlin International Film Festival is premiering German director Christian Petzold's adaptation of *Transit*, which turns out to be faithful to the novel's fleeting alliances and easy betrayals. The movie holds in almost perfect balance boredom and fear, emotions rarely treated in tandem. But Petzold retrofits the story for today's moment, overlaying Seghers's wartime characters and plot on a latter-day Marseille. There's not a smartphone or computer terminal to be seen, and passports and visas come thoroughly analog—but to learn when a consular official will finally see them, refugees wasting away in the lobby, wearing forties-style seersucker suits and big hats and clutching period valises, keep an eye on one of those take-a-number LED displays you'd find hung on the wall of a modern bank or travel bureau. People seize up at the sound of twenty-first-century sirens or the sight of police in modern riot gear, knowing that the improperly papered will be dragged away or, to maintain some control over their fate, take their own lives.

In *Transit*, the ostensible space to be transited is the linear gap between besieged France and the Americas to which everyone is desperate to flee. But it's the diminished y-axis transit space, between past and present, that the director highlights with his adaptation. Petzold has telescoped the Marseille of then and now into a single look, buffeting it with a *mistral* of timelessness, to insist on comparisons across the years. For every frustrated visa applicant in wartime Marseille we're forced to consider an asylum seeker turned away today. Petzold doesn't toggle between time periods. He considers the moment too urgent for that. Instead, he collapses them.

An S-Bahn and a bus take me to the villa where, one morning in January 1942, fifteen officials of the Third Reich decided how to carry out the Final Solution. In a first-floor room overlooking the Wannsee, on the spot where those Nazis enjoyed coffee and rolls, curators have laid out in a glass case the cold-blooded minutes of that meeting.

Here the Nazis discussed the "problem" of "the *Mischlinge*." By leaving intact the Nuremberg Law that exempted Germans with one grandparent of Jewish descent from the worst consequences, they confirmed at least for the moment that my father's life would be spared. Here too they listened as the *SS-Obergruppenführer* Reinhard Heydrich spoke of "our new prospects in the east," a nod to the barren landscapes my father would capture in sepia photographs he sent home from the steppe. Poland, Ukraine, and the western reaches of the Soviet Union featured that "menacing monotony" of Sebastian Haffner's description, a vastness that now seemed to promise impunity.

By the end of the following year, many Germans would have at least a sense of what had been decided at the Wannsee Conference. Home on leave, soldiers talked. "Event reports" (*Ereignismeldungen*) sent back to Berlin by Waffen-SS "task forces" (*Einsatzgruppen*) filtered down to mid-level bureaucrats. It's impossible to seize, transfer, and exterminate millions of people, and expropriate and dispose of their homes and belongings, without engaging substantial numbers of civilians—railway clerks, real-estate agents, middlemen.

When Goebbels spoke of the Jews during a February 1943 speech in which he called on Germans to commit to "total war," the propaganda minister went a couple of syllables into the word "extermination" (*Ausrottung*) before catching himself and pledging simply their "exclusion" (*Ausschaltung*). But rather than misleading his audience, Goebbels was calculatedly implicating everyone who heard him that day. Of all the regime's means of social control, this may have been the most insidious: by the middle of the war the Nazi leadership had let the German people in on just enough to make sure they knew that to lose—to submit to victor's justice—would lead to a fate so grave that under no circumstances would they be able to surrender. Civilians shared the open secret that they knew enough, in the words of historian David Bankier, "to know that it was better not to know more." The reluctance of so many of today's Germans to court pity for their ancestors' suffering, to invoke the Allied bombings and postwar expulsions, is a kind of tacit acknowledgment of how many knew of the Nazi atrocities at the time. To forgo sympathy was a consequence of Germany's shame.

I had come out to the Wannsee believing that only members of Ordnungspolizei (Order Police) units and the Waffen-SS carried out the Final Solution where my father served. And then a panel in one of the villa's downstairs exhibition rooms stopped me cold.

> *The Wehrmacht also participated directly in the persecution and murder of Soviet Jews. The military administration was behind the listing and compulsory identification of Jews and the establishment of ghettos. In addition, it decided on the fate of prisoners of war and was frequently responsible for assigning Jews as forced laborers. Wehrmacht units frequently provided logistical and administrative support for the mass murder and also carried out their own shootings, albeit not on the same scale as the murder squads of the SS and police.*

It turns out that in 1995—unbeknownst to me, and likely also to my by-then thoroughly Americanized father—Germans had finally been forced to confront a long-standing myth: that only units of the SS and the Order Police committed Nazi atrocities. This reckoning came with the *Wehrmachtsausstellung*

(Wehrmacht exhibition), an installation staged by the Hamburg Institute for Social Research, which featured photographs and letters sent home from the front that implicated ordinary soldiers in abuses much graver and more extensive than popular memory let on. The exhibit and its message did not go down well. In Munich, five thousand Germans marched with signs like DEUTSCHE SOLDATEN, HELDEN TATEN (GERMAN SOLDIERS, HEROIC DEEDS). But twice as many counterdemonstrators turned out, and the Wehrmacht exhibition marked the beginning of the slow but steady process of modern Germany fusing its conception of World War II with its conception of the Holocaust.

At the time of the Germans' invasion of the Soviet Union, my father was a grunt, barely twenty-one. He drove a truck, delivering maps and photographs, as he told me and his letters home attest. He was in some oblivious limbo, I'd long wanted to reassure myself, neither directly involved in atrocities in the east nor party to the dawning awareness of them back home. But he had been in Ukraine, an occupying soldier taking and following orders. What those orders might have included, I now knew.

There's a German word, *Lebenslüge*, that means "life-giving lie." It refers to the self-deception that permits one to carry on under the shroud of some grave implication. I will never be able to inventory all that my father knew or when he knew it or to measure the full weight of the war on his conscience. He told me only up to a point, at least the point to which I asked. But Günter Grass addressed this subject in his 2006 memoir, and I wonder whether Grass's words capture how my father felt. "The ignorance I claim could not blind me to the fact that I had been conscripted into a system that had planned, organized, and carried out the extermination of millions of people," Grass wrote. "Even if I could not be accused of active complicity, there remains to this day a residue that is all too commonly called joint responsibility. I will have to live with it for the rest of my life."

As a family we go to the Berliner Ensemble, Brecht's old theater along the Spree, for a stage adaptation of *The Tin Drum*, the Grass novel that Kurt and Helen acquired in translation for Pantheon Books in 1959. For nearly two hours a single actor will stand before us as Oskar Matzerath, the *enfant terrible* of German literature—a boy born in 1924 who vows on his third birthday to stop growing, and instead shrieks and drums when his elders prefer silence.

The twenty-seven-euro ticket would have been worth it if we had seen no more than the production's first thirty seconds. No curtain went up. For the moment, no house lights went down either. The actor playing Oskar simply took several steps out from the wings. Then, lit by a gradually intensifying spotlight, he glared at us. The audience continued to babble. Oskar continued to glare. Only slowly did we begin to quiet ourselves and, finally, fall silent.

In the space of those moments, subjected to that look of indictment, I could feel the full force of an inquisition, as if we had been transported back to the sixties and everyone in that theater now had a younger generation to answer to.

In a few hours I would walk out on the riverside promenade and resume my role as a son posing questions. But for now a perpetual three-year-old had turned the tables, making elders of us all, as if to ask, What had *we* known? When had *we* known it?

SIX
INTO A DARK ROOM
Niko, 1939 to 1941

W orld War II broke out—*Hitler Angriff gegen Polen*, in the words of Kurt's diary—just as my father began his final year of boarding school. After graduation in August 1940, Niko was conscripted into the Reichsarbeitsdienst, the Reich Labor Service, which groomed young men for the military. He reported to Tannheim in Austria's Tyrol, where he's pictured here, left, at work on a sports complex.

Conscripts were issued a visored felt cap with a crease down the middle—what they called "an ass with a handle." They alternated chores like painting and roadwork with duty at the rifle range. They sang the Labor Service anthem ("Brown like the earth, our uniform") and sat through lectures on the glory of the Reich. They learned to handle a spade as if it were a weapon, polishing it and shouldering it in turn.

In October 1940, having been formally drafted, my father reported to an induction center in Bavaria, then returned to Austria for basic training—three months of infantry, another three of driving instruction. When his mother insisted he take along a suitcase, Niko tried to explain to her, as he once told me, "the quality of linen there isn't what you're accustomed to." Poor vision in his left eye spared him flight duty and landed him instead in the motor pool. As a driver and mechanic in the Luftwaffe, he wore a blue uniform graced with an embroidered sleeve patch—two wings sprouting from an automobile radiator.

Every week or two Niko wrote his mother back in Munich. His letters are marbled with small-bore longings and requests— for chocolate, cigarettes, cash, boot insoles, a raincoat, his beloved Leica, and the donuts of Kuni, the family cook, as well as his violin and (for he loved jazz too) an alto sax on loan from his uncle Hanne. The war is well underway, but like the German people at large he seems oblivious that it might come home. Just turned nineteen, he sounds like a kid sent off to summer camp, regretting what he forgot to pack.

November 10, 1940: "I'm made to feel as if I've never driven before. We have at our disposal a Mercedes passenger car and an extraordinary truck. It has seven gears, three driven axles, and goes almost anywhere off-road. That would be something for Auntie Joe [his sister], who's too lazy to shift three gears."

January 26, 1941: "I've finished my driving tests. I'm now in possession of licenses one, two, and three. Once it gets a bit warmer we'll go on a rally, i.e., we leave base in a car with instructions to hit certain checkpoints. . . . At each checkpoint they'll monkey with our car, introducing some mechanical flaw. It's our job to troubleshoot quickly and continue on. Best time over the course is the winner."

February 2: "Consider the disaster I've been spared: The other day it was announced that privates such-and-so, four men all told, are being transferred tomorrow. Sent off to become parachutists. Those poor souls . . ."

February 16: "Mid-March we finish our training. On the fifth and sixth we go as a convoy to Graz. Over the Packsattel and Bruck an der Mur. That should be fun. Everybody gets a turn driving a passenger car, a truck, and a motorcycle. Each about fifty or sixty kilometers."

That trip was cut short when a soldier died of head injuries after being thrown from his motorcycle while negotiating a curve. The entire unit traveled to his Tyrolean hometown for the funeral. The young man, twenty-one, had been expected to take over the family flour mill.

A postcard from Kurt—mailed in Spain, forwarded from Munich—reached my father at his base in Klagenfurt. Kurt had no way of receiving a reply, but perhaps that's why, on February 23, Niko sent a letter to the closest paternal figure he could, his stepfather, Hans Albrecht. "The main thing is not to think at all but mechanically do what needs to be done," he wrote. "That way everything is a bit easier. The worst part is that one's brain is essentially shut down and little by little one forgets almost everything. I think I'd have to start from scratch after my time in the military. It's so stupefying.—

"... One just lives from day to day.—"

In April 1941, his unit finally moved out. After a stopover in Vienna, he landed in Brünn in the Sudetenland, Brno of the latter-day Czech Republic. He remained dutiful about alerting his mother to his movements, with allowances for military discretion.

My grandmother seems to have asked about "the kind of people" he was serving with. Niko replied, clearly irritated:

> It's something I couldn't care less about. Nobody asks after anyone's background. The duties we share level us all, and you can no longer distinguish whether someone is smart or stupid. . . . Who really cares with "whom" we are? What bonds us here is the monotony of our daily routine, the boring military life. And believe me, after half a year you just begin to vegetate. The mind has gone to sleep. A deep, deep sleep. I couldn't pick up a book and read. At this point I have no interest in any intellectual pleasures. I would have to thaw out first in different surroundings in order to experience life. To think about and live for all that interests me, all my hobbies, music, technology, theater, etc.—I hope you'll understand or at least try to.

Niko's response contained a kernel of what frustrated him about his mother—her preoccupation with class and prerogative. His rejection of that attitude would help lead him to emigrate after the war.

He went on: "Some of us have been transferred already to Romania, Bulgaria, or Greece. They have their car or truck, and they're independent. We too will soon follow."

In early June my father was issued a Ford truck with a V-8 engine. On June 17 he wrote a cryptic letter home, revealing only that he had driven some thousand kilometers to an airbase. Otherwise, "You must use your imagination about my activities."

He was about to take part in one of history's most consequential events. Not two years after signing a nonaggression pact, essentially granting Stalin permission to seize the Baltic states and a greater share of Poland, Hitler would betray him and invade the Soviet Union.

The *Führer* vacillated over this decision, which the Nazis code-named Operation Barbarossa. Hitler called it "child's play," predicting that German troops would reach Moscow by harvest time. But privately he seems to have harbored doubts. He once confessed that the invasion was like "pushing open a door to a dark room never seen before, without knowing what lies behind it."

On June 22, 1941, Hitler nonetheless ordered his troops to break down that door. Driving a truck with target maps and

reconnaissance photographs, my father became one of three million soldiers to participate in what was then the largest offensive in military history. He did so in support of an air squadron called Edelweiss, whose encampment he captured in the watercolor on the previous page. Niko's unit made up part of the southernmost of the Wehrmacht's three major thrusts, advancing through Poland, Galicia, and Ukraine: Krakow, Lvov, Zhitomir, Vinnytsia, Belaya Tserkov, Poltava, Kharkov. By the end of September the weather had already turned bitterly cold. At one stopover Niko placed a tarp covered with straw over a dug hole, carving out a ledge for a jerry-rigged fireplace. "It will be a disaster when winter comes," he wrote home on October 1.

On Christmas Eve he reached the river city of Dnipropetrovsk, just west of the long north-south line where the Nazi advance had stalled out. There my father hunkered down for the winter—indeed, for a world-historical winter.

Several months earlier, from New York, Kurt's second wife had sent a letter to his first wife about my father. "I think especially of Niko, whom I include in all my prayers," Helen wrote Elisabeth in Munich. "You know how much I have taken into my heart this quiet creature, so happy to stand on the sidelines with his 'inner boundlessness,' and how much I wish he could come into his own completely, to his profession, his calling—that in doing so he might find inward and outward freedom."

I had seen the huge working-class apartment block on previous trips to the outdoor market on Winterfeldtplatz in the Berlin district of Schöneberg. Thrown up like a barricade against east-west traffic, the building has a balconied facade graced with TV dishes and Turkish flags. This journey of a couple of miles usually comes with appetizing thoughts of my destination—*Wurst* and *pho* and *gözleme*; scrapes of raclette drizzled over country bread; fresh vegetables still encrusted with soil from the Brandenburg plain. But those associations became differently charged after I stopped at that housing complex to read a plaque I noticed for the first time.

Until Allied bombs destroyed it in early 1944, a sports arena stood on this spot. The *Sportpalast* hosted prizefights and six-day bicycle races and, when the Nazis wanted to assemble the largest possible indoor crowd in the capital, mass rallies. One gathering, held in October 1942 and broadcast throughout Germany and the occupied lands, marked the Reich's harvest festival. That night Hermann Göring not only promised that no German would go hungry during the coming winter; the deputy führer also pledged that every civilian would enjoy a boost in rations.

Germany had indeed just enjoyed a good harvest. But, as I would learn, Göring was referring to something sinister. The Nazis had already begun to implement "the Hunger Plan," the mass expropriation of food from Poland, Russia, and Ukraine, as ordered by SS chief Heinrich Himmler and Herbert Backe, the state secretary for food and agriculture. In his declaration that every "Aryan" German would eat more, Göring left unsaid the chilling corollary—that Jews, Poles, Ukrainians, and Russians would, by design, starve.

Since June 1941, Nazi invaders in the east had been under orders from Göring to live off the land and send any surplus back to Germany. One memo prepared by the bureaucracy made clear the consequences: "If we take what we need out of the country, there can be no doubt that many millions of people will die of starvation." Before the launch of Operation Barbarossa, Backe referred to a "surplus population" to be liquidated as German forces advanced. "Through military actions and the food problems," Himmler predicted, "twenty to thirty million Slavs and

Jews will die." For Ukraine specifically, a readout of a decision Hitler made during the summer of 1942 declared that "the feeding of the population is a matter of complete indifference." The Nazis considered this collateral damage to be a feature of their démarche in the east, not a bug, and of a piece with their vision of a manifest destiny in which conquered lands—cleansed of Jews, scattered with indentured Slavs, resettled by German farmers— became a de-modernized colony. Ukraine would no longer be the breadbasket of the Soviet Union but of an ethnically pure Reich. In *Bloodlands*, by the historian Timothy Snyder, I find material that fits with family papers like the final pieces in a puzzle. Snyder documents at length and in detail what Niko never spoke of, and I never knew to ask about—genocide by starvation in Ukraine under Nazi occupation during 1941–42.

Yet the Hunger Plan—to starve to death up to thirty million non-Germans by diverting food to soldiers in the field and back to the home front—didn't go according to schedule. The Wehrmacht failed to meet Operation Barbarossa's goal of reaching Moscow by the end of September. With supply lines stretched, the Germans fell victim to rain and mud and, eventually, Russia's great historical friend, winter. It was as if the chapter on Napoleon had been ripped from their officers' field manuals.

Snyder defines "the Bloodlands" as that swath of Poland, Russia, the Baltics, Belarus, and Ukraine, east of the Oder and west of the Don, where both Hitler and Stalin regarded the inhabitants as subhuman pawns and, in the end, disposable. The fourteen million people to die there between 1933 and 1945, on territory controlled by those two dictators, "were all victims of murderous policy rather than casualties of war," he writes. "Most were women, children, and the aged; none were bearing weapons; many had been stripped of their possessions, including their clothes." He goes on to call the invasion of the Soviet Union as portentous an event as any in the history of Europe—"the beginning of a calamity that defies description."

Snyder attempts instead an enumeration of scale. As a result of Hitler's choice, more than ten million soldiers, German and Soviet, died in combat. A comparable number of civilians were killed by bombs, hunger, disease, or exposure. Yet another ten million people—including six million Jews and three million Soviet prisoners of war—were simply murdered by the Nazis. "Right after the invasion began, the Wehrmacht began to starve its Soviet prisoners," he writes, "and special 'task forces' called Einsatzgruppen began to shoot political enemies and Jews." A soldier of the Wehrmacht hardly needed to be conscripted into some *Einsatzgruppe*, much less pick up a gun, to find himself implicated: "If German soldiers wanted to eat, they were told, they would have to starve the surrounding population. They should imagine that any food that entered the mouth of a Soviet citizen was taken from the mouth of a German child."

Snyder's narrative is a sobering corrective to someone like me, conditioned to think of Nazi genocide as having been perpetrated largely at death camps in the Polish woods. From his book I more fully understand what the Third Reich put my father's youth in service of.

Niko wasn't in the Waffen-SS or the Order Police. "The cosmos of the army and the cosmos of the Nazi apparatus were totally divorced from each other," he once told me. And that may have been his experience. But from my visit to the villa on the Wannsee, I knew that the Wehrmacht lent support to every type of Nazi activity in the east. And now I had discovered how circumstances on the ground introduced an entirely new category of complicity. "It was the lack of victory in the Soviet Union that made the Wehrmacht inseparable from the Nazi regime," Snyder writes. "In the starving Soviet Union in autumn 1941, the

Wehrmacht was in a moral trap, from which National Socialism seemed to offer the only escape."

On October 13, 1941, when Einsatzgruppe C, Einsatzkommando 5, machine-gunned twelve thousand Jews forced to stand on the lips of pits dug at the southern edge of Dnipropetrovsk, my father was still more than two months from arriving there. His letters home place him in Kharkov in mid-December, around the time more than ten thousand of that city's Jewish residents were rounded up and imprisoned at a tractor factory on the outskirts of town; in January, Sonderkommando 4a, another unit of Einsatzgruppe C, would join Order Police battalion 314 to shoot them in batches. I'm going to assume that Niko's duties as a Luftwaffe driver kept him clear of the first stage of this atrocity, and I know he was encamped in Dnipropetrovsk by the time the second took place. But from growing up at his table, I also know that a meal set before him could surface animal instincts in this otherwise surpassingly gentle man. If soldiers had been given orders to feed themselves first, my father would not have been inclined to disobey.

His letters make clear that he and his fellow troops are eating well. There's also the occasional hint that Ukrainian peasants and Soviet prisoners aren't. "We have everything aplenty," he wrote on June 29, a week into the invasion. "So much and of such quality, it's almost like being at home, e.g., yesterday we got pork chops with potato dumplings!" June 30: "We get real coffee for breakfast and black tea at suppertime. We feel quite spoiled." August 8: "Once we were driving to a Ukrainian village to buy food, and without any effort could purchase five hundred eggs, eight gallons of cream, twelve pounds of butter, and forty pounds of honey. We paid: three pfennig for an egg, fifty pfennig for a quart of cream, sixty pfennig for a pound of butter, and one mark for a kilo of honey."

Among the targets of the Hunger Plan were Soviet prisoners, like the ones in the photograph opposite, which my father took during Operation Barbarossa over the summer of 1941. Around the same time, writing his mother about POWs who have been put to work in the mess, he betrayed the kind of anti-Slavic sentiment then common among the German people: "You could scrape the dirt from their skin, and they drink water from puddles, though they do get fresh water to drink. At chow time they line up and start fistfights among themselves. Only a shot in the air by the guards can get them to stop."

"I'm not starving," he reported on September 6, 1941. "No need to worry." September 22: "Yesterday we requisitioned meat for *Schnitzel* from the kitchen. A real Sunday treat. . . . Delicious!" November 11: "The construction crew has built us a brick stove. It is nicely stoked now, and we fry ourselves potatoes at night."

On November 19 he described a scene with a final sentence that makes me wince at its callousness. "There is a dead horse outside, half-putrefied and frozen," he wrote. "A [Ukrainian] stands there, hacking himself chops with a pickaxe. Next to him, a little dog chews a bone. *Bon appétit!*"

And so it went, through December 13 — "The midday meal is usually a stew, evenings a third of a loaf of bread, a bit of fat, and either soup or some cheese or *Wurst*, or canned fish" — and on to Christmas Eve dinner in Dnipropetrovsk, where he had just arrived: "Potato salad and *Bockwurst*, a substitute for turkey."

In wondering "What did you do in the war, Daddy?" I hardly expected the answer to come back, "I ate well."

Growing up, I'd heard my father tell stories about the city where he would spend a year and a half. He said that Ukrainians at first welcomed the Wehrmacht as liberators from the Stalinist policies that had engineered famines through the thirties. He and his fellow soldiers would go for leisurely swims in the Dnieper; in Dnipropetrovsk, in Poltava, and Zhitomir too, they thought nothing of staying out past midnight, leaving their sidearms back in the barracks. Only after the Nazis began to ship Ukrainians back to the Reich as forced laborers, he told me, did partisans ramp up their activity.

He once mentioned a girlfriend named Lidiia. She taught him some Russian and would join him for walks along the Dnieper. And he mentioned another woman, Tania, who lived near the barracks and called him "Pushkin" for the way his hair kinked up if he failed to comb it after a swim or a shower.

Perhaps Lidiia is at the left edge of this photograph, half-visible in the white dress, all but sitting in my father's lap. "Fraternizing," Niko has written on the back. Snyder reports that starvation hit peasants in the countryside the hardest. As city dwellers who have befriended German soldiers, these young Ukrainian women and their families likely made out better. Niko told me he gave Lidiia food to take home and sometimes joined her family for picnics. He said this late in his life while suffering from cancer, and now that I've read *Bloodlands*, I can't help but wonder whether the conscience I know he had led him to make

a point of telling me. With Lidiia, did my father drive some bargain in what was likely a transactional relationship? Did an urge for atonement lead him to become active in a group devoted to US-Soviet cultural exchange, Bridges for Peace, during the late eighties?

In those letters home, one of the few gruesome things Niko shared is a scene in Kharkov from mid-November 1941: the corpses of ten or so locals killed by the Germans, dangling from the balcony of a building, each hung with a sign in Cyrillic lettering listing their crimes. "There were more as we drove on," he wrote. "There are still many partisans in this city who blow up buildings, kill soldiers, or engage in other sabotage. Thus these drastic measures of discouragement." But my father surely saw other things that he chose not to tell a mother he knew struggled to adapt to the real world. Family letters and conversations with relatives lead me to believe he had secrets to keep—in a letter Maria would send Kurt after the war, in which she referred to the abiding weight on her brother of "all the things he saw"; in

Niko's preference not to speak with my historian cousin Marion Detjen about his time in Ukraine.

Why did he never go into such things? He wanted to spare us, of course. But the question, tacked on to an ever-lengthening list, suggests an answer in the form of another question: How *could* he have spoken of them? Although that hardly keeps the back half of the refrain from coming round, the companion to *He never told me: I never asked.*

I think back to what he wrote his mother shortly before Operation Barbarossa: "The mind has gone to sleep. A deep, deep sleep. . . . I would have to thaw out first."

That was deliberate, the keeping of soldiers in a state of psychological and emotional permafrost. "From now on you belong to the *Führer*!" German boys were told upon induction into the Hitler Youth. As Hitler once said, "I want no intellectual education. Knowledge will spoil the young for me. It is self-control they must learn; it is the fear of death they must conquer; this is what creates true freedom, creativity and maturity."

And prepares them to accept anything.

*   *   *

The process of sifting through Niko's letters home comes with a heart-stabbing moment. Until opening that box, I had never seen the photograph opposite, of my father in uniform with a swastika on his chest, taken in Klagenfurt shortly after he reported for basic training. Despite the censorship to which he sometimes alludes, and which surely colors what he chooses to share, I read his letters in the hope of stumbling across some subversive thought or political solecism, evidence that he might have been fighting his own private rearguard action—that her Opa, as my nine-year-old daughter wished that day at the Cabinet War Rooms, really did have his heart in the Allied cause.

I find none. But I find nothing horrific either—just prejudices socialized into Germans of his generation and the occasional hyperbole of a ravenous grunt barely out of his teens.

He had told me he passed through Auschwitz during the war, spending a night there in transit, unaware that industrialized murder was taking place behind the walls of Birkenau. But I'm hardly prepared for the sight of my father's handwriting—the same script I know from birthday endearments or a check to tide me over a college break—on an envelope from a letter sent home in late 1944, the stamp depicting Hitler in profile, the postmark AUSCHWITZ.

SEVEN
A DEBT FOR RESCUE
Kurt, 1941 to 1945

"The first days of a European in America might be likened to a re-birth," Kafka wrote of the emigrant protagonist of his novel *America*. "One must nonetheless keep in mind that first impressions are always unreliable, and one shouldn't let them prejudice the future judgments that will eventually shape one's life here."

This might have served as a cautionary note to Kurt, whose diary describes the whirl in the spring of 1941 after he, Helen, and Christian set foot on American soil. On day one they checked into the Hotel Colonial on Columbus Avenue, where Thea Dispeker put them up. A week later they met their co-sponsor, Robert Weinberg, and visited the offices of the Emergency Rescue Committee to ask after the vanished money. Within a month Kurt had filed "first papers" to start the clock, so they could all apply for US citizenship five years later.

But the doting attention quickly fell away. The kind of people who in Europe would have instantly recognized Kurt's name now asked him how to spell it. Invited to a dinner party at a home on Long Island, he and Helen were struck that no American guest asked about what they, eyewitnesses to the rise of the Nazis and the fall of France, had lived through. They were physically safe.

But new circumstances threatened their sense of identity, and identity is bound up in one's native tongue, so essential to fully expressing one's personality. Kurt knew he needed to improve his English, but with Christian he insisted on speaking German. "I do not," he told his wife, "wish to communicate with him in a rudimentary fashion."

As book publishing was the only way he knew how to make a living, Kurt hastily began to prospect for advice and capital. He met with publishers Alfred A. Knopf and W. Warder Norton, and reached out to his ex-wife's cousin George W. Merck, the CEO of New Jersey–based Merck & Co., a prosperous pharmaceutical firm that had grown out of the American subsidiary established by the Darmstadt family in 1891 before being seized by the US government during World War I under the Trading with the Enemy Act. Figuring that the United States would soon join the war and, as in France, they would be rounded up, Kurt and Helen had packed overalls and work boots, the better to survive an internment camp. But that fear gradually receded. For the first time they could remember, they didn't know where the nearest police station was. "We've made some friends and acquaintances here, and we're also getting to know many new people who are good-hearted and friendly," Kurt wrote Maria two weeks after their arrival. "But it will all be very, very hard, and we must very, very quickly find possibilities for work."

Just turned fifty-four, Kurt had been out of the publishing game for more than two decades. He and Helen spent much of the summer and fall holed up in the New York Public Library, trying to identify foreign literature that could interest American readers. They haunted concerts, lectures, and galleries and, means permitting, entertained—"inviting people for dinner if their guests were indigent or for a drink if they were not." They spent that first Christmas with an old friend from Munich, the bibliophile Curt von Faber du Faur, who had also taken up gentleman farming outside Florence during the thirties. *Verlag besprochen*—publishing firm discussed—Kurt's diary reports of that visit to Cambridge, where their friend now lectured at Harvard. Soon Faber du Faur and his stepson, Kyrill Schabert, agreed to put up $7,500 if Kurt and Helen could raise a matching sum. Weinberg, George Merck, and Gerard Neisser, a friend of Helen's brother, all ponied up, and by February, not a year after alighting from the *Serpa Pinto*, they were back in the book business. They named the firm Pantheon after Kurt's old art-book house in Florence, Pantheon Casa Editrice, and in September moved into a grungy seventy-five-dollar-a-month apartment on Washington Square South. The living room, dining room, and bedroom served as Pantheon's office, mailroom, and reception area. "If I wish that these efforts might find some material reward in the not-so-distant future (out of the question for the time being), I do not say this because we want to get rich," Kurt would write shortly after the firm's founding. "All I wish for is improvement of our working conditions—an additional room and some professional assistance."

It seemed unwise for Kurt and Helen, enemy aliens since the United States had joined the war against Nazi Germany, to formally head up the new business. So the original documents listed Schabert as president. The investment agreement further called for neither Wolff to be paid a salary until the house broke into the black. Eager for the New York literary world to take them and their enterprise seriously, Kurt and Helen sometimes strained to project an illusion of bourgeois arrival, as in the preposterous photograph opposite, where they posed with a dog that wasn't theirs in someone else's apartment. In early 1942 they caught a break when Kurt successfully crowbarred several thousand dollars out of his account at Barclays Bank in London. Otherwise, the émigré joke—"America, Land of Unpaid Opportunity"—obtained. As Thomas Mann would write Kurt in 1946, "You know yourself how these times and this country nip and gnaw."

Pantheon, Helen later recalled, "operated on a combination of tightrope and shoestring," out of a "crazy office" marked by "a Babel of languages." She and Kurt spoke French with one editor, the Russian-Jewish refugee Jacques Schiffrin, and German with another, the Bavarian anti-Nazi Protestant and Emergency Rescue Committee volunteer Wolfgang Sauerländer. Their order clerk was Albanian; their bookkeeper, Portuguese. "Grotesque as it may sound," Helen wrote Maria in 1946, "I am the only person in the editorial and production department who knows some English (about father's English the less said the better)."

Despite the firm's unsteady footing, Kurt refused to abandon his standards. One day the staff took up the question of

whether to use real or fake gold leaf to emboss lettering on the spine of a book. Kurt argued for real. A salesman made the case for fake, pointing out the savings on each copy. Kurt replied that fake would fade. The salesman countered that by then the buyer would be stuck with the book—a point that, as far as Kurt was concerned, settled the issue. Only real gold would do. "One has to learn this country like a new language," Helen wrote her sister in Bavaria. "It doesn't come naturally like a dream come true, like my oh so beloved France. There are no affinities to bridge the differences; everything has to be done by experience and intellect."

Years later Kurt captured his ambivalence over being an entrepreneur in exile: "This wasn't a gift from heaven, but a kick." The nippings and gnawings of experience had also helped lead him to drift further from his onetime vow to embrace the new. In an unpublished document, Kurt sketched out a different mission for Pantheon—not to espouse the narrow interests of an *Exilverlag*, not to engage in politics or pamphleteering, not to flog the merely topical at the expense of the timely, but rather "to present to the American public works of lasting value, produced with the greatest care and stress on quality. Our editorial concept is to help spread knowledge and understanding of the essential questions of human life and culture."

In the meantime, he and Helen benefited from a paradox, an auspiciousness of timing that my cousin Marion Detjen captures well:

> *A range of factors made the time not altogether unfavorable for starting a small, intellectually ambitious but financially modest new publishing house. The U.S. economy had just recovered from a recession, boosted by government spending and rearmament. Roosevelt had finally managed to overcome the isolationist attitude of the public, and there*

*was a growing public interest in European culture, espe-
cially when the information seemed bipartisan, apolitical,
and beyond any suspicion of fostering socialist or communist ideas. Furthermore, the immigrants that had recently
arrived and settled in New York and on the West Coast
had, though small in number, brought about a massive
cultural transfer, bringing with them new ideas, academic
knowledge, intellectual concepts, artistic creativity, and a
general curiosity which created a market for [their] own
cultural objects.*

Decades later Helen would recall those early years in Manhattan, "with Europe still a killing ground and the miracle of not
just resettlement, but a flourishing business":

*I lost my German identity and realized how irretrievably
European Kurt and I were, for the simple reason that our
experience and education, visual and intellectual, had mil-
lennial rather than centennial roots. That, however, made
it all the more urgent to try and transmit some of what
seemed valid and communicable from the old continent to
the new. It was something one owed to one's new country,
a debt of gratitude to be paid for rescue, a vow never to
underestimate America's stunning capacity for understanding, support and response.*

In 1943 Pantheon published an anthology of the poems
of Stefan George in translation. A year later, amidst more and
more reports of Nazi atrocities, *The Complete Grimm's Fairy
Tales* became an unlikely holiday-season hit, even as its publication brought screeds from critics about the brutality of the
German soul. To Pantheon's good fortune, W. H. Auden wrote

a countervailing endorsement for the front page of the *New York Times Book Review*, declaring that "these tales rank next to the Bible in importance." If French-themed books figured to win more sympathy than German ones, Kurt and Helen—Americans-in-waiting, to be sure, but also proudly Francophile—obliged. With Jacques Schiffrin helping light the way with his contacts and editorial confidence, they published André Gide, Albert Camus, Paul Claudel, and Charles Péguy. A bilingual edition of the work of Péguy, an essayist and poet, was Pantheon's first-ever narrative publication.

Helen had Péguy on her mind in March 1942, several months after the Japanese attack on Pearl Harbor drew the United States into the conflict against the Axis powers. "I like this country much better since the war began," she wrote the Countess Colloredo-Mansfeld in Saint-Lary. "Everything is done with a grandiose one-sidedness, which is what you want under such circumstances, and the civilian isn't worth a damn and gets steamrolled. It reminds me of Péguy: 'When one fights, one should engage the fight in good earnest, according to its own fashion, as all work must be done, earnestly, according to its own fashion. . . . Do not commit the falsehood of waging war as if it were peace.'"

If America's resolve to destroy the Nazi regime by any means necessary cheered Helen and Kurt, it left unspoken a sobering corollary. When Helen gave voice to those sentiments, Kurt's ex-wife was in Munich. His daughter was in Freiburg, soon to be bombed out of her apartment. And his son—my father—was on the Russian front.

Before arriving in Berlin I hadn't given this any thought, but the question arises: How did Kurt feel about leaving a son and a daughter not just behind, but in circumstances fraught with the kind of danger Kurt himself had already experienced firsthand?

It's hard to fault Kurt for not taking Niko and Maria with him into exile during the early thirties, when the horror of the regime hadn't fully revealed itself. By 1940, flight would turn out to be perilous enough with Helen and one child in tow. Further, Niko and Maria were more "Aryanized" than their father—as emblemized by the *Nachweis* each held and Kurt didn't—and a sense of security had likely been socialized into them both, for they lived in comfort with a Merck mother and a physician stepfather. After war broke out, Niko was expected to report for duty; Maria was married to a man who would be sent to the front himself. As Kurt and Helen made their escape from Vichy France, Nazi Germany still appeared invincible.

But Kurt had a record of sometimes failing to make good on assurances. In the summer of 1917, Kafka tentatively asked how much support he could expect from his publisher if he were to take a three-way leap of faith: quit his day job as a civil servant, get married, and abandon stultifying Prague for the Berliner *Luft*. "To be sure, I will not depend entirely on the proceeds of my writing (or so I still have reason to believe)," he wrote. "Nevertheless I—or the deep-seated bureaucrat inside me, which is the same thing—have an oppressive fear of this future. I do hope that you, dear Herr Wolff, will not quite desert me, provided of course that I halfway deserve your kindness."

Kurt reassured him. "As far as your plans for the future are concerned, I wish you all the best, from the bottom of my heart," he wrote back. "It is my sincerest pleasure to assure you that both now and after the war is over you will receive continuous material support; we will certainly have no trouble working out the details."

It was a brazen promise, all the more so because Kurt of all people knew of Kafka's fragile artistic constitution. World War I introduced further variables. "While people feared that the coming winter would bring the chaos of hunger revolts, he was promising an author like Kafka, who still lacked widespread name recognition, very costly deckle-edged paper and half-leather covers," the Kafka scholar Reiner Stach points out. "The delighted author understandably hoped it could be accomplished, but the publisher's optimism was downright reckless."

"You really have to scream," Kafka would write a friend in December 1918, "to be heard by a publisher drowning in authors."

Niko and Maria might have formulated a variation on that cry: you really have to scream to be heard by a father drowning in authors and colleagues and friends and mistresses.

They had their differences, Kurt and Niko. They were different, after all. Kurt was not, in his son Christian's words, "a reflective or philosophical person. He was an aesthete. And very social." Niko, by contrast, would remain content in what Helen had called his "inner boundlessness"—a knack for living in the wings. It would take my father's relocation for the two to reconcile themselves to each other as men in full. As Niko told me, "In New York I got to know my father for the first time."

If Niko carried a complicated relationship with his father to the United States, my father never foisted that inheritance on me. Our differences rarely led to sustained conflict. For that we can perhaps credit the hard break of emigration, which ensured that Niko's experience diverged enough from mine to dissolve many potential lines of scrimmage. But strangely, here in this country that raised him, I find myself almost regretting the placid quality of our relationship. Niko is the most reticent character in this account. It's as if his calling is to be that person who stands by, ready to tamp down the outer boundlessness of performatively emotive family members like his sister—to be "secretive," as Maria once described him to me, "never talking, always feeling."

That relative muteness has drawn me closer to him, to try to pick a signal out of the historical noise so I might leave for my own son and daughter the accounting Niko never fully left for me. In some ways, I realize, it's only after his death that I'm getting to know my father for the first time.

EIGHT
AN END WITH HORROR
Niko, 1942 to 1945

For all of 1942 and much of '43, Niko remained in Dnipro-petrovsk, billeted in a building with a field kitchen in its courtyard. He tended to chores around the barracks and delivered maps and photographs throughout eastern Ukraine, usually driving alone over muddy or rutted roads. He was promoted to corporal. And by his own account he continued to eat scandalously well. He wrote his mother in December 1942: "After a decent breakfast with honey, *Wurst* and butter, I'm so hungry by ten o'clock that I can eat a large pan full of fried potatoes. Yet more at lunch, and at night a solid meal, washed down with beer." The following August he wrote home: "We eat as well as at any *Gasthof*. Today we'll have pea soup, *Sauerbraten* with new potatoes and gravy, tomato salad, and vanilla ice cream! . . . For supper real Portuguese sardines in olive oil, butter, jam."

But their correspondence soon reflected the turn the war was taking. His mother described air raids on Munich, and Niko indicated that Soviet overflights of Dnipropetrovsk—he called them "visits from Ivan"—had become more frequent. By early February 1943 the Germans had been routed at Stalingrad. News of bombing raids back home coincided with a temporary halt to his mother's letters, and he worried that there was a connection.

In the spring of 1943 my father spotted a notice in the barracks that the Institute of Technology in Munich was looking to fill openings for students in its chemistry department. His application for a study leave was approved for late that year, and on November 14, his mother's birthday, he arrived home. It would be a temporary reprieve, lasting not even five months, and he had always wanted to be an architect, not a chemist. But this interlude scrambled his destiny, setting him on the course that put him in a lab and ultimately sprang him from Germany. More immediately, it probably saved his life. He soon realized what it would have meant to be in the path of the Soviet onslaught of January 1945, an offensive even larger than Operation Barbarossa: death or captivity in the gulag. "There," he told me years later, "went one of my many lives."

With the changed circumstances of the war, Niko's return to duty in April 1944 led to reassignment within Germany proper, to a paratroopers' squadron in Thuringia. "Please don't imagine me jumping from the sky," he wrote his mother. "But the six of us will be assigned to a driving pool, since our old outfit no longer exists and a new group is being formed." Two months later he was redeployed again, to Württemberg for training as an 88mm gunner with a flak battery. By August his unit had been sent to the Beskid Mountains of Upper Silesia. At the end of the month he was to begin officer training near Besançon, in France, but my father was skeptical, for this was the third such course to be scheduled after two previous ones had been canceled.

Niko can say only so much in his letters, but I recognize an incipient pacifist, appalled by the destruction of the war. His mother surely heard echoes of Kurt's dispatches from the front during World War I. "It's so unspeakably sad that so much beauty is being destroyed, all that was once dear and familiar to me from previous travels," Niko wrote. "Who knows if I will

ever see these places again? Also Elba, Saint-Tropez, Florence—
everything is part of the war now and gone."

Nor was he still at large in a land of unlimited caloric extraction. "Please send food, like bacon," he wrote on September 12,
1944. "Most of the time I'm hungry." The day before, American
forces had taken their first steps on German soil, across the River
Our from Luxembourg.

On September 24 Niko began five weeks of training to
become a sergeant. But the course was called off two weeks in,
and he was sent with his regiment to a succession of postings—
first in Dux (now Duchov in the Czech Republic), then coastal
Holland, then back to Dux, and to Holland again, and finally,
in early December, to what would be his last theater of the war.
"A brief greeting en route," he wrote his mother from near the
Rhineland town of Münster. "Who knows where we're going."

His destination became clear within days, when the Nazis
went into what would turn out to be their death spasm. In German the offensive was known as Wacht am Rhein, or Watch on
the Rhine, although histories of the victors call it the Battle of
the Bulge, after what the Germans' initial incursion looked like
on a map. Niko's unit was deployed to the Eifel, the wild hills
of Germany's western borderlands. There, somewhere between
the German town of Geichlingen and Vianden, in Luxembourg,
he hunkered down in an antiaircraft emplacement, on a ridge
exposed to the pounding of American artillery.

On Christmas Day he scratched out a letter home. "It's so
dreadfully difficult for all of us, but we must stick with it and
endure," he wrote. "I'm lying in a dugout, barely covered by a
tarp. It's freezing cold outside and a feeble sun relieves the long
moonlit nights. It's dark now, which means no attacks from
above. The artillery barrages provide the only Christmas music.
When it stops, it feels eerie. I hadn't counted on being in the

midst of this again this year. But if God wills it, I'll get out of here in one piece."

Niko may not have realized the extent, but the western Allies were steadily recapturing territory lost to the initial Nazi advance. Exploiting beachheads from the Normandy invasion, they had massed almost eight times as many men in France and Belgium as the Germans, and held an even greater advantage given how much matériel and manpower Hitler now had to send east to fend off the Soviets. Meanwhile, each winter-clear day reminded Niko that the Luftwaffe had been bombed and strafed into irrelevance. "All day long fighter planes circle about, sweep down on us, over our heads, like vultures after their prey," he wrote. "Beginning at dawn we lay in wait at our cannons to defend ourselves when they get too close. In between we take on the role of regular artillery and shoot across the front line. Thus the days go by . . ."

Over the following weeks he and another soldier dug themselves a better position. They lined it with fir branches and fit it with a small stove, only to discover an infestation of lice, 135 of which he harvested from his sweater one day. "It's so terribly difficult just now, and sometimes hopeless," he wrote on January 26. Then he seemed to refer to his inner boundlessness: "It's easy to lose faith that one might get out of here alive. But I'm amazed over and over again by my protective, lucky star, considering the horror around me."

By January 29 his unit had abandoned its ridgetop position and retreated to a nearby village to await further orders. "What lies ahead I don't know, but I believe it's going to be rougher yet," Niko wrote.

> We've had several dark days already. Being in this village
> is a bit more quiet. But heavy artillery lands here every so

often. When I started this letter a direct hit struck the house
next door. And having been spared, there's this feeling of
gratitude that envelops you, displacing the gripping fear
just passed. You know, when life gets to be so primitive—
(another shell exploded just now)—and we're constantly
seeking shelter, like homeless people, shelters that often
seem bizarre, that's when a simple room with a warm
stove, and a bit of straw to rest, makes you as happy and
content as a small child.

My father's unit seems to have stayed in this village for
another week or two, when he realized he was only a short hike
from Grünhaus bei Trier, home to the winery of the von Schubert
family, whose son Andreas had been a classmate at boarding
school. Niko and another soldier walked the few kilometers
from their encampment, and Frau von Schubert fed them a meal
and shared news of her son, then off serving with a tank division.
German officers had commandeered the property and were "loll-
ing around amidst the antique heirlooms of the family," Niko
reported in what would be his last letter home. "The fate of this
lovely castle will be sealed soon too, as the Americans aren't far
off. Now and then an artillery shell comes crashing in."

A short hike from Trier, this direct descendant of that city's
chief rabbi, wearing the swastika of the Wehrmacht, finished his
finest meal in months and resumed his retreat.

Over the next few weeks, Niko and his unit struggled to
outrun the American advance. They had long since abandoned
their 88mm guns to more easily lose themselves in the woods.
Formal units dissolved and small bands of soldiers carried on in
random fashion. Niko spent one night on an island in the Rhine.
On March 29, after crossing a field to reach the square of the

village of Wehen, just outside Wiesbaden, he was taken prisoner by Americans in jeeps.

But before that, my father was witness to an episode he never spoke to me about. I learned of it only after his death, and then only because he had shared it with my brother-in-law, whose insistent way in conversation had a way of breaking down obstructions in the Human Flowchart.

By early 1945, as it became clear that they faced a choice between "an end with horror and horror without end," more and more Germans resigned themselves to the first. Nonetheless, in mid-February, Martin Bormann, Hitler's private secretary, issued a directive ordering "summary courts martial"—rough justice to cull the Wehrmacht of defeatists. "Anyone not prepared to fight for his people but who stabs them in the back in their gravest hour does not deserve to live and must fall to the executioner," the order read.

Sometime during those bleak days before capture, my father and a half dozen or so others in his unit concluded that the fight was lost. But as they mulled over how best to turn themselves in, the ranking soldier among them, a true believer, began to draw up plans for guerrilla warfare. Their differences led to an angry argument.

It became clear that this ranking officer was committed to a fight to the death. "What we're going to do," this officer began, turning his back—whereupon one of my father's fellow soldiers raised a pistol and shot him dead.

In early April the Americans transported Niko west to France, to a camp on the outskirts of Le Mans, a tent city where sixty thousand prisoners slept under shared blankets on bare ground. They were fed bread and ersatz coffee for breakfast, a pint of tomato or green-bean soup for lunch, and two ounces of cheese or canned pork for dinner. The Allies would eventually take into captivity some five million POWs, a total that overwhelmed them. But rations amounting to 850 calories a day, barely a third of what the average male adult needs to maintain his weight, were intentionally punitive. And although this was an American camp, many of the guards were French and, my father recalled, particularly hostile. The Geneva Convention mandated that signatories feed and care for POWs at the same standard as their own troops, but a trick of nomenclature got the Americans off the hook by defining captives like Niko not as POWs but as DEFs—disarmed enemy forces. My father once told me the fate of a fellow German prisoner caught stealing chocolate. He enjoyed nothing but chocolate every day until he died.

Niko would always be grateful to one of the first soldiers to process him, a GI from Chicago, who confiscated his Leica but insisted on compensating him with several cartons of cigarettes—a cache my father would dip into over the coming weeks to barter for food. He soon caught another break, in the unlikely form of an ear infection and a temperature of 104 degrees Fahrenheit. This won him transfer to a US Army hospital, where he was given morphine for the pain and had the ear drained. During his convalescence he slept in a bed with sheets and pillows and ate meals on trays. After Germany's surrender, he was shuttled from camp to camp, eastward through France, until finally, in midsummer, he joined hundreds of other POWs on a train, in open cattle cars where prisoners could only stand or squat.

From the terror of aerial bombardment to widespread hunger, the Allies visited on the Germans a succession of turnabouts during the final months of the war and its aftermath. Here it was the dehumanization of transport by cattle car. Over three days, Niko and his fellow POWs made halting progress or found themselves shunted onto sidings to await a new locomotive. Confined to the cars at all times, they were left exposed to the elements, as well as to the waste and stench that rose around them and, as they discovered one day while left on a siding in Strasbourg, something potentially worse.

A transport filled with drunken French soldiers had pulled alongside the prisoners' train. When the Frenchmen recognized this adjacent gallery of Germans, several raised their rifles and began to fire, below, above, and for all the prisoners knew, right at them. The American guards were almost as panicked as their captives. The GIs couldn't speak French, didn't have time to procure an engine, certainly couldn't let their prisoners go. A reprieve came only when the train carrying the French soldiers pulled out of the station. "Another of my nine lives," Niko called it.

On August 13, Kurt wrote in English to Maria in Freiburg: "What weighs on our hearts is of course Niko's fate. Elisabeth has heard no news from him since February, when he was in the east. There is very little chance of getting news from him for an indefinite time to come, and it will not even be possible to find out in the near future whether or not he is alive."

A few days after Kurt wrote that letter, Niko was routed through a US processing center in Heilbronn. He was given clean clothes, a small sum of money, and discharge papers. It took more than three months after Germany's surrender, but he was now officially free to go home.

On the morning of August 17 he arrived at Munich's main station and hopped a tram for Nymphenburg, where my grandmother still lived in an essentially intact home on the Südliche Schlossrondell, one of two gently curving roads that lead to the palace. In her pocket calendar Elisabeth made a note of his arrival. *10 Uhr: Niko kommt—sehr erschöpft, 121 Pfund!* (10 a.m.: Niko arrives—extremely exhausted, 133 pounds!)

The next day: *Niko ausschlafen, hat Dysenterie.* (Niko sleeps in, has dysentery.)

He survived the war with no apparent psychological malady, and no physical ones other than that dysentery, the ear infection, and a permanently discolored toenail from having dropped a 450-pound V-8 engine on his right foot.

And yet, a detail my father shared about his return to Munich, on a morning he recalled as sunny and warm, sticks with me. When he reached his mother's house, he didn't simply walk through the door. First, he rang the bell.

Another day, another revelation to wrestle with.

The bookstore is tucked away off Friedrichstrasse in central Berlin; the book, a 2015 account called *Blitzed: Drugs in Nazi Germany*, is a chronicle of depravity and delusion. Historians differ over the soundness of some of author Norman Ohler's arguments. But he makes the case that a methamphetamine called Pervitin put the blitz in the Blitzkrieg, allowing the Wehrmacht to go without sleep over three days in June 1940 and breach the borders of France and Belgium before either country could mount a defense. Later, desperate to penetrate the Thames estuary during the waning months of the war, the Germans built torpedo-bearing mini-submarines and doled out cocaine-infused chewing gum to poorly trained teenage pilots, many of whom wound up drowning after prolonged sleep deprivation. And most pertinently to me, *Blitzed* contends that in July 1943, Dr. Theodor Morell, the beefy Hessian who served as the *Führer*'s personal physician, began to dope up the man he referred to in his notes as "Patient A." Morell kept Hitler under the influence for most of the rest of the war. If he hadn't fortified him by doing so, the doctor claimed, "Germany would have been brought to its knees."

The family of my grandmother Elisabeth Merck founded and still runs the world's oldest drug and chemical company. Among the substances Hitler apparently took, Merck produced two. One was the cocaine for which the firm was world-renowned. The other, an opioid called Eukodal, had a particularly insidious effect. Beginning in late 1942, Morell seems to have administered more than a thousand doses of Eukodal to Hitler over an eight-hundred-day span. This regimen, the book contends, turned the *Führer* into a junkie. After US Air Force B-17s destroyed the Merck factory in Darmstadt in December 1944, Hitler's doctor could no longer procure Eukodal and Patient A went cold turkey.

All of this leaves me swimming in a cloud of implications.

In 1826, my great-great-great-grandfather Emanuel Merck isolated the active ingredient in poppy seeds in his Darmstadt pharmacy and began to mass-produce alkaloids of standardized quality. Merck soon became famous for the purity of its morphine, and by the 1880s the firm enjoyed a virtual monopoly on the world's legitimate cocaine trade. By the early twentieth century Merck flake had such a reputation that counterfeiters in China would slap phony labels on vials to make them look like the real "Red Capsule" thing, pictured in an advertisement overleaf.

Pharmaceuticals stood out as one of Germany's few thriving industries during the economic uncertainty between the wars. One reason was Eukodal, essentially the same opioid as OxyContin, that scourge of America today. Merck had introduced the drug in 1917, marketing it as a painkiller and cough suppressant, but Eukodal caught on through the hedonistic twenties for its euphoric qualities. Twice as effective at relieving pain as morphine, capable of delivering a loftier high than heroin, Eukodal was a favorite recommendation of doctors, some

of whom became regular users themselves. The drug wasn't so much a cousin to morphine as a sibling—"Little Sister Euka," in the words of one of its devotees, Thomas Mann's son Klaus. Or as a connoisseur of later vintage, William S. Burroughs, put it in *Naked Lunch*: "Like a combination of junk and C [heroin and cocaine]. Trust the Germans to concoct some truly awful shit."

Morrell began to treat Hitler with Eukodal in July 1943, on the eve of a high-stakes meeting with Mussolini. The Allies had just landed in Sicily, and the *Führer* was desperate to keep Italy in the Axis camp. Under the influence, Hitler performed: he filibustered for almost three hours, until Il Duce reconfirmed Italy's solidarity with Germany even as Allied bombers were pummeling Rome. By October, Ohler reports, Hitler was receiving up to four times the typical therapeutic dose.

Merck drugs figured again in July 1944, in the aftermath of the failed Valkyrie plot to kill Hitler. The explosion of a bomb in a briefcase, planted by the officer Claus von Stauffenberg beneath

a table at the Wolf's Lair in East Prussia, left Hitler with a perfo-
rated and bleeding eardrum. Another doctor was summoned—an
ear, nose, and throat specialist named Erwin Giesing. Officially,
the Nazis regarded cocaine as a degenerate sacrament of Weimar
values. But Giesing prescribed Merck's finest in a 10 percent topical solution, and Hitler was pleased with its effect.

Norman Ohler describes the onset of overconfidence and
megalomania over the next few months as the *Führer*, even as
losses mounted in the east, proposed a counteroffensive in the
west. Giesing swabbed cocaine on Hitler's nose and throat each
morning, Ohler writes, while Morell continued to administer
Eukodal, now at twice the dosage of a year earlier. The result was
"the classic speedball—the sedating effect of the opioid balancing
the stimulating effect of the cocaine."

By the time of the December 1944 raid that destroyed the
Merck factory, Hitler, in the picture Ohler paints, has become
distracted and sleep-deprived, with needle marks tracking up and
down jaundiced, tremulous arms.

> *In fact, Hitler's bunker mentality had discovered in Euko-
> dal the ideal end-time drug for the hapless final battle.
> His numbness, his rigid view of the world, his tendency
> towards the fantastical and the unscrupulous transgression
> of all boundaries—all of this was ominously supported by
> the opioid that he used so frequently in the last quarter
> of 1944. During this time, when the Allies were entering
> the Reich from both east and west, the powerful narcotic
> erased any doubts about victory, and made Hitler even
> more unfeeling about both himself and the outside world.*

By January, Morell could no longer administer Eukodal
because Merck could no longer produce it. Two months later

Hitler issued his so-called Nero Decree, the order that every last shred of German infrastructure—highways, railroad tracks, bridges, power plants, factories, banks—be destroyed.

I had hoped to discover that Merck pharmaceuticals got Hitler hooked, clouding his judgment so that, as the Wehrmacht suffered reversal after reversal and German cities were destroyed from the air, withdrawal helped send him into a spiral that hastened the end of the war. Instead, *Blitzed* makes the case that cocaine and Eukodal propped him up and amped him up. The high from the drugs, then the crash from Eukodal's sudden unavailability, inured him to reality and encouraged his basest instincts. Merck alkaloids ensured that the Nazi war machine would remain deployed at full force, where a sober leader might have folded his hand.

To hear Ohler tell it, my ancestors not only contributed to Hitler's descent into that psychological bunker of madness and delusion. They also profited from it. Some truly awful shit indeed.

NINE
BLOOD AND SHAME
Kurt and Niko, 1945 to 1948

With America's entry into the war in late 1941, mail service between New York and the Reich ceased. Kurt and Helen could no longer reach my father, aunt, or grandmother, and vice versa. "Tell [Niko] that I always think of him with a love that's great and deep, that I hope for a future for him in which he will be able to live out his true purpose, and I hope at that time to be a good, helpful, and supportive friend," Kurt wrote his ex-wife in one of the last letters between New York and Munich before Pearl Harbor shut down the mails. "Please do not forget to tell him this—I would like him to know how much I, and Helen too, hold him in our thoughts, how very dear he is to us."

Soon afterward Maria wrote Kurt: "You must not dwell on how Niko is doing; he is protected, protected by his nature, and he will surely return undisturbed from all the horror to the life he knew before. From his letters one gets the feeling that he has become much more mature, more mature in his heart, and has learned to appreciate things which until now have seemed to him immaterial, things besides ravioli and technology."

With peace came a flurry of letters filled with three and a half years of pent-up news and sentiments. In the fall of 1945 Kurt finally reached Elisabeth again, writing this time in English,

a choice of language that seemed to acknowledge the new order
that would prevail for the rest of his life.

> *Now, at last, we hear through a letter from [Helen's sis-
> ter] Liesl that Niko has come home to you. I can imagine
> what this must have meant for you, and I am immeasur-
> ably happy for us both that he is safe. . . .* Embrasse-lui de
> ma part, très tendrement. *And tell him to learn English;
> seriously, I mean it. Perhaps, one day, I may be able to do
> something for him and his future.*
>
> *The memory of the past makes the bitterness fade and
> whatever beautiful days and things were shared stand out
> brightly. As time advances, I often feel the ghostliness of
> existence. We become houses inhabited by shadows and
> echoes, which co-exist hauntingly with the near and bright
> reality. . . .*
>
> *I have tried to send parcels to various addresses, in
> the hope that one or the other may reach you, though this
> is like throwing one's bread upon the water. (Each time we
> sit down to a good meal we say, How much rather would
> we send this to Europe.)*

Maria was living with her toddler son, Jon, in Freiburg, a
university town of little strategic importance whose medieval
center had been flattened one night in November 1944. Late in
January 1946, she wrote Kurt in New York about my father:

> *I've got a beautiful photo of Niko, but I don't dare send
> it, as he's in uniform, looking like a medieval knight with
> his casque de fer. Niko looks very much like you now, only
> he's much smaller, smaller than I am, in fact, and very
> fragile. His face looks quite transparent sometimes, and*

he has beautiful eyes and a lovely forehead. You would
find him changed a lot after all he went through. When
he came for his first leave from the east, having been away
for twenty-two months, I was so startled at the sight that
I nearly cried. He came late at night, quite unexpectedly.
I opened the door and found a strange, tired, grown-up
man, and he had left as a boy, fresh from Schondorf. I
can't imagine what I would have done if something had
happened to him. I used to dream about it and wake up
with a terrible fright. And the last months of the war were
pure agony.

These letters were written and read in wildly divergent con-
texts. Those whose war consisted of one set of experiences could
only imagine what other family members lived through. For all
of the Franco-Prussian War, which it won, and even World War
I, which it lost, Germany kept the conflict confined mostly to
foreign stages. Now death and destruction had come home. Half
of the country's military casualties—up to four hundred thousand each month—occurred over the final ten months of the war.
Almost unique among losers of a major conflict, the Third Reich
never surrendered, which left the Allies to prosecute their victory
by destroying whatever Hitler hadn't, from Germany's armed
forces to its sovereignty.

As evidence emerged of the death camps, the suffering of
German civilians rightly took a back seat to a full airing of Nazi
atrocities. But the German people had suffered too. British and
American bombs had leveled German cities. The advancing Red
Army had plundered German homes and raped German women.
Some twelve million Germans had been driven from their ances-
tral lands in eastern Europe, the expellees condemned to survive
amidst the rubble alongside their ethnic brethren in the west. The

world could muster little sympathy, for so many had cheered Hitler on. But that didn't diminish the scale of the misery—some twenty-six million Germans made homeless from destruction, expulsion, or flight.

Only scattered voices objected to the suffering, an oversight the novelist W. G. Sebald, writing decades later, would call a "scandalous deficiency." During the war Victor Gollancz, a Jewish publisher in London, had been among the first figures in the Allied lands to amplify early reports of the Holocaust; now he warned that the indiscriminate bombing of civilians had imperiled "the values of the West." Gollancz would be joined by the Swedish writer Stig Dagerman. "Deserved suffering is just as heavy to bear as undeserved suffering," Dagerman wrote, after touring a defeated Germany in late 1945. "It is felt just as much in the stomach, in the chest, in the feet, and these three very concrete pains should not be forgotten in the raw draft of bitterness blowing from a rainy post-war German autumn."

My family in Germany had not escaped that unrelenting aerial bombardment, from the Americans by day and the British by night. The Allies began steady raids in 1943, attacks that would target 131 German cities and towns and continue almost daily until the end of the war. The bombings wound up killing six hundred thousand German civilians, more than twice the number of military casualties suffered by US forces in Europe. But the Allied calculus—that death, injury, and homelessness would demoralize German civilians and turn them against the regime— failed to prove true. People the raids failed to kill were likely to be left too traumatized to function, much less take up sedition. One night, back in Munich on leave, Niko had joined his mother and sister in the cellar during an air raid. "Never again," he told Maria afterward. "We're like rats in a trap. I'd rather die at the front."

Among my ancestors, these radically different wartime experiences—Kurt and Helen's flight and exile, Maria and Elisabeth's fate to be "rats in a trap," Niko's service on two fronts—played out in their letters.

As Maria awaited the return of her husband Hans Baumhauer from a POW camp in France, she held down a job in Freiburg as a secretary and interpreter with the French Occupation Authority. In mid-February 1946 she wrote Kurt from that office.

> What's still hardest to bear is absolute silence. Over the past few years, during which there never was any real silence, moments of relative quiet were in fact filled with a horribly intense kind of waiting, which made those "silent" moments seem much more enlivened than the so-called animated ones. The silence we sometimes have now seems alien and horrible. It crackles, bearing strange thoughts, an impenetrable mass loaded with unknown elements of what's to come, like the electrified air just before a heavy thunderstorm. Which leads you into a strange state, full of disquiet and a sense of the surreal. . . .
>
> Imagine being afraid to be among people from your former life, because all that has transpired, and can never be adequately explained even to those closest to you, stands like some impassable wall between yourself and those who weren't there. . . .
>
> The charge now being lodged at us by outsiders—that what happened behind the iron curtain that separated Germany from the rest of the world is our fault—can only be brought by someone who was behind that curtain at the time and knows how it was. . . .

> *Determining guilt or innocence can only be done by
> those who have thoroughly tasted the bitterness of the past
> twelve years—all the way, to the end.*

Maria is no longer an insecure adolescent. She now courts her father's empathy rather than his approval, sharing what it's like to be a rat in a trap:

> *No one who hasn't actually experienced it can imagine
> that feeling of helplessness and vulnerability. No one
> can fathom the sensations packed between the sound of
> the air-raid sirens and the "all clear," and no one knows
> how it is for someone who must swallow those emo-
> tions not once, but day after day, night after night. Until
> your first big air raid, you still have the courage of the
> clueless. . . .*
>
> *Tired and sleep-deprived, you tumble down the
> stone cellar steps into a dank darkness. Into an illusion
> of safety. No light. A candle stump in a bottle. On the
> ground, crouching figures in grotesque guises. Light carves
> out tired, dull faces in the blackness, as if making an etch-
> ing by Rembrandt or Goya.*
>
> *The air begins to tremble faintly from the vibra-
> tions of the airplane engines. The quaking extends into
> the walls, creeps over the cellar floor, continues into the
> crouching bodies. The barking of the flak begins, a bar-
> rage of artillery fire from the heavy batteries. Through
> the trap door of the cellar "escape hatch" you can see a
> rectangle of velvety night sky split by searchlights. Sud-
> denly, flares: the city is being target-marked—"Christmas
> trees" have been deployed. The "escape hatch" slaps shut.
> And so it begins.*

In cellars all over Germany, the courage of the clueless went to die.

> We lie flat on the basement floor so as not to be knocked over by the force of a blast. The damp, icy cold slowly creeps through thick clothes and coats down to the bone. Yet you don't freeze: your glowing, hot face is pressed against the dank floor.
>
> You sense a strange, wavelike tremor, eerily silent and threatening. The first "carpet." Now it comes: a rushing blast of air pressure, and you swear your eardrums will burst. The house sways, as if a huge hand is squeezing it from above. Within the walls, plaster rains down. The tinkling of glass. The smell of rubble and fire. Then quiet. After a few seconds it begins all over again. In between, the heavy-caliber weaponry, howling. You crouch there like a target with an arrow trained at it, an arrow that bores into your heart. . . .
>
> Suddenly, silence. Still unbelieving, no one moves. Then consciousness gradually returns, life slowly flows back into your shocked body to shake it loose from its torpor. Tired and battered, you crawl up the cellar steps. . . . The sky is red from fire. The house is filled with cold air and the acrid smell of smoke pouring through broken windows. The walls are cracked, and plaster lies in shards on the ground. . . .
>
> Drained, shivering, and deathly exhausted, you dump yourself back into bed and sink into an abyss of confused sleep and restless dreams.

Maria deploys this description in service of the main points she wants to make to her father: that "we're not the same people you left behind in 1939 . . . those versions of ourselves are buried beneath the rubble"; and that Thomas Mann has no grounds to "cast stones at us and claim we're all implicated in blood and shame."

Maria fingers Mann, the exiled novelist who lived out the war in Princeton and Pacific Palisades, for having asserted, "It is impossible to demand of the abused nations of Europe, of the world, that they shall draw a neat dividing line between 'Nazism' and the German people."

Kurt tries to comfort his daughter in a carefully scripted reply. But he winds up confirming Maria's charge that an "impassable wall" has gone up between them.

> *Your letter of February 17th moved me very much and weighs on me still. I answer you with hesitation, as two things make it difficult: One, I feel that you all must be treated very tenderly and gently after the horrific experiences of recent years and in light of all that you're now going through; thus I must avoid saying anything that could further hurt you in your fragile state. And the other reason is that I hate nothing more than to play the role of judge or Pharisee. But I think there's no danger of the latter, for I feel one with you as a native German. We Germans begat Hitler, not Hitler the Germans. I had already cut the cord with Germany as early as 1930, as you know, but no one can absolve oneself of one's responsibilities simply by booking passage to another country. After all, I lived in Germany into my forty-third year and have as much responsibility as anyone to answer for this country by dint of my ancestry and past. "We are our brother's keeper."*

Kurt nonetheless calls out her description of "the bitterness of the past twelve years."

Oh, Maria, you should know better. You and the majority of Germans had it only too good until 1939. . . . There were no martyrs then, and during those same years, which we spent serenely, there was suffering, pain, and horror within Germany that we failed to recognize and take seriously. . . . And from 1939 on, you and I saw things through different eyes—or rather you, nearly all of you, didn't see them, didn't want to see things as they were.

In France, I crossed paths with many victims of the German concentration camps, people with shattered bones, men who had been emasculated, turned into physical and psychological wrecks. . . . And as the dear German soldiers were sending you silk stockings and chocolates from Paris, French civilians had taken to back roads to flee the taunting of German dive-bombers, and I, your father, ragged and harried, with a heart filled with fear, was escaping on foot, marching all day, so as not to fall into the hands of those same dear German soldiers. . . .

Oh, Maria, you describe the hell of 1944 and '45. Where was your conscience between 1939 and '43? Warsaw, Rotterdam, Coventry, Lidice, the extermination of hundreds of thousands of Poles, Czechs, Jews, Russians, you didn't lose any sleep over that. . . . It took more than three years for the boomerang to return, for Germany to become one of the victims. In a metaphysical sense, the Germans brought their suffering upon themselves. . . .

In this ash heap, people now talk of guilt. And you confront the dead, who tell old tales as they climb from their graves. My child, no one can absolve oneself through suffering unless suffering is freely chosen.

Kurt then turns to the German roots he and Maria share:

The guilt you refer to is an old guilt, much older than the war. The Germans will only reconcile with themselves and the world if, out of their own fear and suffering, they recognize the suffering of others—those whose mortal fear was no less than yours, only more senseless, more hopeless, thanks to the capriciousness of their tormentors, tormentors who were Germans. No one can absolve us of this, not you, not me.

How cowardly the Germans were. To understand, consider the behavior of others: Brave Italians and Frenchmen hid and saved many of their Jews, protected them from their own secret police and the Gestapo, and thousands of others saved and fed German, Austrian, and Polish Jews, fed them throughout, putting their own lives at risk to do so. . . . The Germans in Germany looked the other way when their friends committed suicide, when they disappeared into the camps—they didn't know anything or didn't want to know. But, again, we are our brother's keeper. "The tormentor and the tormented are one and the same. The former is mistaken in thinking he's not party to the torment; the latter in thinking he's not party to the guilt," says Schopenhauer. . . .

For goodness sake, don't think I see all Germans as black and guilty, and others as all white and innocent. . . . In the main, however, I believe that we Germans are complicit in any injustice that others now commit. For the Germans unleashed the dogs of hell upon the world—hatred, wickedness, evil, cruelty—so that all of Europe is infected and sick, and another boomerang lands back whence this plague came.

Ultimately, Kurt sides with Thomas Mann.

A fresh start for the Germans is possible only by acknowledging our immense guilt. Thomas Mann is right: all of us are covered in blood and shame. We must acknowledge this fact, no ifs, ands, or buts, and accept it unreservedly. This is the task for the present and the future. God has kept us alive to address this problem, and only the prospect of its solution gives the next generation hope for a life worth living. Whether someone is as young as you or as old as I, our lives will hardly be long enough to complete this task, and how long we get to engage it is up to God's grace. Change in the world will not come through the United Nations, nor from the outside; individuals, you and I, we must transform ourselves until it leads to wisdom and enlightenment in us. In this light, children will grow up to be better, more responsible people. ("The child learns not from what parents say, but how they live."—C. G. Jung.)

I've been trying to show you that we see through different eyes, because you were on the inside and I was on the outside. This geographical difference should cease to exist. We should now see through the same eyes. We are bound by fate with the same task before us.

Father and daughter have each staked a claim to the truth as he or she lived it. Maria gave birth during an air raid, and her son, Jon, wasn't yet ten months old when another night's bombardment left their apartment uninhabitable. In believing in the singularity of a still-fresh "end with horror," she shared the perspective of millions of shell-shocked Germans. At the same time, Maria was only beginning to learn the particulars of Kurt and Helen's flight with Christian from France—a trauma that led seven-year-old Christian, after the separation and escapes of 1940 and '41, to tell his parents, "All I hope for is that the whole family perishes in the same catastrophe."

Any extended back-and-forth over guilt and shame, or pleas for empathy or self-criticism, would be cut short. Maria pushed back only feebly in a subsequent letter, and both she and Kurt signaled that some things were best taken up face-to-face. After engaging in a similar exchange with her sister back in Bavaria, Helen too concluded that this wasn't a subject to be pressed, not from afar, not with the memories of war so raw.

The day after Kurt wrote Maria that letter, she sent him one of her own, in which she refers to a photograph of my father she had shared earlier—perhaps the one here, on the back of which Niko has written "Hungry Summer." If her words seem excessively pitying, I'd attribute that to her sisterly compassion and an incomplete sense of the scale of Nazi atrocities.

That photo of Niko, alas, is an accurate one. His expression
captures two and a half years of the Russian campaign and
the lethal exhaustion from which we all suffer. Aside from
the physical hardships, the icy winters in the east, all the
things he saw, and the hunger, Niko felt the terror of it
all. At the end of his furloughs I'd be the one to take him
to the train station to head back to the front, and the sight
of his face, pale and distracted, and his body, buffeted by
that sea of field-gray in the half-destroyed station, will
always remain unforgettable to me. The last time, with
those trains overflowing with lambs to be led to slaugh-
ter, the pointlessness was so cruelly clear to us both that
no words of consolation had the slightest effect. The last
thing Niko said to me was, "It's all over, and now they're
sticking pistols in the backs of our necks and driving us to
certain death."

There's a subgenre of German literature called the *Heim-
kehrerroman*, the novel that deals with the soldier back from the
front. My father's *Heimkehr*—his homecoming—was smoother
than that of many others. Occupants of the house on the Südliche
Schlossrondell could still count on a working stove. But Allied
forces had commandeered the little available wood and coal. Toi-
lets and water lines froze. My grandmother's home quickly filled
up with boarders, assigned there by authorities desperate to house
the homeless. Niko and Elisabeth consolidated themselves in the
dining room, clear of their uninvited guests—the woman who
taught Slavic studies at the university; the avuncular gentleman
from the Bavarian countryside; the married couple, both psycho-
analysts, whose four-year-old son my father came to call *le fils
expérimental*. As they prepared to face that first postwar winter,
the American officer in charge, Lieutenant General Lucius Clay,

put the locals on notice: "Some cold and hunger will be necessary to make the German people realize the consequences of a war which they caused."

For Niko, it all became too much. One morning he showed up at breakfast with a cardboard sign hanging from his neck. *BITTE NICHT ANSPRECHEN*, it read—PLEASE DON'T SPEAK TO ME.

In Munich in early 1946, a German civilian could expect an allocation of 1,330 calories per day. To supplement these rations, Kurt and Helen sent regular CARE packages, as well as food and clothing. In the meantime, Niko found ways to make some money. The Archdiocese of Munich-Freising hired him to take measurements and draw sketches to help restore the Bürgersaalkirche in the city center. A training film called *Your Job in Germany*—written and produced by Theodor Geisel, the American grandson of four German immigrants, who would go on to become Dr. Seuss—had warned occupying soldiers not to fraternize with locals. But that policy proved impractical and was quickly abandoned, so my father would loiter outside an American PX with a camera, offering to take photographs of GIs and make prints they could send home. Sometimes he took payment in food or cigarettes instead of cash.

As soon as the Institute of Technology reopened in March 1946, Niko returned to the chemistry department, where he and fellow students improvised a lab in one of the buildings still standing. As he heeded Kurt's advice to improve his English, nothing helped more than the midday jazz show on the American Forces Network, *Luncheon in Munchen*. When a woman with the American Occupation Authority swung by the Schlossrondell in her jeep one day to drop off aid packages, Niko chatted her up. He eventually procured photographic paper for her; in return, she posted letters to Kurt in Manhattan, including this

one, dated September 19, 1946, in which he too wants to make
sure his father knows what life has been like.

> *We're currently living in the age of the questionnaire. You
> have no idea what you can be asked and what people are
> interested in. There is the standard questionnaire with
> 132 entries, about one meter long, which serves to ascer-
> tain one's past, political and otherwise. You don't have
> to fill that one out too often, but almost every couple of
> weeks come extensive instructions on how to correctly fill
> something out. You are registered, you get a new identity
> card, you need a registration card from the employment
> office, and food ration cards . . . and then there are the fuel
> ration cards, which must be brought to the coal dealer,
> and you have to make sure, when a quarter cubic meter
> of wood becomes available, that you get it home imme-
> diately. . . . They record your marital and occupational
> status, and then come more questionnaires pertaining to
> the upcoming elections . . . and just when you think you're
> getting a brief break, a man shows up in the doorway. Says
> he's from the housing office. He's usually very kind and
> polite, for this unhappy man is desperate to find places for
> poor people living in shelters or like pigs in the street, and
> you show him all your rooms and the dear subtenants who
> live in them, and how you regret not being able to help
> him. . . . I'll spare you any more.*

At seven a.m. on fair-weather days, an eighty-four-year-old
handyman named Joseph would show up at the house on the
Schlossrondell to cut wood and rake leaves. "Unfortunately he's
half-blind and can't be trusted with the vegetable garden," my

father reports. "One time he pulled up and threw out the onions and left the weeds in place. So with my help, Mutti does the gardening more or less alone. . . . For a few weeks now we've had cool autumn weather. I look ahead with horror at the winter to come, without windows—now the third year like that—with little to heat the house. But we survived last winter, and so it must be."

The first questionnaire my father mentions was for the de-Nazification process, administered by courts known as *Spruchkammern*. Ex-Nazis could be assigned to one of five classes, ranked V, IV, III, II, and I, in ascending order of guilt: exonerated or non-incriminated; collaborators or fellow travelers (*Mitläufer*); lesser offenders; activists or militants; or major offenders. Unless he had been implicated in serious crimes, a common soldier born after 1919—my father cleared this cutoff by two years—was presumed, absent evidence otherwise, to be not worth prosecuting.

In early October 1946, Niko sent his father another letter, this time describing a trip to Darmstadt, where he saw his uncle Wilhelm for the first time since the war.

Wilhelm Merck was Elisabeth's younger brother, a Merck Darmstadt director with a dandy's sense of style and a passion for racing cars. Little Niko had idolized him. In a deal the firm struck during the twenties with Mercedes-Benz, Merck would buy only Mercedes cars for its company fleet. In return, Wilhelm received the use of two automobiles, one for personal purposes and another to race in rallies—an SSK-300 Sport Kabriolet with chrome tubes sprouting from both sides of the hood and headlights bugging out from beside each front fender.

Until her suicide in 1927, his wife, Ernesta, shown with Wilhelm in this photograph, had been an automotive celebrity in her own right, featured in the pictured Mercedes ad campaign as the

flapper-like "Lady in Red." Huge trophies in the living room of their Darmstadt home attested to the success of them both. During visits Niko would slip into the driver's seat and grip the wheel of that Kabriolet, with the black finish of the chassis setting off red leather upholstery. He imagined himself negotiating the storied Nürburgring, bagging a trophy of his own.

Those days were long gone, as Niko reported to his father upon returning from Darmstadt. "The streets are spick-and-span, completely undamaged, but . . . you pass the oozing rubble from the once-pretty shops of the Wilhelminenberg," he wrote. "It pours out on to the sidewalk like thick porridge." He found Uncle Wilhelm's home in ruins. Nothing had prepared Niko for the sight of his hero, who now lived out back in a garden shed.

> *Uncle Wilhelm looks terrible. He has a tiny bird's head, very thin hands, and a back thoroughly hunched from spinal arthritis. He doesn't look like this because he hasn't had enough to eat; he had a complete nervous breakdown and is*

> *totally at wit's end. What with moving from the Löwentor*
> *to [the home of the distant cousin he had married, Lisbet]*
> *and concern over the construction of this emergency lodg-*
> *ing, and all the other worries about the [Merck] factory,*
> *Manuel [Wilhelm's son Emanuel, still imprisoned in the*
> *Soviet Union], and etc., he has been laid low.*

Niko's return trip turned into an odyssey. "When we got back to Munich, exhausted and dead tired, we had to wait in the rain for an hour for the tram," he wrote. "But it had stopped running, so we had to walk a half hour in search of another. All thanks to our *'Führer.'*"

After a war's worth of my father's letters, each drafted with an awareness that it would have to clear the censors, finally, a slap at Hitler.

That German winter of 1946–47, the one Niko feared, turned out indeed to be epically cold. Barges loaded with provisions froze fast in the ice. Desperate women climbed atop the coal cars of slow-moving trains to toss off lumps for later collection. Germans cut down any standing tree for firewood, wrenching stumps from the frozen ground. Pictured opposite, in an almost barren Tiergarten, a Berliner hacks away within sight of the husk of the Reichstag.

In the meantime, in Freiburg, Maria's bitterness abided. Kurt's daughter was now a single parent, as she and her husband split up soon after his *Heimkehr*. A complicated relationship with her mother—Elisabeth never fully accepted Maria's bohemian ways or her artist husband—foreclosed for the moment the option of moving back in with her in Munich, even if there had been room in the house on the Schlossrondell. Still not sure her father in New York fully understood, she felt alone.

   For his part, Niko wanted more than anything to join Kurt
in the United States. And it turned out his father was indeed
"able to do something for him." My father soon held the equivalent of a bachelor's degree, and the head of the chemistry department at Princeton, the soon-to-be-knighted English atomic
chemist Hugh Stott Taylor, told Kurt that he needed only to
see a transcript to offer Niko a place as a graduate student and
arrange for financial aid. "Professor Taylor was an immigrant
too," my father told me once. "He was willing to admit me sight
unseen." Taylor's guarantee allowed Niko to apply for a student
visa. In the meantime Kurt, a US citizen since December 1946,
swore out an affidavit pledging that his son would not become a
public charge.

During air raids, my grandmother had descended the cellar stairs, posture erect and lit candle in hand, wearing a French World War I helmet Dr. Albrecht had brought back from the front as a souvenir, "looking like she stepped out of a Delacroix painting," as Maria put it. One Allied bomb had left a crater in her garden; another, which came through the roof and landed on the dresser in her bedroom, failed to explode. Now Elisabeth was reluctant to accept that Niko, despite the hold placed on his own life, would not stay indefinitely at her side. But on Christmas Eve in 1947, in a short poem acknowledging that this would likely be their last together, Elisabeth seemed to accept his need to leave for America. She invoked the word *Heimat*, which can mean home, and homeland, and a broad range of things besides—from the community familiar to you to the landscape you were born into. And she deployed the imagery of the forest, *der Wald*, a place so sacred and powerful in German culture that more than a thousand longer words are built on it, words like *Waldumrauscht*, the rustling sound of leaves in the woods:

> *You want to swap your* Heimat *for foreign things,*
> *The New World lures you,*
> *The red maple forests powerfully rustling . . .*

> *Europe is dying, the weary people yearn for death's sleep,*
> *Seeking only rest and balm for their wounds,*
> *Since they encountered the god of war*

In June 1947, Kurt finally returned to Europe, where he saw Maria and Niko for the first time in nearly nine years. Niko came over from Munich to meet his sister in Freiburg, and together they took the Basel Express south, to Weil am Rhein, on the

Swiss border, to meet up with the man they called *der Greis*, the Old One.

Maria worked through the tangle of emotions of that visit in "Wiedersehen und Abschied: Selbstgespräche mit dem Vater" (Reunion and Farewell: Interior Dialogues with Father), a reminiscence published anonymously in Germany the following year. She and her brother abandoned their compartment to stand in the corridor of the railroad carriage, trying somehow to will the train to go faster. But they made the trip having "grown deeply mistrustful of fortune," Maria writes, "that anything happy might break our way."

They alighted at the train station in Weil, then followed a winding road that led finally to a customhouse at the border. As soon as they made out the figure standing behind a wooden barrier, waving at them with outstretched arms, they fell into a trot. Of that moment Maria writes:

> *I'm at the end of a marathon lasting nine years, with only a few hundred meters before the tape, and I feel Niko next to me, as if a part of me, and the tears run down my face so I can't see a thing until, with my last strength, I stumble against the barrier and feel an arm around my shoulder and Niko's head close to mine and rough wool fabric on my wet cheek and a voice above me, completely unchanged, I could pick it out from a thousand, cheerfully saying:*
>
> *"But don't get all excited. What have you done with your bags?"*

Niko never mentioned this reunion to me, and I wouldn't want to impute to him everything his sister was feeling. But I'm certain my father would recognize many of the brushstrokes in the portrait of Kurt that Maria goes on to paint in her piece—of

a man strong and substantive but elusive too, a serial escape artist who somehow escaped harm, escaped Europe, and, whatever
his intentions, for long stretches escaped his fatherly obligations.
For all the strings Kurt would pull to help Niko start a new life
in the New World, he could do nothing to get him or Maria out
of Nazi Germany.

Kurt drove Maria and Niko back to Freiburg in his rental
car. On the outskirts of the city, Maria describes how "the first
real evidence of war and destruction begins to reveal itself" — "[a]
half-destroyed building, like a dollhouse, revealing its secrets up
to the attic. Homes where people lived and died, were happy and
suffered. Cellar holes full of filth and rubbish . . ."

> *You look out the window and, seeing a German city for
> the first time, interrupt your stories for a moment and
> say, "Actually, I've made up my mind not to look at the
> rubble."*
>
> *And these few words, they hurt me somewhat, a mix-
> ture of anger and fright rises inside me, but then I think,
> Yes, you don't need to look at it, just wait a bit and it will
> look at you — it'll grab you by the throat, and you'll sud-
> denly realize that this was once your life as much as ours.*
>
> *We drive through a welter of streets, none of them
> undamaged, and . . . I too force myself not to see the destruc-
> tion, and think that maybe I've become too sensitive.*
>
> *We finally reach our destination and try to drive the
> big American car through the garden gate, to more easily
> unload the luggage, but it can't be done, the gate is too small.*
>
> *The gate is too small. Probably not just in this par-
> ticular case — no, here everything suddenly seems too small,
> too cramped, too tired. Even language, the possibility to
> express oneself.*

Maria had returned to the same theme she broached in that letter to her father sixteen months earlier, in which she privileged those who actually lived through the horror, "all the way, to the end."

In fact, Kurt was well aware of the destruction. A year earlier Pantheon had published *Lost Treasures of Europe*, a volume with more than four hundred plates of masterpieces now damaged or ruined—"from Coventry to Kiev, from Cassino to Rotterdam," he had written Maria, "that part of Europe's cultural heritage destroyed by this war and the human eye will not see again." A year after this reunion, Kurt would be back in Germany on assignment from Washington, with letters of introduction from the National Gallery of Art and Library of Congress. He would spend four weeks furiously chasing down the fruits of what was known as the *Führerprojekt*, a professionally shot, full-color photographic survey, ordered by Hitler in 1943 as the Allies ramped up their air raids, so that frescoes, statuary, and other immovable and jeopardized works of art could be restored or reconstructed after the victory of the Reich.

Yet to Maria, it seemed her father was busy taking inventory of what the war had forever changed, not who.

At the end of their father's visit, Maria and Niko put Kurt on an overnight train from Freiburg to Paris, from which he would go to Le Havre to board a ship back to New York. "Oh, horrible, agonizing train stations," Maria laments on the platform, as she recalls leave-takings going back to the early thirties. The *Bahnhof* recurs in her account for a reason. During the immediate postwar, railway stations became the hub of life, "the focal point of an often miserable, transient, provisional existence: the place where, despite the collapse of rail transport in the spring of 1945, refugees arrived, notes were left by people seeking lost family members, and the black market thrived," the historian Richard Bessel writes. "The entire country seemed to be waiting for a train to arrive: a train that would bring their families together, a train that would enable them to go home."

But for the Wolffs there would be no permanent reunion.

Through the window I see you negotiating with the sleeping-car conductor, and I see your lips moving as if in a silent movie, and even though I can't hear your words, I know you're bribing him so you can have a compartment to yourself. I see you in the most exaggerated detail: gray coat, pale profile, dark hat. . . . And a thousand things I want to say sit in my throat in a strangling lump, and I know I can't say them anymore.

You pull the window down and lean out toward me, give me a lost look, and I feel you close to me, because I sense that you're just as mute as I am, yet at the same time . . . already in Paris, already on the ship, the vastness of the ocean distancing you farther and farther from me, that other part of the world absorbing you—the foreign, the busy, the living.

And the train starts up and pulls your hand from mine, and your face, sad and pale, floats above me, and I see in it a weariness that's bound up in our overall fatigue, and I feel it's high time you get away, away from all this horror, before you understand it completely, fully understand it.

And finally, finally, I can turn around and cry as the train tolls out of the station behind me: away, away. Past, over. . . .

Now I realize what I wanted so desperately to say to you in those last seconds by the train, when the lump in my throat wouldn't let me: "Get us out, take us away

from here, soon. . . . Only over there, in another country,
can we find a common language once again!"

I get off at the train station in Fürstenberg an der Havel, halfway between Berlin and the Baltic, and follow a path I imagine
prisoners walking seventy-five years ago. The route comes way-
marked for tourists now, with ideograms painted on the sidewalk
—concentration-camp stripes here, a filament of barbed wire
there. It's a bit more than a kilometer from the station to the camp
itself, but even without the blazes I could have found my way
at the final fork in the road, where Ravensbrücker Dorfstrasse
veers off to the right. That's where a lilac bush in full bloom spills
over a fence to cast shade on the sidewalk. After a fall and winter
I've spent immersed in my father's family, spring is here, with the
scent of my mother on the breeze.

In 2016, a historical novel called *Lilac Girls* began an
unlikely climb up US best-seller lists. It tells a story of three
young women: a German detailed to the Ravensbrück concentration camp as part of a team of Nazi doctors carrying out grotesque medical experiments; a Polish prisoner on whom those
procedures are performed; and a well-born American actress-
turned-philanthropist, who after the war learns of the plight of
the camp's victims, champions their cause, and brings them to the
United States for treatment.

The German doctor was a historical figure convicted at the
Nuremberg trials. The Pole is the novelist's invention. And the
American, Caroline Woolsey Ferriday, appears in the book as
herself. The first cousin of my mother's father, she cultivated the
lilacs of the novel's title at her country estate in Bethlehem, Connecticut, between her bouts of activism.

Caroline, shown here around mid-century, shared the social status, physical stature, politics, and restless spirit of the countess in Saint-Lary. Though barely twelve at the outbreak of World War I, she was moved to write a relative that the kaiser had gone "rank mad." Caroline's father, Henry McKeen Ferriday, along with her aunt, Henry's sister and my great-grandmother Elizabeth Ferriday Neave, spent several of their formative years in France, and Henry passed along to his only child a Francophilia that would last her life. Caroline had learned French from private tutors and was volunteering at the French consulate in Manhattan when the Nazis invaded France. After the war she led fundraising appeals to benefit the families of Free French fighters who had lost their lives.

Caroline never married or had children, but she recognized in my mother—her cousin Alex's daughter Mary—a kindred spirit of the next generation. After being told as a teen that she couldn't take a Jewish friend swimming at the family's country club, Mary Neave let her WASP parents know that "it's just not done" was no good reason. As an adult my mother lived a

defiantly private life, believing one's name should appear in the paper three times only, upon birth, marriage, and death, but that didn't keep her from leaving a public footprint. Whether playing the piano for shut-ins, or recruiting and training volunteers to teach adults how to read, or dragging us to services after Martin Luther King Jr.'s assassination, one child in her arms and another clinging to her skirt, she drew her line and made clear on which side she stood. As she grew older she gave to many of Caroline's causes, and not just because her lilac-cultivating cousin had left her some money to do so. And my mother made sure we knew that her grandparents came from Louisiana, Tennessee, North Carolina, and that northernmost Southern town, Cincinnati—places that together made for a weighty historical inheritance in their own right.

Upon reaching the grounds of Ravensbrück, the only camp the Nazis built exclusively for women, you see the old SS quarters first—a scatter of vernacular villas with pitched roofs set amidst pine trees. Near them sits the modern visitors' center, from which you can catch the shimmer of Lake Schwedt, where the Nazis dumped the ashes from the crematorium. The first structure to interrupt this idyll is the main administrative building, the *Kommandantur*; beyond it rises the massive camp wall, with its main gate issuing directly on to the *Appellplatz*, the roll-call square, where prisoners stood to be counted, humiliated, beaten, and selected for work or mutilation or death.

Just off the *Appellplatz* lies the site of the old *Revier*, the infirmary, where the Nazis turned a cordoned-off ward into a torture chamber. Doctors deliberately wounded the legs of prisoners selected for their youth and health. They introduced pus, soil, glass, or splinters into exposed areas to induce infection, which they treated with sulfonamides—although some prisoners in a control group received no treatment at all. Of the seventy-five women subjected to these experiments, all but one of them Poles, at least five died as a result and another six were killed at the conclusion of the protocol. The rest were left to hop around the camp on one good leg. Repurposing as a badge of honor the German term for laboratory rabbits, *Versuchskaninchen*, they called themselves "the Rabbits."

The Nazis didn't fully appreciate that some of their captives, imprisoned in the first place for resistance activity, knew the arts of espionage. Using a camera smuggled into the camp on a prisoner transport from Warsaw, inmates surreptitiously took photographs of the Rabbits' wounds and deformities, then hid the film until a released prisoner could smuggle it out. With a urine-based invisible ink, they wrote on envelopes of letters home what was being done to whom; by applying a hot iron, family members could read each message, whose gist the Polish Resistance relayed to the world beyond. An August 1943 edition of a Polish underground newspaper carried the headline HORRIFIC ATROCITIES IN RAVENSBRÜCK and detailed the experiments, even naming the doctors involved, including the one featured in *Lilac Girls*, Hertha Oberheuser. Not until April 1945, in a deal brokered with the Nazis by the Swedish Red Cross and the Danish government, did a fleet of white buses transport the surviving Rabbits to neutral Sweden.

Caroline learned of the Rabbits from women of the French Resistance who had been imprisoned at Ravensbrück and became her friends after the war. For years she and others tried to exact reparations from the West German government. But Ravensbrück was liberated by the Red Army, not the western Allies, so the Rabbits' story remained little known in the west. Bonn claimed it had no influence because of its lack of diplomatic ties with Poland, now in the Soviet Bloc. And a camp for mostly

non-Jewish women didn't fit neatly into the Holocaust narrative
the world had been processing since the end of the war.

Caroline finally won a breakthrough in 1958, when she
prevailed on *Saturday Review* editor Norman Cousins to write
about the Rabbits' plight. In response, readers donated enough
money to bring thirty-five of the victims to the United States that
December. Those who needed surgery or therapy received it, and
Caroline hosted four of the women at her Bethlehem home over
Christmas. In the meantime she engaged Benjamin Ferencz, who
had prosecuted leaders of the *Einsatzgruppen* at the Nuremberg
trials, to lean on the Federal Republic of Germany. As the Rabbits generated steady publicity during their US tour, the West
German government finally agreed to help cover the cost of their
treatment. Five years later the Germans paid out reparations too.
Upon learning that Dr. Oberheuser was practicing as a pediatri-
cian in northern Germany—she had been released only five years
into a twenty-year sentence—Caroline successfully led a pres-
sure campaign to strip her of her medical license.

Among the ancestors my mother and I share with Caroline is a
slaveholder named William Calvin Ferriday. He took possession
of four-thousand-acre Helena Plantation in Louisiana's Concordia Parish as a gift from the family of his bride, Helen Catherine
Smith, of Natchez, Mississippi, upon their marriage in 1826. One
of their sons, J.C., granted rights-of-way through the plantation
to a succession of railroad lines before his death in 1894, and soon
this depot carved out of the family landholdings took the name
Ferriday.

According to a census J.C. himself conducted on the eve
of the Civil War, the Ferridays then held in slavery 149 people.
Two years later J.C.'s brother, William Calvin Jr. (Caroline's

grandfather and my great-great-grandfather), an ordained Presbyterian minister who had gone north to study at Lafayette College and Princeton Theological Seminary, volunteered as a chaplain with the Pennsylvania 121st Infantry. He did so in defiance of the family's several generations of investment in "the Southern way of life."

Unsettled by her slaveholding ancestors, Caroline drew instead on the righteous heritage of her grandfather, as well as the abolitionism championed by a long line of Woolseys on her mother's side. Her activism doubled as atonement for the actions of her forebears. In taking inventory of Caroline's contributions to the black freedom struggle—from helping to found the first African American–owned bank in Harlem; to providing financial support for civil rights organizations and historically black colleges; to supporting racial justice in the Louisiana town that carries the family name—I can hear Kurt's injunction to Maria: *Whether someone is as young as you or as old as I, our lives will hardly be long enough to complete this task, and how long we get to engage it is up to God's grace.*

Readers of *Lilac Girls* know a fictionalized Caroline—a woman who has an affair with a married Frenchman and, when she discovers her paramour's lost daughter in an orphanage after the war, only grudgingly reunites the girl with him and his Jewish wife. A novelist might be excused these plot devices to keep a character from coming off as too saintly to be believable. But Caroline lived a real life beyond the pages of that book. She really did say her prayers before breakfast each morning. Born just before midnight on a July third, she celebrated each Fourth of July as if patriotism were congenital.

If we're looking for character flaws, there would be plenty to count. We could start with stubborn and be sure to include "impatient," a word one Rabbit, Stanisława Śledziejowska-Osiczko, employed to describe Caroline, explaining, "She wanted to change the world in one day." But if indeed "our lives will hardly be long enough to complete this task," that's surely the tempo we should adopt, every day.

What Caroline did, what my mother did too, is nothing more than complete the transit to adulthood. As Susan Neiman puts it, "Growing up involves sifting through all the things you couldn't help inheriting and figuring out what you want to claim as your own, and what you have to do to dispose of the rest of it."

There is no better staging ground for this exercise than the city I now board a train to return to. Berlin, Neiman adds, "makes ethics a grounded, constant presence; any concrete slab or bullet hole could remind you of moral questions."

TEN
CHAIN MIGRATION
Niko, 1948 to 1952

O n August 5, 1948, the SS *Ernie Pyle*, a converted cargo ship, left Southampton for New York. Its passengers included hundreds of Americans returning from visits to the United Kingdom, a handful of Yiddish-speaking Holocaust survivors, and my father. The western Allies had introduced currency reform only a week earlier, which made virtually worthless the 10,000 Reichsmarks, once worth about $1,000, that Clara Merck had long ago bequeathed to her then eight-year-old grandson. Thus Niko carried ten dollars in his pocket and, with no formal German government to claim citizenship of, was listed on the manifest as "stateless."

Assigned to the lower deck, he took a bunk beneath a young priest from New Jersey who had been visiting relatives in Germany. The priest practiced his German on Niko, who tried out his English in turn. One night Father Joe introduced him to that foundational rite of American Catholicism, bingo, the lone entertainment on board. Niko began playing the twenty-five-cents-per-card minimum with his grubstake. He quit one dollar in, after finding himself ten dollars ahead. "My first investment," he would call it.

It was five a.m. and still dark when the *Ernie Pyle*, captured by my father in the photograph here, sailed into New York harbor after eight days at sea. Niko stood on the foredeck, bathed in the humid air of an August dawn. The tip of lower Manhattan loomed like the prow of another ship. To his right lay a line of lights, cars already thick on the Brooklyn Bridge. Then, above the outer boroughs, a huge orange orb—the sun rising to illuminate the skyline on this dawning Friday, a Friday the thirteenth. The welter of sensations left him feeling as if he were under the spell of a fever.

For my father, who had turned twenty-seven one month earlier, this was his very own *Stunde Null*, or zero hour, as Germans would come to call the reset brought by the Allied occupation. His father had been a man in a hurry: Kurt went into publishing at twenty-one and founded his own firm five years later, marrying in between. But Niko's childhood had been jolted by divorce, his adolescence disfigured by Nazism, his adulthood stayed by war. Because of armed conflict, disease, or death in captivity, half of his demographic cohort, German males born shortly after World War I, failed to survive their twenties. In 1773 the political philosopher Johann Georg Schlosser wrote a letter to one of my ancestors, the writer Johann Heinrich Merck, with a few lines Kurt liked to cite: "There is still something between joy, suffering, and indifference. I do not know what to call it, but whatever it is, I know I would like to find it. It's something like a child's life." For Niko, precisely this kind of ordinary existence—the life Kurt knew he wanted more of and the one I would take for granted—could at long last begin.

Upon disembarking from the *Ernie Pyle*, many of the Holocaust survivors were met by family members who worked in the diamond trade on Forty-Seventh Street. Niko could count nineteen dollars to his name as well as American family to fetch him at the pier. He was about to benefit from what would one day be contemptuously called "chain migration."

Kurt and Christian escorted him to the apartment on Washington Square. A week later, with Helen, they took a train north to Albany, where they were met by Kurt's exile friends Richard and Editha Sterba, pupils of Freud's from Vienna, who drove them to their summer home in Glastenbury, Vermont. Gaining altitude, feeling the humidity fall away, watching the sky get bluer and the landscape greener, Niko marveled that a place so much like Bavaria could be among the United States.

The Sterbas spent the rest of the year in Grosse Pointe, Michigan, where they had become prosperous by renting space on their couch to doctors, children, and auto executives. But every summer they relocated to Vermont with their two daughters, a cook, a housekeeper, and several horses. A parade of friends filed through their compound, with its wood-clad buildings and swimming pool, mostly fellow refugees, many of them musicians, including the pianist Claude Frank, who might join Richard, an amateur violinist, to play after meals. With music, nature, three meals a day, and enough spoken German to keep him from feeling lost, the setting cushioned my father's landing.

Before leaving the Sterbas at the end of that summer, Niko was driven the ten miles to the Bennington office of the Vermont DMV, where his Luftwaffe-honed skills behind the wheel proved sharp enough for him to pass the state driver's test. Over Labor Day weekend he drove Kurt, Helen, and Christian back to Washington Square in Kurt's 1948 Ford, which would ordinarily be garaged near the Sterbas' property over the winter, but Niko would now use to shuttle between Princeton and Manhattan on weekends.

In addition to helping his son get that position as a graduate student, Kurt had worked his exile connections to find Niko a place to live—in the shambling home off Nassau Street of Erich Kahler, a German Jewish cultural historian who had come to America in 1938. Kahler held a position at Princeton's Institute for Advanced Study, where he was friendly with Albert Einstein, who held the mortgage on Kahler's house. On these several floors Kahler re-created the Prague in which he had lived before the war, hosting a cast of regulars and boarders that came to be known as the Kahler Circle. At one time or another the group included the logician Kurt Gödel, the painter Ben Shahn, and the art historian Erwin Panofsky. With his broad interests and love of good conversation, Kahler presided at mealtimes. His wife, Lili, prepared breakfast and dinner for anyone in residence. The germophobic Gödel supplied his own cutlery.

Into this Old World biosphere dropped Niko, who was assigned a tiny bedroom-bathroom suite on the top floor. Its previous occupant had been Hermann Broch, who holed up there to finish *The Death of Virgil*, the epic begun in a concentration camp and just published by Pantheon in a dual-language edition. Here Niko passed through a way station Broch captured in that book with the paradoxical phrase *noch nicht und doch schon*— not yet and yet so. In the morning my father would walk down Nassau Street, then left up Washington Road to the Frick Chemistry Lab. Lectures there demanded that he learn on two tracks— chemistry, to be sure, but English too, as he tried to separate the New England honk of this professor from the Southern twang of that one, and both from the *Schweinerei* of English spoken by the Delphic Dr. Furman. Soon fellow grad students began tearing him away from the books, which he's seen with below, to take him across Nassau Street for a lunch of a pork roll sandwich and a vanilla shake. Then it was back to duty in the lab, where twice a week he taught a course in exchange for a tuition waiver. Niko wearied quickly of the premeds who wanted to know how little they could do and still get a passing grade.

One February night in 1949, my father drove Kahler in that Ford to the Institute for Advanced Study for a lecture by the Danish physicist Niels Bohr. Robert Oppenheimer introduced the evening's guest, while Einstein sat in the audience. To Niko, Bohr's forty-minute presentation on quantum mechanics and epistemology was incomprehensible. Afterward, asked to give Einstein a lift home, my father panicked. What if the Great Professor wanted his opinion of a lecture Niko hadn't understood? My father realized he had only one recourse: to ask Einstein first what *he* thought. It seems Niko hadn't missed a thing. *Wenn der Bohr redet, kommt nur Blödsinn raus*, Einstein replied. *Er soll lieber beim Schreiben bleiben.* When Bohr speaks, nothing but nonsense comes out. He should stick to writing.

After that first year Niko became financially independent of his father by landing a $3,500-a-year position as a lab instructor. He moved into a dorm at the Graduate College and bought his first car. He paid forty dollars for a yellow 1938 Dodge, then spent another twenty-five on seat covers and a new battery, salvaged a gray fender from a junkyard in Trenton, and spray-painted the whole ungainly mess green. On his trips to Washington Square he would traverse the north Jersey badlands over the Pulaski Skyway, a steel-and-concrete monument to an immigrant: the Polish exile officer Casimir Pulaski, who was awarded honorary citizenship after the Revolution for having saved George Washington's life.

My father soon had a new reason to make that trip. Thea Dispeker—the exile who had sworn out one of Kurt and Helen's required affidavits and induced her friend Robert Weinberg to provide the other—now enjoyed a thriving business in New York as a musicians' representative. Her husband, Lolo Greig, a banker, knew my mother's father, who practiced law in the city. It was decided that Niko should meet Alex Neave's daughter Mary, who was studying piano at Manhattan's Mannes School of Music.

It would seem to be an unlikely match. Only several years earlier, as a teenager growing up in New Canaan, Connecticut, my mother had hoped for the annihilation of the army of which my father was a part. But trusted introductions and music, which they both loved, smoothed the way. The breakthrough came at Thea and Lolo's holiday party, where the brunette with the long pianist's fingers and Gibson Girl silhouette turned Niko's head. When my mother knocked a tray of hors d'oeuvres onto the wife of Felix Salzer, the Mannes dean who would soon be grading her finals, my father rushed to her side.

Eleven
Late Evening
Kurt, 1947 to 1960

The New York literary world soon embraced Pantheon Books and celebrated its efforts. An encouraging early sign came when illustrators and translators, eager to attach themselves to the growing prestige of the firm, began to discount their customary fees. The house eventually fared well enough to begin paying Kurt and Helen salaries of $500 and $400 a month, respectively, and in 1949 rented proper office space on Sixth Avenue with views of the Hudson. To the business, the Wolffs supplied complementary talents: Kurt, public and instinctive, comfortable with the sweeping gesture, set the course; Helen wrote sensitive letters and eyeballed manuscripts and translations. "My father was immensely cultivated, but he could bluff," Maria told me once. "He never would have line-edited four volumes of [Karl] Jaspers." Helen dug into the Jaspers.

But even with such green shoots, the business was woefully undercapitalized and often left Kurt scrambling. In 1947 he sold the papers of the old Kurt Wolff Verlag to Yale so the family could live off the proceeds. During trips to Europe he would buy up artwork, usually in small, easy-to-transport formats, that people desperate for food or other staples were willing to pawn. In his own way, he was desperate too. Back in the United States, consigning these treasures to Manhattan art dealers, he would accept a few hundred dollars for pieces that today would fetch tens or hundreds of thousands. He eventually liquidated the prizes of his own collection—works by Paul Klee, Käthe Kollwitz, Ernst Ludwig Kirchner, Pablo Picasso—and at one point auctioned off nearly two thousand Honoré Daumier lithographs, pumping the proceeds back into the publishing house. "I remember my father once saying, 'I want to show you something,'" Christian recalled. "He called me into a room where he had laid out a large Renoir pastel nude. The next day it was gone."

A sentence in a novel Kurt and Helen would publish to much acclaim—*The Leopard*, by the Sicilian nobleman Giuseppe Tomasi di Lampedusa—captured the conundrum Pantheon Books faced with the turn of the decade: "If we want things to stay as they are, things will have to change." Peace had failed to deliver prosperity. Kurt judged the fortunes of nearly half of the fifty titles Pantheon published between 1949 and 1951 as either "bad" or "disastrous." Rising costs of production and shipping failed to meet with the public's willingness to pay more for a book. My step-grandmother would recall: "I remember Kurt's coming into the bedroom one day—I can still see him, standing there in the doorway, looking elegant and elegiac—and saying, 'Helen, do you realize how close we are to bankruptcy?'"

Two things helped tide the firm over, both extraneous to Pantheon's season-to-season acquisitions and sales efforts. One was the occasional selection of a title by the Book-of-the-Month Club, which by the end of the war counted almost nine hundred thousand members. The other was the agreement struck in 1943 with the nonprofit Bollingen Foundation and its patroness Mary Mellon, wife of the philanthropist Paul Mellon, to publish a series of lavish books on Jungian themes and the arts, archaeology, literature, mythology, psychology, and religion. The agreement called for Pantheon to be paid a $250-per-month retainer, which during the early years wound up serving as the Wolffs' sole "salary." Forty years later, looking back on those days, Helen said flatly that Pantheon "survived because of Bollingen. No more, no less."

Pantheon's board nonetheless heard alarm bells. "The accountant representing our major shareholder, faced with the bottom line of a particularly lean year, admonished management, *id est* the Wolffs, to look around for greener pastures," Helen recalled several years before her death. "The arid year was 1954. Then the rains broke."

In 1955 Pantheon published *Gift from the Sea* by Anne Morrow Lindbergh, the wife of the celebrity aviator Charles Lindbergh. For Kurt and Helen, the book was a departure twice over. A slight collection of lessons learned during a life lived under public scrutiny, it seemed to hold out little lasting literary value. But the book signaled that Pantheon had gone native. An author from an iconic American family entrusted her thoroughly American story to an immigrant publisher. Knowing what advance orders foretold, Kurt could scarcely contain his gratitude when he wrote the author on the eve of publication.

> *I am thinking of you and your gift to us with an undivided heart, weighing it and what it has meant to me, Kurt Wolff, with . . . a sense of the miraculous. I had long since resigned myself to do my work in this country under the sign of Péguy—that is, in relative obscurity, one's efforts disproportionate to their tangible results, braced and exhausted simultaneously by swimming against the stream. Whenever books were offered us by authors, agents, foreign publishers, they were inevitably the "difficult" ones, with the ones*

*promising success going to the old-established, large Ameri-
can firms. . . . It seemed a fateful, if irrevocable pattern. And
that is why, in thinking of your gesture in giving us* Gift from
the Sea, *I used the term "miraculous." It was just that to me:
the free, trusting, generous gift of an uncalculating heart.*

Gift from the Sea sold six hundred thousand copies in hardcover and two million in paperback, certifying Pantheon's naturalization in the world of American letters. Three years later came
confirmation that this breakthrough had done nothing to diminish the firm's reputation as a safe harbor for imported literature.
The Russian writer Boris Pasternak granted world rights to *Doctor Zhivago* to an Italian publisher, Giangiacomo Feltrinelli, who
in turn reached out to Pantheon through a British go-between
with an offer of US rights. At the height of the Cold War, Kurt
and Helen were entrusted to position the book as a literary title,
not a political one, for in addition to selling the novel short, any
false marketing step could imperil the author, a dissident in the
Soviet Union.

Kurt would never meet his Russian laureate. After *Doctor
Zhivago* became a global best seller, the Soviets kept Pasternak
confined largely to his dacha outside Moscow and ultimately
refused to allow him to accept the Nobel Prize. But my grandfather did his best to jerry-build a relationship on that favorite
place of his, the page. Like Kurt, Pasternak had studied in Marburg, with many of the same professors, including the Kant and
Plato scholar Hermann Cohen. Before the hammer of the Krem-
lin came down, Kurt wrote his author with the hope that they
would soon have a chance to meet and reminisce about Marburg
and Cohen—"perhaps," Kurt suggested, "in Stockholm toward
the end of 1958." Meanwhile, he updated him on the reception of

Doctor Zhivago in the United States, where a reviewer at a Chicago TV station had highlighted the novel's lessons for Americans, who might now be inspired to stand up to oppressions built into their own system: "How quickly do we give in—to the boss, to the main chance, to the quick buck. How readily do we 'play it safe, not half-safe'? What excuse do we find—in our personal life, in our business life, our life as Americans not to 'rock the boat'—to relax, to conform, to play along."

Fishing for endorsements for the book, Kurt had sent copies to William Faulkner and Ernest Hemingway. But he tamps down expectations that blurbs will be forthcoming. "Both are great writers, of course," he told Pasternak. "But both are unreliable, seldom or never write letters, and both are alcoholics."

In 1942, Pantheon had originally listed Kyrill Schabert as president of the firm because he made for a more sensible face of the company during wartime than an enemy alien like Kurt. By the late fifties, the two had become estranged. In the run-up to the publication of *Doctor Zhivago*, Kurt and Helen watched Schabert side with the sales manager, who insisted that Russian novels didn't sell. Now, as readers worldwide bought more than a million copies in a matter of weeks, Schabert took a victory lap as Pantheon's titular head. Kurt and Helen seethed at what they saw as hypocrisy.

Several years earlier Kurt had come home from the office one day "shaken and white-faced," in Helen's words. He had just been told he wasn't Pantheon's publisher, but its editor, even as the original letter of intent, drafted in 1941 by Schabert's stepfather, Curt von Faber du Faur, stipulated that Pantheon would be "headed up" by Kurt Wolff. "This is the first time in my life I've been told I'm not a publisher," he said to his wife.

In a November 29, 1958, letter to John Lewis, chairman of Pantheon's board, Kurt takes up the distinction, surely with an assist from his spouse.

Some misunderstanding may have arisen for semantic reasons: what and who is a publisher?

First and foremost, it is a man of literary tastes with a sound knowledge of world literature and of contemporary writing, with a feeling for quality and style, and with both judgment and intuition as to what may appeal to the reading public. Publishing is both a business and an art, that is why it is such a fascinating and challenging profession, demanding the whole man, the whole life. A publisher in my definition of the term must be sympathetic to the creative process and to that most difficult and neurotic creature: the creative artist in the throes of production. But that is not all: he must have a sound knowledge of book production and its various techniques, a taste for book design; he has to keep in touch with the intellectual opinion makers, critics and scholars, and speak their language; he must know where to go for advice.

This over-all knowledge distinguishes a publisher from an editor. Editors as a rule do not determine policy; they rarely have a knowledge of production; they are relieved from the burden of coordination. It is the publisher who sees to all that, who carries the ultimate responsibilities for this intricate business beset by deadlines. He has to have the experience and the ability to work with such different people as authors, artists, printers, designers and, in a house such as Pantheon in particular, he also has to have a thorough knowledge of the European publishing scene and its leading figures.

Whether he had been a success or failure as a publisher, Kurt added by way of conclusion, he would leave to others. But he had

> *tried to live up to this definition, and to create for Pantheon a certain prestige, not only by the books we published but also by those we did not—no crossword puzzles, no mysteries, no lurid sex stories, etc.*
>
> *To me, the division between Kyrill's and my own functions . . . has always seemed reasonable and logical: Kyrill kept up contact, and very ably, with people in the book trade and with various publishing organizations and committees in the U.S. I devoted myself to what I consider the hard core of publishing. We moved in different circles; but that does not mean that Kyrill was the publisher and I the editor. The final responsibility for what Pantheon stands for is with me.*
>
> *But that does not mean that I was unable and unwilling to work with Kyrill as a team. We have done it in the beginning, and successfully. It was only when I realized that Kyrill was no longer promoting Pantheon as a firm built by the three of us, but as his personal platform, that he appointed himself head and delegated to myself and Helen the status of "his staff," that my sense of justice and equity became outraged.*

For all his written flatteries, Kurt could fire off a good *j'accuse*, like the letter he sent Schabert that same month: "You are not a publisher and you never will be. You are an illiterate in literature, you cannot differentiate between a good book and a bad book, not even between a marketable and an unmarketable one. . . . I am not in need of publicity, but I refuse, at my age, to be ridiculed by your conceitedness and your craving for recognition."

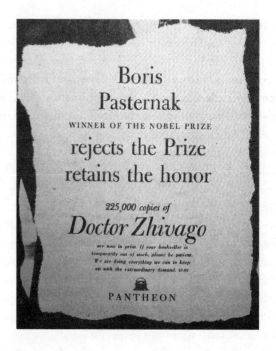

Boris
Pasternak

WINNER OF THE NOBEL PRIZE

rejects the Prize
retains the honor

225,000 *copies of*

Doctor Zhivago

are now in print. If your bookseller is
temporarily out of stock, please be patient.
We are doing everything we can to keep
up with the extraordinary demand. $5.00

PANTHEON

Members of Pantheon's board shared legitimate concerns about Kurt's age, health, and lack of a clear successor. And Schabert himself had plenty of skin in the game, having personally loaned the company $15,000 and mortgaged some of his own assets on its behalf during the lean years. But the triumph of *Doctor Zhivago*—vaunted in ads like this one pictured, from the *New York Times*, with copy Helen wrote—brought to a head something more fundamental: a philosophical split within the house. Pantheon suddenly found itself with a windfall, and the prospects for a firm long content with its particular "physiognomy," as Helen liked to say, were no longer a matter of theory. American publishers now competed for the rights to sell textbooks to the school districts beginning to educate the baby boom generation.

This would lead Wall Street to take more interest in the sector, sparking mergers and takeovers; publishers were fated to become merely one division within a conglomerate, expected to supply a healthy contribution to the greater bottom line. Kurt and Helen championed the idealistic side in this incipient debate, arguing that high literary standards would deliver adequate financial returns over the long term. But Schabert and two like-minded board members wanted to take Pantheon down a more modern, commercial path—and they held the cards. The irony was especially bitter. A best seller, delivered to the house because of trust in the Wolffs' discretion and reputation, forced a confrontation that Kurt and Helen would lose. In a sense, history foretold it. The cultural historian Anthony Heilbut likens German refugee intellectuals in the United States to the European court Jews of old, men like Kurt's ancestor Salomon von Haber. "They exerted great authority in some areas, but in other places they remained vulnerable," Heilbut writes. Life on both sides of the Atlantic ultimately delivered "alarm and betrayal."

The internal tumult over *Doctor Zhivago* caused Kurt to suffer a flare-up of a heart condition diagnosed a decade earlier. His papers include a spiral-bound notebook with several sentences scratched out in pencil, undated but clearly from 1958 or '59. "I'm in the late evening of my life, and take leave of the work that has consumed me completely for the past seventeen years, activity in which I have invested more time, diligence, passion than even during the European chapter of my career," he writes. "I'm sick. Of course K[yrill] isn't to blame for my illness. But I regard him as its cause."

Kurt and Helen decided to abandon the poisonous atmosphere in the New York office for Switzerland, ostensibly to set up a Pantheon European branch. They had personally shared in the profits from the Lindbergh and Pasternak best sellers, and to help fund a new chapter chose to cash out their stake in the firm, even at the cost of seats on the board and a sharp reduction in salaries. But the move wasn't all retreat and defeat. "My father was a great conversationalist whose English was never that good," Christian once told me. "In New York he always felt at a disadvantage." Back in Europe this most gregarious of men would once again find himself on the social front foot. In April 1959, Kurt dashed off a note to Hermann Hesse to let him know that he and Helen would soon be his neighbors. The enthusiast-on-the-page was back at it, telling Hesse how much he enjoyed rereading an essay of his on the consolations of old age. That spring Kurt and Helen relocated to Locarno in the Italian-speaking Ticino, taking an apartment in the Hotel Esplanade overlooking Lake Maggiore. They formally left Pantheon a little more than a year later.

In 1970, Helen would respond to a friend who had proposed a book to enlighten Americans about her late husband's life and work. "I cannot help feeling that Kurt would not want it, because of his traumatic experience in this country as a publisher," she wrote, recapitulating the conflict that led them to leave New York.

> Kurt left America a broken man, physically and psychologically. (I'm not being hysterical or exaggerating. When he shuffled to the plane that was taking us to Zurich, Niko and Christian were convinced that this was their last time to see their father.) . . . Under his gentle and dignified manners he suffered acutely. In July 1960, after his resignation from the firm, he entered into a commonplace book a series of quotations which culminated in "An old man always is a King Lear." This was ten years ago, but I still can hardly bear to read or write it.

In exile in New York, my grandfather had longed for a world where he wouldn't have to waste his breath arguing that gold lettering shouldn't fade from the spine of a book. Yet, as Marion Detjen points out, continental origins clung to Kurt in success and failure alike. Forced to make a living at the only thing he knew, he did so against the odds and with great flair. Ironically, in Germany before World War I, Kurt had rankled rival publishers with "American" book-selling tactics—colorful jackets, popular prices, bold designs in newspaper ads and kiosk placards. But something Old World at his core put him at loggerheads with the business culture of his new homeland. The East German daily *Neues Deutschland* would allude to the Pantheon endgame in its description of him as a man who had been "betrayed by his class." In the end, it all took a toll on his heart.

Kurt saw no choice but to flee again, back across the ocean, to Switzerland—literally, to a neutral corner; once more, he couldn't help but conclude, to save his life.

I owe my being here, at the Bundesarchiv in the nondescript Berlin district of Lichterfelde, to a Bavarian factory foreman named Hanns Huber.

On April 15, 1945, at the Josef Wirth paper mill in the Munich suburb of Freimann, a Nazi official arrived in a dark sedan to issue a command. Over the coming days the factory would take delivery of truckloads of paper that was to be immediately pulped. Given the prevailing shortages, Herr Huber was delighted by this news. And sure enough, trucks soon began to turn up. They delivered bale upon bale, some twenty bales a day over nine days, fifty tons of paper in all. Curious, the foreman peeked inside a few of the first bales and realized what they contained: the membership records of the Nazi Party—cards with names, in some cases photographs, even notations to indicate reliability, of millions of followers of the *Führer*, hastily evacuated from the party treasurer's office in central Munich as American forces closed in from the west.

Nazi officials had handed over their incriminating records to the wrong man. Hanns Huber despised National Socialism and made sure the bales remained undisturbed in a corner of the factory yard. When another Nazi turned up several days later, demanding to know why so much had yet to be pulped, Huber bluffed. *Those bales? They're from other customers bumped by all this urgent party business.* Huber stalled successfully until the fall of Munich two weeks later.

For decades after the war, the US government secured those membership records in its sector of Berlin. Only after reunification did the Federal Republic of Germany take possession and make them publicly available, in this archive in whose reading room I find myself.

The NSDAP-Kartei (National Socialist German Workers Party files) of the Bundesarchiv contain much more than records of Nazi Party members. From affiliated professional organizations to auxiliaries for boys, girls, and women, every by-product of the Nazification of German society generated its own paperwork. Frau Gresens, the researcher assigned to me, has pulled anything that matches the names and birthdates I've submitted. She hands over a stack of folders. I take a seat, a deep breath, and an inventory of what I find.

It turns out that Ernst Reisinger, Helen and Niko's headmaster at Landheim Schondorf and protector of "first-degree *Mischlinge*" there, joined the National Socialist Teachers' Bund in 1933 and four years later applied for party membership. His application seems to have been turned down—perhaps because, petitioning so late, he was regarded as an opportunistic *Märzge-fallene*, or "March violet." Or perhaps because of an April 1933 letter I find in his file, in which a woman from Berlin denounces Reisinger to a *Hauptamt* in the teachers' bund, bemoaning that the "Horst Wessel Song" is "something foreign" to her younger brother, a Schondorf student. "You will understand how painful it is for us to put the education of Ernst-Georg in Dr. Reisinger's hands, which deprives him of the great experience of our times," she writes. "In Schondorf it's said that one wants to keep politics separate from school."

But every other file I sift through contains something more sobering.

Maria once told me that Hans Albrecht, her and Niko's viola-playing, magic-trick-performing stepfather, was "as likely to hobnob with Nazis as with the July twentieth plotters," and the evidence confirms him to have been a line-straddler. He never joined the party. But he held membership in the Reichsärztzekammer (the nazified National Medical Association) and appears in the records of the Reichsministerium für Wissenschaft, Erziehung und Volksbildung (Ministry of Science, Education, and National Education). And in 1933 he became a *förderndes Mitglied der SS* (FMSS), a supporting member of the SS, making regular financial contributions in lieu of taking a commission and a uniform. If these payments constituted a kind of protection money, they apparently worked, according to an exchange I come across between two Munich-based Nazi bureaucrats in late 1938, in which they discuss my step-grandfather. "His political attitude so far gives no cause for complaint," concludes the last of these memos marked HIGHLY CLASSIFIED. "With collections, etc. [i.e., FMSS contributions], lavish generosity can be confirmed. It can be expected that he will always be committed to the movement and the state. The *Gauleitung* [the Nazis's regional administration] raises no concerns." Without at least some party engagement, Dr. Albrecht would likely never have become obstetrician to the wife of Deputy Führer Rudolf Hess.

A folder for Mathilde Merck attests that my distant cousin, known within the family as Tante Tilla, was a fanatical party follower. For more than eighty years she kept a diary, and by the thirties it had become seasoned with the Nazi beliefs she clung to until her death in 1958. As a generous patron of the Ahnenerbe, the SS-administered institute devoted to "Aryan" pseudoscience and history, she wrote often to the *Reichsführer* Heinrich Himmler and Ahnenerbe general secretary Wolfram Sievers. Only Hitler surpassed Himmler as a war criminal; Sievers was convicted at the 1948 Doctors' Trial at Nuremberg and hanged for his role in the murder of 112 Jews, selected at Auschwitz so their skulls and corpses could be used for the kind of twisted anthropological "research" to which the Ahnenerbe dedicated itself. The Bundesarchiv includes a letter in which Sievers informs Himmler that Tante Tilla has offered to leave her Darmstadt home to the Ahnenerbe so it can be turned into a museum of comparative art. Beyond her journaling, most of Tilla's writing consisted of privately printed monographs and doggerel shared with family. But in 1941, at Himmler's urging, she applied to join the Reichsschrifttumskammer, the Reich Chamber of Literature, so a play she wrote and dedicated to him, *Die Letzte Volksmutter*, could be published and performed.

Yet the fattest folder by far contains the file on my grandmother's brother Wilhelm Merck, the company director and onetime Mercedes-sponsored race-car driver my father had so looked up to. Uncle Wilhelm joined the party on May 1, 1933, the same day as his cousin and fellow company director Karl Merck—shortly after Hitler's seizure of power and just before the Nazis began to limit admissions. Yet it turns out he wasn't just a Nazi. That same year Wilhelm became a member of the SS, the organization that would be implicated in every atrocity perpetrated by the regime, from supervising the Gestapo to running the death camps.

Himmler had issued an order prohibiting any SS man from marrying unless both he and his bride could document "Aryan" ancestry back to 1800. Sitting before me is an inch-thick stack of Wilhelm's correspondence with the SS Race and Settlement Main Office, the sub-ministry charged with safeguarding the "racial purity" of the membership. In 1936, Wilhelm—SS member No. 73089 and at the time a middling *Unterscharführer*, the equivalent of a corporal—begins plying the bureaucracy with a blizzard of birth, death, and baptismal documents. Maybe this is because he has been back on the marriage market since his wife Ernesta's suicide. Or perhaps (for he submits genealogical information for his late wife too) he is trying to clear the way for their sons, Emanuel and Peter, to pull on black uniforms someday. The records he forwards are exhaustive, the cover letters cloying. And the typewritten replies from the reptiles in the bureaucracy come studded with a chilling keystroke: a runic SS, executed by engaging the shift key and typing the numeral five.

Taken together, these documents make up the bed in which my father's uncle chose to lie. And they put a frame around the scene Niko described after his 1946 visit to Darmstadt, where he found Wilhelm a broken man, living in that garden shed behind his bombed-out house.

Here in Lichterfelde I realize that, like Caroline Ferriday, I too have a cross to bear in the form of a great-uncle. And I'm led back to the late seventies, when my father was stunned to learn that, as a family shareholder in Merck Darmstadt, he owed the US government tax on all paper gains of his stock, despite having never cashed in a pfennig. He hired a tax attorney, negotiated a settlement with the IRS, and—I remember his relief as if it were yesterday—found a family member in Germany to buy him out. He reinvested the proceeds, then rode the rising tide of the US stock market through decades of mostly steady growth.

That initial sum, which grew to help send me to summer camp and college, owed itself to West Germany's *Wirtschafts-wunder*. But while Merck has been a largely respectable corporate citizen since the war, much of the company's intellectual capital and brand positioning can be traced to the nineteenth century and the decades before World War II. For that reason it's impossible to simply overlook the interceding Nazi era. How did Merck survive the Third Reich? Beyond using forced laborers from the east, apart from supplying drugs to which Hitler apparently became addicted, what did the company—what did my family—do under or with or for the most shameful and warped regime in history?

Die Recherchen zu Ihrem Vater, Nikolaus E. Wolff, verliefen negativ, Frau Gresens reports. Niko, in the clear. But if there's a lesson I'm drawing from this deep pile of paper, it's the interconnectedness of implication. No one is in the clear, least of all anyone held to modern standards of accountability. And those standards lead me to an excruciating place. For while it's easy to judge my step-grandfather harshly for having been a supporting member of the SS, who am I to hold against Dr. Albrecht what he might have done to conceal Niko's Jewish roots, if doing so helped save my father's life?

A day later we meet Wilhelm Merck's grandson, my cousin Niko Merck, and his family for dinner in our *Kiez*. He's a former dramaturge who now edits a theater website he helped found. His wife, Ute Frings-Merck, is a journalist whose life in Berlin dates to the earliest days of the Kreuzberg squats. They've adopted two

Vietnamese-born children, a son from the south about to head to college in the United States and a daughter from the north who shares a homeroom at that international school with our son.

Cousin Niko has a direct, sometimes Socratic manner and enjoys posing the probing question. Today 70 percent of Merck Darmstadt remains in the hands of the family, whose *Familienrat*, or family board, still has a say in Merck policy. Niko and Ute belong to a feisty subset of family shareholders, mostly artistic or progressive, who see themselves as checks on the hidebound thinking that can sometimes drive company decisions. During a recent visit to Darmstadt to congratulate Merck on its 350th birthday, Angela Merkel made sure to mention the company's use of forced labor, and her callout pleased the faction with which Niko and Ute align themselves.

Cousin Niko knows all about Tante Tilla and her friendship with Himmler. Apparently everyone in the family does. Her outsize personality amplified her political beliefs, and the attention she attracted filled a void in her life after she became a widow in 1932. Cousin Niko believes other family members found Mathilde Merck to be a useful foil, a kind of crazy aunt in the attic. "With her being the black sheep and such a forceful person, everyone else could say, 'Oh, Tilla over there, *she's* the Nazi,'" he tells me.

To illustrate Mathilde's blend of imperiousness and obstinacy, cousin Niko shares a story: Well into the war, with coffee more and more scarce, Himmler had sent her a portion of his private supply. Mathilde returned it with a note that read, "I drink tea."

What cousin Niko did not know, until I tell him now, is that his grandfather had been in the SS.

Wilhelm Merck never served as a soldier in World War II, his grandson tells me after taking a moment to absorb this. He bore the designation *uk.*, for *unabkömmlich* (indispensable), meaning the regime considered him most useful to the war effort at the Merck factory. But that detail makes his apparent enthusiasm for National Socialism seem only more craven. And there's this: If the point of getting right with the SS Race and Settlement Main Office was to smooth his sons' futures by attesting to their "racial purity," Wilhelm's efforts would have been pointless. After finally returning from captivity in the east, his son Emanuel, cousin Niko's father, married Ursula Lange, one of the "first-degree *Mischlinge*" that Schondorf headmaster Ernst Reisinger took pains to protect.

I try to soften the blow of this news about his grandfather by telling cousin Niko that the Bundesarchiv also supports my father's—and, it turns out, cousin Niko's mother's—memory of Reisinger as a man who tried to keep the worst of the regime at bay. But cousin Niko's mind is elsewhere. He takes several beats before deploying his mordant sensibility. "A grandmother who was Jewish," he says. "And a grandfather who was in the SS." Then he repurposes a Nazi word that means "people's community": "Victim and perpetrator in one family makes me a full member of the postwar *Volksgemeinschaft*."

Cousin Niko's maternal grandmother, Käthe Silbersohn, was born in Königsberg in 1891 into an East Prussian Jewish merchant family. By the outbreak of World War I she had begun working as a physician and soon married a non-Jewish psychiatrist named Johannes Lange. They divorced in 1934. Three years later, considered a "full Jew" under the Nuremberg Laws and prevented from practicing medicine, she committed suicide in her Munich apartment. Käthe's ex-husband died a year later, leaving the orphaned Ursula Lange and her younger brother Ernst to be shuttled between boarding school and various clergy and family friends.

After her graduation from Schondorf in 1939, Ursula moved to Berlin, where she lived out the war under the protection of a former colleague of her father's, the neuropathologist Hugo Spatz. Decades later it emerged that Spatz had been a Nazi Party member who, at the Kaiser Wilhelm Institute, performed research on the brains of corpses from concentration camps.

This news had so shattered cousin Niko's mother that she wrote the reporter who broke the story to press him: Was he certain?

He was indeed certain, the journalist wrote back regretfully.

Ursula Lange Merck, who lived through the Third Reich thanks to the mercies of a Nazi brain researcher, spent her adult life fearing nothing more than mental illness. In 2003 she died of dementia.

TWELVE
SECOND EXILE
Kurt, 1960 to 1963

"U ltimately it all depends on whether I, à *la fin des fins*, have become a halfway decent person, at least insofar as the modest raw material I'm working with makes possible."

So Kurt wrote his old friend Curt von Faber du Faur shortly before the move to Switzerland, with mortality clearly weighing on his mind. He went on:

> *I am completely happy to have grown older (you too?)—I'm always astounded that one doesn't really age gradually, at least not at all for many years, but rather from time to time with violent jolts. (The beginning of this year delivered to me just such a jolt.) Then you look around searchingly and make interesting observations, like: the weight of important things has shifted, and agreeably so. And as far as the business of "being a good person" is concerned: since you've never achieved this desirable state, you remain pleasantly occupied with working toward it until the end. I so love the words of Péguy: "I know that I'll die. I just don't believe it."*

The verb is *abbröckeln. Man bröckelt ab*, Kurt liked to say—"one crumbles away," especially after the heart trouble and general aches and pains of his seventies. And then, as if he had suddenly discovered the cure for piecing himself back together and undoing the damage from those serial jolts, came "the great miracle of my later years," Kurt wrote Faber du Faur several years on. "A man whom I had never met before, younger than Niko, suddenly turns up and seduces Helen and me (the 74-year-old!) into a collaboration that [is] fully satisfying . . . [and he] turns out to be a personality of exceptional intelligence, vitality, enthusiasm, open-mindedness, integrity, and *noblesse*. . . . For me, *the* American miracle."

Late in 1960, an unprepossessing piece of mail turned up at the Hotel Esplanade, addressed to Kurt and Helen both. William Jovanovich had scrawled a simple query on a postcard: "Would you like to publish with me?" The president of Harcourt, Brace & World must have known that no other verb would stir their blood just so. During a visit to Locarno after the new year, Jovanovich filled in the details. He wanted Kurt and Helen to join his firm as publishers under their own imprint. Working from Switzerland, they would report to him alone, while Harcourt Brace handled back-end tasks and assumed all risk. The Wolffs would have complete control over whom and what and how to publish, and share in the profits from every "Helen and Kurt Wolff Book" regardless of how their eponymous imprint list performed for Harcourt overall. After being beholden to the Pantheon board and clashing with Kyrill Schabert, they could hardly fathom their good fortune at finding themselves independent intrapreneurs under the aegis of this "American miracle"—a man born in a Colorado coal camp to a miner from Montenegro and his Polish immigrant wife.

On a fall morning in 1962, a little more than a year after striking this arrangement, Kurt and Helen awakened in their room at the Hotel Beau Rivage in Lausanne.

"I had a strange dream," he told her.

"So did I," she replied.

"I dreamed I wrote a novel," he said.

"So did I."

"I remember the first sentence."

"So do I."

"*There are days of which we say they don't please us.*"

"*Some days are more dreadful than others.*"

Helen repeated this story often after Kurt's death. I'd long been baffled by her willingness to excuse his philandering—"One can't expect a virtuoso to play for an audience of one," she would say—but here is proof that they shared a connection much more intimate than the simply carnal. Ever the close reader, she took care to point out the subtle differences in their respective opening sentences. "Kurt's is, I believe, a quote from Goethe, or at least in the style of Goethe," she wrote in recounting the episode to Günter Grass. "Mine, quite notably, is in English. I often dream in English, especially if I wish to formulate something (in my dream) concisely."

That detail underscores how, two decades after their emigration to the United States, Helen had adapted to the New World while Kurt remained bound to the continent that formed him. Indeed, Kurt's final years were marked by an odd mixture of restlessness and contentment. For two people who had lived so much of their life together on the move, a hotel in yet another country made for an emblematic domicile. The Esplanade permitted them to furnish a three-room suite with their belongings, and they hung the walls with a Matisse and a Guardi. I imagine them finding consolation in the lilt of spoken Italian, the rustle of palm fronds, the view from the terrace. In Locarno, a friend of Kurt's would write Maria after his death, "I found a Kurt I had never known before—not only charming as ever, but relaxed and buoyant, and animated with his own special élan." That spirit suffuses this portrait, taken by my cousin Niko's father soon after consummation of the Harcourt partnership.

But Switzerland can be inhospitable to a foreigner who isn't a full-fare tourist, and their setup was hardly a home. "I've often wondered why Kurt Wolff . . . was living in a hotel at the end of his life," Wolfram Göbel mused in a 1987 lecture to mark the hundredth anniversary of Kurt's birth. "Had he had his fill of books, of possessions? No, I believe—this followed from the wise insight, made at the end of a bitter but rich and full life, that the real value in literature lies not in the preservation of treasures but in their constant rediscovery."

In much the same way he carried his home around with him, Kurt existed within a kind of force field. "He's treated with

respect without having to throw so much as an elbow," Helen wrote Maria in 1962, "simply by dint of the confidence of his bearing and the silver spoon that since birth has protruded unmistakably from his mouth."

Of course it helped that Helen had his back. "It's great that you have your lioness," wrote Faber du Faur, the original Pantheon investor and Schabert's stepfather, not without admiration. "She would attack a herd of elephants if it wanted to do something to you."

When Kurt would travel to Germany, usually in the fall around the Frankfurt Book Fair, he enjoyed introducing himself as *ein Amerikaner aus Bonn.* In fact, a new generation of literary Germans was rediscovering and claiming him. In 1960, after accepting an honor from the German Booksellers Association, Kurt affirmed his determination to continue "to strike out on new paths, even if they prove to be detours or dead ends," and to involve himself "with more than sales figures and production costs."

In October 1963 he met with Grass in Paris, where the two worked over passages in the English translation of *Dog Years,* which Harcourt Brace would soon publish as a Helen and Kurt Wolff Book. Days before, at the Frankfurt Book Fair, Kurt had feted Grass and his forthcoming novel with a lavish dinner at the Frankfurterhof. The author stands with Kurt in the photograph from that event shown here—perhaps the last taken of my grandfather.

Members of Gruppe 47, the organization of postwar writers in which Grass was active, wanted to honor Kurt's record of supporting fresh literary voices, so they invited him to a meeting later that month, in the spa town of Bad Saulgau, in Germany's southwest. On October 21 he and Helen came up from Locarno to Ludwigsburg. The next day they planned to travel

the few miles onward to Marbach am Neckar, to visit the Schiller National Museum and German Literary Archive, and from there backtrack to Bad Saulgau. After checking into their Ludwigsburg hotel, Kurt decided to stretch his legs.

Years later the *Independent* of London would get almost everything about Kurt's death wrong, describing him as having been "crushed by a tram against the railings of a Frankfurt bridge." What happened took place elsewhere and wasn't nearly as dramatic. A tanker truck began to back into a narrow driveway between two buildings, and Kurt, loping along the sidewalk, thought he could clear the opening by picking up his pace. He miscalculated, and the truck pinned him against a gate post. It was the kind of tragic pratfall that would have been rich material in the hands of, say, Günter Grass.

Kurt was taken to an adjacent children's sanatorium, and Helen was summoned from the hotel. They had several final hours together before he died of internal injuries. The end bore out what he had said of himself: *Ich werde an meiner eigenen Leichtsinnigkeit sterben.* "I will die of my own carelessness."

Word reached us early the next morning in Princeton, to which we had moved from Delaware four years earlier. I found out from my father, who had taken the phone call in bed and still lay there. It was the first time I remember seeing him cry.

Tributes began to roll in as news spread. "He had one special quality that is very rare," wrote the *Times* of London. "His gaiety, intelligence and cultivated learning were so freely imparted that when one was with him one felt one was equally (or almost equally) gay and intelligent and learned, so sympathetic and understanding was his approach to his guests."

The German catastrophe had unfolded during the prime of Kurt's life, between 1914 and 1945—what Fritz Stern called the second Thirty Years' War, "more frightful even than the first." The passing decades, the intercession of World War II, West Germany's fixation on laying down a marker at *Stunde Null*—all had so obscured the details of my grandfather's early career that the next day's *Ludwigsburger Kreiszeitung* reported the death in town of the "American" publisher Kurt Wolff. Technically true—though in a subsequent issue the newspaper did clarify that he was "closely linked to the history of German Expressionism."

Helen elected to have Kurt buried in Marbach, a short stroll from the manuscripts of so many of his early authors. Hannah Arendt took note of the "uncanny" symbolism in his final resting place. "It's lovely and comforting," she wrote Helen from Chicago. "He never really experienced the rootlessness that is the fate of us all. To go back where he came from, it seems to me, is the last link in a chain of felicity, as if Dame Fortune had smiled again, horrifically, on a life that always remained blessed in both happiness and adversity, and radiated this blessing."

Bernhard Zeller, director of the Schiller National Museum, delivered the graveside remarks. "He was able to discover and attract the boldest voices, the most restless spirits, the most hidden talents—among them more than a few whose rank would only be recognized by a later generation," he said. "Not even disasters and collapses could rob him of the strength and spirit to start over again and again. He dreamed big, and the effects of his work were felt far and wide, combining his sense of value and measure with an entrepreneur's daring but at the same time an artist's imagination."

Helen dropped Zeller a note shortly after the funeral, thanking him for a eulogy that "put the emphasis on what was essential and lasting in him—his passion for publishing, his love of books and their design. I have you to thank for your assistance on the twenty-first, on that calamitous day, and for your immediate response to my request for assurance that Kurt be buried in Marbach, the only place in an international sense he could call a spiritual home."

It had been a literary-state funeral. But for Niko, the trip to Marbach entailed more than burying his father. Maria would later tell me that, surveying the many women among the mourners, he had muttered something about "false widows." And for the first time as an adult my father came face-to-face with his half brother Enoch Crome.

From Kurt's diaries I know that, as a seven-year-old, Niko had played with Enoch, born on his own birthday in 1926 and thus precisely five years younger. But my father never once mentioned Enoch to me. When Niko saw him graveside and registered the resemblance that marked them as kin, my aunt remembered, he went ashen. During a long walk one summer day during the

nineties, my mother told me that Niko had returned from Marbach "shaken."

Always better equipped than Kurt to cope with change, in
better health and command of English, Helen decided to move
back to the United States. With my parents having just welcomed
their third child, and Christian beginning to make a life in New
England as a husband, father, academic, and composer, Helen
could now count as much family stateside as in Europe. For
another thirty years she would continue to publish Helen and
Kurt Wolff Books with Harcourt, Brace & World and then Harcourt Brace Jovanovich. "The false widows pretty much leave
me alone," she wrote my father from Locarno three weeks after
Kurt's burial, appropriating Niko's epithet. "Only [Hermann
Hesse's wife and the Wolffs' Swiss neighbor] Ninon will come
over, on the twentieth, which should be a bit exhausting even if
not worth avoiding. She sent me a very beautiful poem by her
husband to cheer me up for my fresh start in New York, with
these two lines":

> *Every beginning offers a magic power*
> *That protects us and helps us to endure.*

A few weeks afterward, the two women once married to
my grandfather exchanged letters. From Switzerland, just before
Christmas Eve, Helen wrote Elisabeth in Munich.

> *You have written such a lovely letter to me, so noble in
> spirit, and I've thought about it often. One thing you don't
> really see, I believe, is your role in Kurt's life. You were with
> him in the most glorious times, in his youth . . . that happy
> time in which his enthusiasm for publishing coincided with
> the poetic zeal of an era in which everything was new. In*

many ways you were much closer to him than I—in shar-
ing a sense of the aesthetic, the social, the grand gesture of
life. You supplied him a setting he never found again, of
beauty, of scrupulousness, of indulgence, for which I, com-
ing from a destroyed world, had neither an aptitude for
nor a model to follow. Kurt spent the best, most beautiful
years of his life at your side.

When I first met him he was in the process of disso-
lution, like time itself. Those were tremendously fraught
years, in which he made no promises to himself about the
present or the future, and actually lived in a state of des-
perate but dulled resignation interspersed with bouts of
lethargy. Maybe he was just looking for someone he could
rely on unconditionally, who accepted him as he was—
who expected nothing and demanded nothing. Given my
generation and difficult family relationships, I offered a
kind of guide to living: the fragility and unreliability of
things and people, the disintegration of any structure one
might have held on to. I loved Kurt above all else . . . just
never with confidence. He could never disappoint me.
I did not love him like God or like a mother . . . but as
a magical, amiable, and unpredictable child. As if I too
were a child, I feared for him and would try to protect
him, especially from himself. His radical unreasonableness
often drove me to despair, and yet that was part of his
nature, without which he wouldn't have been nearly as
carefree, as radiant. . . . In recent years he often accused
me of "incapacitating" him, for that's how he felt about
reminders and worries, and would say my every second
utterance was "Don't do that!" We were so profoundly
different in character that he surely often suffered under
me, from my sobriety and caution. . . .

In the old days widows went into the monastery,
which housed many others of their kind. I shall go into
the asceticism of work and hope that helps.

This photograph brings back my lone vivid memory of Kurt. He passed through Manhattan and paid us several visits during the summer of 1963. (Warm weather and family company couldn't get him out of that dark blazer and tie, and I'd been dressed to match.) In Princeton one afternoon Kurt set himself up in a chair on our screened-in porch and did something that seared itself into my six-year-old mind.

To drill some frugality into his boy, my father had given me a tin cash register that functioned as a piggy bank. Place a coin in its slot, pull the arm, and it would record the value of the deposit and display the running total, with the drawer set to pop open once the register held ten dollars. Months passed without a digit moving. Something—soda pop, jawbreakers, baseball cards— always claimed my pocket change. From the bedroom dresser that red sentinel reproached me, its arm raised high as if ready to give me the back of its hand, a proxy for my father and his war-forged belief in thrift.

That day Kurt discovered this tin box and, realizing its constitution, set about to subdue it as he would any stubborn person. A man whose life's purpose had been to disburse pleasure threw off any shackles of "sobriety and caution," feeding the register with change until it disgorged its full ten bucks. I watched, entranced, as this incorrigibly social man, so eager to make the human connections he craved, reeled me in.

That was in July. Three months later Opa Wolff would be dead.

THIRTEEN
SCHWEINENEST
Niko, 1952 to 1978

After growing up in a world where people knew their place, my father found himself launched into one where you took your place. He collected a succession of assents—from Princeton, which granted him the thing his father had failed to earn, a PhD; from DuPont, which offered him a job as a bench chemist in its labs in Wilmington, Delaware; and from my mother, who agreed to marry him.

At Princeton, Niko wrote a dissertation having to do with cholesterol derivatives under controlled conditions. At DuPont, he interviewed with a Mr. Cavanaugh, who worked in explosives and walked with a limp, a combination that led my father to entertain notions of cause and effect. Niko found the smell of tetraethyl something-or-other overpowering. "You'll get used to it," Mr. Cavanaugh assured him.

Niko bristled at the paternalism American companies practiced during the fifties. But in the spirit of the lone compliment thrown his way in that miserable Max-Gymnasium report card long ago—"His behavior was on the whole commendable"— my father could be counted on as a member of a team. Twice he would win DuPont safety awards for his fastidiousness in the lab. The man who now introduced himself as Nick was pulling down a serious paycheck. Deciding to upgrade from that Dodge into which he had sunk a little more than sixty-five dollars, he turned up at a sales lot in downtown Wilmington.

"Got anything to trade in?"

"Not really."

"What'd you drive over in?"

My father gestured meekly at his green machine.

"I'll give you $250 for it."

What a country, he thought.

Getting my mother to yes took more doing and as much physics as chemistry. Smitten by this woman Maria would call *Schmetterlingaugen*, Butterfly Eyes, and captivated by her dedication to the piano, my father pressed his interest. She was hesitant: barely out of her teens when she met him, living an independent life with roommates in Manhattan, my mother knew that if she hitched herself to this man nine years older and much more experienced, there would be no going back. In the fall of 1953, just as he began at DuPont, she insisted on not seeing him. He continued to write her just the same.

By the end of June 1954, she was all in. They set a wedding date for that October and discussed what a life together would be like. Parenting would not be subcontracted, and my father pledged always to be faithful. As my mother told me years later, "My reaction to that was, 'Well, of course.'"

She would come to learn why my father felt the need to make that promise so explicit.

Before Niko became a US citizen in December 1957, my mother helped drill him for the exam. At the ceremony at the federal district courthouse in Wilmington, he was handed a copy of the Constitution, compliments of the Wilmington Lions Club and the American Legion. With that and his latest set of wheels, shown overleaf, he was a fifties American archetype come to life.

Niko's closest friend at DuPont was Karl Frensdorff, another German emigrant chemist, who had been in his graduate class at Princeton. Before the war Karl's Jewish family sprang him from Hanover on one of the sealed *Kindertransport* trains bound for Britain. His parents soon escaped on their own to England, where the family reunited before sailing together to America.

For all their gratitude at being taken in by the United States, Niko and the man I knew as Uncle Karl shared the same distrust of authority, conformity, and enforced patriotism. The closer you had brushed up against the Third Reich, the more vigilantly you kept an eye on McCarthyism and its by-products. Both men had the playful way with words common among people forced to master a second language later in life. After that citizenship ceremony, Karl gave my father a mock memo, copying the "Turpitude Division, FBI; Espionage Division, CIA; Patriotism Subcommittee, DAR; 'America First, Americans Second!' Committee, American Legion; and the Contributions Committee, Republican Party." It was a collection of "regulations," a guide "promulgated to render more smooth the transition of the new citizen to the American Way of Life," that read like the lyrics to a Tom Lehrer song. Best to avoid

> *hidden pitfalls and chasms*
> *Be non-political as protoplasm*
> *Be wary of enthusiasm*
> *Abhor like plagues iconoclasm!*

In this artifact over which Niko and Karl bonded, I have one of the founding documents of my father's formation as an American. He staked out the center with a revolutionary's zeal, cheering anyone in public life who called the powerful to account or demanded that government work better. He loved the political performance art of Senator William Proxmire, the Wisconsin Democrat whose monthly Golden Fleece Award turned common sense into a cudgel. Senator Lowell Weicker, the indignant Republican renegade from Connecticut, was among Niko's favorite Watergate characters. And he would fall into a lifelong habit of voting for moderate, internationalist Republican senators with alliterative names, casting ballots for Clifford Case and Jacob Javits and Jim Jeffords as he moved from New Jersey to New York to Vermont.

"Home is the land of one's childhood and youth," the Resistance fighter and Auschwitz survivor Jean Améry wrote in 1966. "Whoever has lost it remains lost himself, even if he has learned not to stumble about in the foreign country as if he were drunk."

Kurt may have remained a kind of stumblebum, but not my father. Niko navigated the New World sober, mastering the language and practicing his new citizenship with the discipline of a twelve-stepper. He wasn't quite like the German immigrants of

Kurt Vonnegut's *Palm Sunday*, eager to be "ignorant and root-less as proof of their patriotism," for my father loved his *Wurst* and a proper beer, and delighted in a cassette of oompah-pah music Maria once sent over on a whim. But he had no interest in unpacking his past, not in front of us, least of all before friends and neighbors, many of them Jewish, some of them ex-GIs. Lucky for him, in the same way no Long Island dinner guest of the early forties could be bothered to ask Kurt and Helen about the continent freshly collapsed around them, Niko was rarely asked about his origins. He came to regard this as an unspoken gesture of welcome.

In 1959, after RCA hired Niko away from DuPont, we made the move to Princeton, into a split-level home within an easy commute of the company's research park on Route 1. My father understood that the thing that had so beguiled him as a child, technology, was now changing the world—and no country more profoundly than his new one. At a conference during the sixties he listened to a physicist give a talk about one of his inventions, a component called the integrated circuit. When Niko approached Robert Noyce afterward to slip him a business card, it wasn't to lobby for a job. Instead my father asked Noyce—who would cofound Intel—to get in touch if he and his business partner ever decided to go public.

Our life in Princeton included the standard incursions of the sixties—images of moon shots, riots, assassinations, in black and white on TV in the den, in color in *Life* in the living room. But reminders of how we were different surfaced from time to time. We exchanged gifts not on Christmas morning but Christmas Eve, after singing "Silent Night," in English, in the flickering of real candles clipped to the branches of the tree, a practice neighbors considered reckless in spite of the water bucket Niko was careful to keep nearby. Mr. Iverson next door worked in New

Brunswick at the national headquarters of the Boy Scouts of America, and he would sometimes slip me copies of *Boys' Life*, which fired dreams of finding a place in some pack or troop, wearing the uniform, flashing the insignia, taking the oath. My father would have none of it, and I couldn't then understand why.

But I never felt like a child raised post-traumatically, or even under a firm Teutonic hand. There was no parenting intermediary, no nanny or cook; my father would summon us to the living room sofa for the close-quarters ritual he called *Schweinenest*, to affirm that he and my mother, my sisters, and I were pigs in the same sty. "Niko wanted to be like that statue of Father Nile in the Vatican," Maria told me once, "with all his tributaries crawling around him."

At the end of 1968, Xerox lured my father away from RCA with an offer to be a manager at its research facility outside Rochester, New York. Just before Christmas we moved to the heavily Jewish suburb of Brighton, which my parents decided would deliver the best public education. Here the Wolffs had to do the acculturating, and we used markers of the old *Bildungsbürgertum* to pull it off—cello lessons, an expectation of top grades, and membership in that locus of social life, the Jewish Community Center. I felt not at all Jewish. If anything, I was sensitive to any residual German-ness, anxious that it might foreclose friendships and, soon enough, romance. But I found my people—kids whose parents were University of Rochester professors and doctors at Strong Memorial and engineers at Kodak or Bausch & Lomb. Our move came just short of my twelfth birthday, so I was thrown into bar mitzvah culture, logging time as a forager at the *kiddish* and a wallflower at the roller rink.

If I sensed German authoritarianism at all, it wasn't from a martinet father but a rigorously enforced cultural correctness. My parents might idly ask each other whether the town we were driving through had "a good music station," which of course meant a classical music station. Overhearing them, I was reminded that one could be forgiven ignorance but never poor taste.

Pollyannaish attitudes unsettled my father almost as much as lowbrow culture. At Xerox he led a research team detailed to a new line of toners for copiers.

"You going to make deadline?" a supervisor asked him.

"Fifty-fifty chance," Niko replied.

"Great!"

My father didn't think it was, particularly. "You know what fifty-fifty means," he told me later. "You cross the street, you make it to the other side. You cross back, and you're dead."

The Human Flowchart was nonetheless grateful to be able to impose order on this world in a way he never could on the old one. In the basement of our Tudor-style home he would whip out his Dymo gun, the Luger of label makers, and dial up words on plastic tape he affixed to the jars over his workbench dedicated to WASHERS and BRADS and PHILLIPS-HEAD SCREWS. In a letter to the editor published in *Country Journal* magazine, Niko geeked out over the differences between American scythes and the ones he had used as a boy in Bavaria, making his points with single-syllable English words I'd never seen before and haven't since: *snath, nib, bead,* and *peen,* as a verb. I can imagine his joy at later finding any one of them in the *New York Times* crossword, which he would turn to and complete more and more often. He griped about the clues drawn from pop culture and sports; I'd let him vent, then ask if he wanted help—an offer that, in the end, he would accept with grace.

To be a wary consumer was part of flexing one's citizen muscles, of empowering the individual so politicians and tycoons couldn't consolidate wealth and influence at the expense of the little guy. The spines of year after year of the *Consumer Reports*

Buying Guide, Niko's own *Britannica*, took up a swath of our bookshelves. When Eisenhower warned of the military-industrial complex, my father had surely nodded along. I would return from school to reliably find on the hallway credenza DC-postmarked mail from Common Cause or Ralph Nader's Public Citizen or some other goo-goo nonprofit. Oh, the idealism in those names— Weimar names! Yet Niko had faith that America could shear even woolly-headed best intentions of their fecklessness.

From time to time I'd see evidence of my father trying to backfill his understanding of what had gone so horribly wrong. William Shirer's *Rise and Fall of the Third Reich* held pride of place in the living room. Niko read Albert Speer's memoirs, and not just as an architect *manqué*. And the latest book from Grass lurked around his nightstand. My father admired the playfulness of his imagination and the impudence of his characters but also the task Grass so insistently turned to, even as Niko himself left his own past unexcavated. On those occasions when his ancestry came up in conversation with a neighbor or colleague, he had a way of leaving it unclear that he had emigrated after the war. Years later I asked about those consistent elisions, and he conceded he would just as soon spare himself the questions. That instinct likely extended to wanting to spare us the burden of answers and probably helps explain why I put off posing many questions myself. One summer during the seventies, while we visited family in Munich, a Swiss friend of mine came up from Zurich, and together we made plans to visit Dachau. Pained, my father had a question for me: "Why would you want to do that?"

He had so wished to put all that behind him and beyond us. When he sold off his shares in Merck Darmstadt, Niko felt relief at being released from tax obligations but surely also at slipping one of the last bonds of the Old World. Yet a few essential things about America always eluded him. I would cringe at his pop-cultural obliviousness, never more so than in the Tampa airport one spring as we made our way back from vacation. When a local TV crew doing man-in-the-street interviews approached him with a question about the state of the economy, Niko grabbed the microphone from the startled reporter and pulled it close—a faux pas no one familiar with the coolest American medium and *Glotzofon* etiquette would make. Later I chalked this up to exuberance over living in a country where the mass media cares what the average citizen thinks and he could say his piece with impunity.

But even in this land he trusted to make just laws and enforce them fairly, I occasionally saw his fealty to rules wobble. Sometime in the early seventies, as aborning adolescents, a few friends and I tried half-hearted juvenile delinquency on for size, engaging in light hanging out that we called "making the precinct scene." One evening, crouching in the bushes along Rochester's Highland Avenue during a lake-effect blizzard, we pelted passing cars with snowballs.

It all comes back to me in a swirl of headlights and blowing snow. The thud against the broad side of a large sedan. The muffled skid of the braking car. The passenger-side door releasing a silhouetted figure, a man, who lit out after the three of us. We scattered, and I was the one he caught. I can still smell the booze on his breath and feel the tug on the wad of my jacket he held in his fist. He frog-marched me back to the car, and I stayed mute during the short ride to our house. At the stoop Niko thanked my captor—assured him that he would "take care of it."

As soon as the door clicked shut, my father exhaled. He turned to me, grinned, and urged me not to get caught the next time.

Each D-Day I'm reminded of when I first surveyed the Normandy beaches years ago. To stand on the lip of the cliffs, to track the gray of the channel to the horizon, to glance back at the bunkers and gun sights of the Atlantic Wall and then over toward the white grave markers describing perfect lines against manicured green—to take all this in—is to marvel not just at the scale and tactical audacity of Operation Overlord but at its lives-for-liberty calculus. The Allies marshaled three million troops for the invasion, the same number Hitler deployed for Operation Barbarossa. Some forty-four hundred Allied soldiers died on June 6, 1944, and another two hundred thousand lost their lives before the Germans were finally chased across the Rhine.

As a boy I must have sensed what this event meant for my family and me. I pulled Cornelius Ryan's *The Longest Day* off my parents' bookshelves before leaving elementary school, and in high school, upon encountering Paul Verlaine in French class, I already knew the lines of verse the BBC broadcast to alert the Resistance to the imminent invasion.

On May 8, 1985, German president Richard von Weizsäcker delivered a speech to the Bundestag to mark the fortieth anniversary of Nazi Germany's defeat. At its heart lay a simple if then-provocative proposition: that Germans should use this occasion not to solemnize their country's loss but to celebrate its liberation. "We must find our own standards," Weizsäcker said that day. "We are not assisted in this task if we or others spare our feelings. We need and we have the strength to look unblinkered at the truth—without embellishment and without distortion. . . . And this must be stated on behalf of all of us today: The eighth of May . . . liberated all of us from the inhumanity and tyranny of the National Socialist regime."

An unbroken line ran from May 8, 1945, back to January 30, 1933, he declared: "It is not a case of coming to terms with the past. That is not possible. It cannot be subsequently modified or made undone. However, anyone who closes his eyes to the past is blind to the present. Those who refuse to remember the past inhumanity will be vulnerable again to new risks of infection."

Anticipating promises of "the end of history" that would come a few years later with the fall of the Berlin Wall, Weizsäcker went on to sound cautionary notes. "From our own history we learn what man is capable of," he said. "For that reason we must not imagine that we are now quite different and have become better. There is no ultimately achievable moral perfection—for no individual and for no nation. We have learned as human beings, and as human beings we remain in danger. But we have the strength to overcome such danger again and again."

From the moment I first looked out from those cliffs and took inventory of the chain of events that led to my existence, I have seen modern German history in precisely the way the German president laid it out. But to Alexander Gauland and Björn Höcke and their co-religionists in the AfD, Weizsäcker had delivered "a speech against his own people."

Here lies the essential question for postwar Germany, one that informs and frames the country's current political life: Are human beings so subject to taxonomy that a modern society can't sprinkle a million from a smaller box within a larger receptacle of eighty million more? Are the German people first Germans or people?

To the son of a Wehrmacht soldier from Munich and the cultivator of a victory garden in Connecticut, the answers to these questions come with nothing less than existential implications. I am alive for the same reason modern Germany prospers—because the world acted on its revulsion at the Nazi regime and then believed it was worth helping future generations of Germans turn to the task that my grandfather, in his letter to Maria, had urged them to take up.

Millions of Germans have done so in good faith. In 1995, a scant decade after Weizsäcker delivered his speech, more than half the country's population regarded the Allies' defeat of the Nazis as liberation, and another 28 percent as both liberation and defeat. The percentage of Germans who considered the subdual of Nazi Germany by force of arms solely as a defeat stood at only 13 percent—precisely, it bears highlighting, the AfD's share of the vote in the September 2017 elections. Further, the rest of the world took approving note of how Germany had remade itself. In 2006 the country hosted soccer's World Cup amidst a healthy equilibrium: Germans had finally hit upon a patriotism that allowed them to cheer and wave flags yet still be gracious hosts— such good hosts, the joke went, that they stepped back to let France and Italy play for the trophy. Visiting fans said they liked the Germans and loved being in Germany, sentiments surely tied to recognition of how far the country had come. As the Green Party politician Cem Özdemir pointed out in a February 2018 speech to the Bundestag critical of the AfD, it is precisely because of Germany's diversity and culture of remembrance that "this country is respected throughout the world."

Rightist populism is indeed on the march around Europe and the globe. But as the country most attuned to its dangers, Germany can make a claim as early-warning system. Thirteen percent is far too large a figure. Indeed, it turned out to be large enough, after Merkel struggled through months of false starts following those elections before finally forming a government, to elevate the AfD to leader of the opposition. But even the AfD wouldn't dare march through a German city chanting "Jews will not replace us," or even "Blood and soil," as American neo-Nazis did in Charlottesville. The rise of the AfD is no reason to give up on the project of vigilance, Susan Neiman argues: "*Vergangen-heitsaufarbeitung* isn't a foolproof inoculation against racism and reaction; the world is unlikely to suffer a shortage of fools." But as she worked on *Learning from the Germans*, Neiman was comforted to discover how many Germans were horrified to learn of the title she intended to use for her book.

Ernie Pyle, the namesake of the cargo ship that would deliver my father to the United States, never filed the column he planned to write upon Germany's surrender. He was shot and killed on April 18, 1945, a few weeks too soon. But among the notes he took while covering more than five years of war—during which forty-four million people, including twenty-six million civilians, died in Europe alone—is this sentence: "Those who are gone would not wish themselves to be a millstone of gloom around our necks."

Pyle's statement sits beside a corollary, not gloomy either: that the GIs who gave their lives storming the beaches, liberating France, and yes, liberating Germany, did so for an idea—that a country's citizens aren't just those people born within its borders. An exile can become a citizen, an emigrant too, by subscribing to a creed. "American" has never been, just as today "German" is no longer, status to which one is bound by blood and soil alone.

By such lights an American-born son of a soldier of the Wehrmacht observes D-Day in Berlin.

FOURTEEN
TURTLE BAY
Alex, 1975 to 1994

I showed up as a college freshman aware of the many ways the Princeton campus bound me to my father. Erich Kahler's widow still lived steps away, in the house where Niko landed in 1948. As campus correspondent for the *Trenton Times*, the local evening paper, I fetched my stories in print by crossing Nassau Street at midday, the same route my father once took to find his luncheonette pork roll. When Niko visited me on campus, we often caught a glimpse of a grad student from his day, a mathematician who had ridden a bicycle around the basement of one of the dorms at the Graduate College while whistling the "Ode to Joy" from Beethoven's Ninth: John Nash, the schizophrenic game theorist of *A Beautiful Mind*, wearing a drab overcoat, still haunting Firestone Library decades later.

The university released me into the world of Manhattan magazine journalism on the cusp of the boom of the eighties. I joined *Sports Illustrated* as a fact-checker, making $16,000 a year plus overtime. Luckily there would be lots of overtime. If my father felt pride at seeing me launched, it probably came mitigated by my literally supplying what Kurt once dismissed as "what makes the sportsman's heart beat faster." As Maria would later tell me, "Sport—it's as if you're a society columnist. It's not quite what your parents expected."

After I spent a year with the roaches in a $400-a-month studio on the Upper West Side, Helen invited me to relocate to her apartment in Turtle Bay. She wanted to spend more time near Christian and his family in New England; if I moved in, she could keep a pied-à-terre. But it turned out New York law didn't regard grandchildren as "immediate family" permitted under the terms of her lease. Soon a stern letter on landlord letterhead appeared under the door, invoking various subsections and subparagraphs. Bureaucrats and official documents had a way of stirring up the past, and Helen suffered through several restless nights until a rewritten lease and bump in rent set things right. These scars of exile would appear from time to time—in some possession she could "always sell if I have to;" in the row of relentlessly sensible shoes in her closet. In an admiring nod at Helen's practicality, Maria called her *die Gestiefelte*—a play on *Stiefmutter* (stepmother) that means "she who is shod in boots."

Over the next dozen years, when she passed through Manhattan on business, Helen and I were the odd couple. She conjured simple suppers evoking impecunious times in France and Italy—a bowl of lentils, a pesto Genovese. Each piece of furniture and artwork came with some backstory. A photograph of Kurt the aesthete graced her desk, his legs crossed and cigarette pointing insouciantly downward. Literary figures—Grass, Uwe Johnson, Max Frisch, various editors and reviewers—came and went, and sometimes I met them in passing, though not when stumbling home, as I often did, when the magazine's Sunday night close bled into a Monday morning, after having discharged my solemn duty to make sure we rendered a certain New York Knick as Micheal—not Michael—Ray Richardson.

I lost my sometime roommate in the spring of 1994. She died in her kitchen in Hanover, New Hampshire, "on her feet," in the phrase of Umberto Eco, author of *The Name of the Rose*, the biggest success she enjoyed after Kurt's death. "Suddenly there is nothing," Grass wrote after hearing the news. "The bridgehead is gone. From this perspective you can sense panic but also a realization of how many authors of my generation are indebted to the German emigrants. Those chased from Germany have done more for us than could be expected or hoped for."

Shortly before she died, Helen gave me a copy of the final entry in Kurt's commonplace book, six lines attributed variously to Stephen Grellet and William Penn—"surely," she wrote in a note, "with his love." To the end my grandfather seemed preoccupied with "the business of 'being a good person,'" notwithstanding "the modest raw material" he was working with.

> *I shall pass through this world but once*
> *Any good thing, therefore, that I can do*
> *Any kindness I can show to any human being,*
> *Let me do it now.*
> *Let me not defer it nor neglect it,*
> *For I shall not pass this way again.*

It's a variation on the pithier advice Helen liked to give: "Always overtip."

Altaf, Hisham, Vedad, Dayot, Ademola: these are the names that populated one of our Berlin Saturdays—young people from points afar who fed us and entertained us, and invited us to consider our good fortune to have a foot in two prosperous countries at peace.

We paid a visit to the Westend home of Helen's grandniece Marion Detjen and her husband, Stephan, who live on a property saturated with history. From their garden the Detjens can see the upstairs window of an adjacent house, the room from which the Gestapo seized the anti-Nazi theologian Dietrich Bonhoeffer. On the exterior of their own home, the metalwork of a window grate includes the Olympic rings, forged to commemorate the house's construction for the 1936 games, which took place nearby. Marion and Stephan have taken a photograph of Jesse Owens rising out of the blocks and burned it into a panel of glass, then hung it in the window of a downstairs bathroom so the African American who humiliated Hitler by winning four gold medals is bathed each day in backlight.

Stephan and Marion relate to all this professionally—he as a political correspondent for Deutschlandradio, she as a history professor at Bard College Berlin, where her classes brim with displaced students from such crisis regions as Afghanistan, Iraq, and Syria. But their neighborhood's ties to Nazi Germany have personal resonances too. Marion long ago took up the *Vergangenheitsaufarbeitung* left to her by her family's business, a Bavarian paper mill that under the Nazis had used forced labor from Ukraine. Today a broader portfolio of motives leads her and Stephan to put up refugees in their home. It's partly to foster conviviality across cultures and partly to slake their own curiosity about the Middle East. It follows from a wish to strike a blow for transnationalism and to help make right the Federal Republic's long reluctance to accommodate immigrants after its founding. The Russian émigré history of the family of Marion's mother,

Marie, figures too. Today her father, Michael, now retired from that paper business but living in the same conservative village, volunteers to help refugees integrate, which leaves Marion beaming with pride.

At Marion and Stephan's, a well-cultivated *Willkommenskultur* makes for second chances all the way down. First came Samer, a Syrian refugee they put up three years earlier as he launched a catering business, the Aleppo Supper Club, to parlay his mother's command of a kitchen into a livelihood for members of their extended family. Now the Detjens host Altaf and Hisham, Yemeni students who have had to flee twice over—first from their homeland, targeted by a Saudi bombing campaign; and then from Turkey, where the universities at which they studied became targets of President Recep Tayyip Erdoğan's crackdown on civil society after the attempted coup in 2016.

In the polyglot *Heim* their house has become, where everyone takes a turn preparing meals, Altaf and Hisham serve us a Yemeni lunch. Afterward we walk to the Olympic Stadium to watch the final game of the season of Hertha BSC, Berlin's Bundesliga soccer club. Within seconds Dayot Upamecano scores for the visitors, RB Leipzig. A few minutes later Vedad Ibisevic equalizes for the home team. Soon Leipzig's Ademola Lookman slots the ball past the goalkeeper, adding to what will be a jubilee of goals in a wildly entertaining 6–2 Leipzig victory. Those first three scorers come from Guinea-Bissau, Bosnia, and Nigeria, respectively. To watch the hardcore fans brandish signs like GEGEN RASSISMUS, FÜR TOLERANZ—AGAINST RACISM, FOR TOLERANCE—is to see how modern Berlin can retrofit a Nazi-era structure with a new narrative.

In 1936 the American writer Thomas Wolfe sat in these same stands for the opening ceremony of Hitler's Olympics. His impressions made their way into his autobiographical novel *You Can't Go Home Again*:

> *The Germans had constructed a mighty stadium which was the most beautiful and most perfect in its design that had ever been built. And all the accessories of this monstrous plant—the swimming pools, the enormous halls, the lesser stadia—had been laid out and designed with this same cohesion of beauty and of use. The organization was superb. Not only were the events themselves, down to the minutest detail of each competition, staged and run off like clockwork, but the crowds—such crowds as no other great city has ever had to cope with, and the like of which would certainly have snarled and maddened the traffic of New York beyond hope of untangling— were handled with a quietness, order, and speed that was astounding.*

Here, on this very day Wolfe wrote about, the Nazis introduced the pageantry of the torch relay. It has been part of every Olympics since, culminating in a runner who ignites the cauldron with a flame lit in Greece. In 1936 a German weight-lifter did the honors, then led the athletes in a recitation of the Olympic oath while he brandished a flag. But that flag wasn't graced with the Olympic rings that protocol called for. Instead, the German standard-bearer waved a swastika flag. In his seat next to Hitler in the *Führer*'s box, the International Olympic Committee president, Count Henri de Baillet-Latour, looked on disapprovingly.

Moments later the Polish ambassador to Germany tapped Baillet-Latour on the shoulder. "We have to be on our guard against a people with such a talent for organization," he said, whispering so Hitler wouldn't hear. "They could mobilize their entire nation just as smoothly for war."

Two poles have fixed our place in Berlin. Look north from our upper-floor apartment, beyond where the wall once ran, and the old East German TV tower commands the Brandenburg plain from its position on Alexanderplatz. To the south, the radar tower at decommissioned Tempelhof Airport pokes its sphere above the canopy of trees in the cemetery across our street. These landmarks hold us in their symbolic symmetry, each representing one side in the Cold War—this one to push information out, the other to pull data in.

The TV tower may be an internationally recognized symbol of modern Berlin, but Tempelhof figures much more in our daily lives. The airport closed in 2008, and since then its runways and taxiways have been folded into Tempelhofer Feld, one of the world's largest and most striking urban spaces. In a scaled-up version of their well-worn squatting tactics, Berliners began to use the airport grounds for recreation before the city could sell the land off to developers. By the time the bureaucracy moved to act, a public park had become a fait accompli. On a whim we'll walk Tempelhof's asphalt and green space, beholding the kitesurfers, breathing deep the kebab smoke from the grills, taking in the apartment blocks that rise hugger-mugger with church spires and the occasional minaret in the cityscape beyond. Our kids might duck out to Tempelhof for an hour, to go for a run or take pictures of urban curiosities for a school project. But it's Vanessa who has the most meaningful relationship with this expanse and the massive National Socialist terminal at its western end. Licensing issues kept her from practicing nursing in Germany, so she began to volunteer with a group that serves Berlin's resettled refugee families, including a few that still call several Tempelhof hangars home.

She and I finally make good on a vow to explore the terminal itself. We walk along the Columbiadamm, past the plaque
marking the site of the old Prussian police building, since torn
down, that became the Gestapo detention center from which
passersby could hear the prisoners' screams. As aviation minister, Göring ordered the Tempelhof terminal's construction in
1935. Workers, mostly forced laborers, assembled Junkers and
Stuka bombers here for the Luftwaffe during the war; afterward,
for the eleven months of the Berlin airlift over 1948 and '49, the
British and American transport planes known as *Rosinenbomber*
(raisin bombers) landed and unloaded their cargo here to break
the Soviet blockade—around the clock, up to one plane every
three minutes, some two hundred thousand landings in all. When
refugees first spotted an old *Rosinenbomber* left on the tarmac
for the edification of tourists, some of them panicked, fearing it
was there to fly them back to Syria.

In a city full of yardsticks by which to measure the new Germany, the Tempelhof terminal is as striking as any. It's built of the
light brown limestone characteristic of Nazi architecture. Red,
black, and white flooring still lines its corridors. Forty-meter-
long steel trusses hold up the roof of each hangar, because the
Nazis wanted to install grandstand seating atop them so as many
as one hundred thousand people at a time could watch party rallies and airshows.

But the fates enjoy the last laugh. Those reinforced roofs
designed to support "racially pure" Germans now shelter several
hundred mostly dark-skinned people, housed here until they can
find a proper home, every one of them a guest of the German
government.

FIFTEEN
MR. BITTE NICHT ANSPRECHEN
Niko, 1979 to 2003

N iko and Mary each brought to their marriage a love for Vermont—my mother from memories of summer camp, where a proper Fairfield County girl found joy in communal living and getting dirty; my father for how the state's pastureland and wooded hills supplied accents of Bavaria-in-America. Both loved the work of Carl Zuckmayer, an exile and author of the Kurt Wolff Verlag, who during the late thirties had landed in the same Vermont town where my parents, in 1963, went in with Christian on an old farmhouse. "We must take one step at a time, as one does in new, unexplored territory, moving ahead with vigor, prudently but with determination," Zuckmayer wrote during his time in this almost literal wilderness. "Then we shall begin to feel . . . that exile is not a flight and a curse but a destiny. And a man must love his destiny."

As an emigrant, not an exile, Niko demanded a brisker pace of himself. But it was his own destiny that he—a freelance consultant now—would find his way for good to this most European patch of the United States. In 1979, while their farmhouse was being winterized, my parents moved into a place across the river in New Hampshire so that my youngest sister could finish high school there. After she went off to college, they spent seven

years on that dirt road in East Barnard, Vermont, until the isola-
tion and their advancing age persuaded them to move closer to
medical care. It was a sound instinct: within months of that final
move, to Norwich, Vermont, Niko suffered a heart attack while
mowing the lawn. The prostate cancer diagnosis came four years
later.

This man who once rode out an air raid in a Munich basement, and thus knew the fate of "rats in a trap," had also, in supplying photographs and maps to the *Edelweiss* squadron, helped
lay rat traps himself. I imagine this played a part in leading him
during the late eighties to demonstrate his avowed pacifism by
participating in the exchange program with Soviet citizens. Niko
credited life with eventually setting him up at some casino with a
comped suite and a pile of house money. But nothing could completely empty him of memories of war and want. The same day
he confided in me that he had once bought fifty thousand shares
of Intel at a cost basis of two cents, he fired off an angry letter to
Verizon, ripping it for raising the price of in-state long distance
by two cents per minute.

He reserved special contempt for any entity—political, corporate, religious—that tried to pull one over on the common
man. After the Eternal Word Network found its way into his
basic-cable bundle, the local daily published his letter declaring
that he was "not a Catholic" and wondering why some creed was
being foisted on him. Lord help the customer-service rep for the
cable provider or the phone company if a hiked rate or new fee
came with even a whiff of bait and switch. Niko had the receipts.
And with telemarketers he took no quarter. He couldn't avoid
them, for caller ID hadn't yet made it to his home, but neither
did he regard hanging up as punitive enough. So he would answer
and lay down the receiver and walk away, leaving the caller to
speak into the void. My mother considered this unpardonably

disrespectful of someone trying to make a living, but I've come to understand its roots. The clinical diagnosis would probably be intermittent, low-grade, late-onset episodes of PTSD. It had been decades since his *Heimkehr*, and still: *Bitte nicht ansprechen.*

Over the summer of 1995 he took my youngest sister, Kathy, on a cruise through the Mediterranean. From the Italy that had redeemed his early adolescence they sailed east, to Istanbul and on to Turkey's Aegean Coast. Their tour group disembarked into the blast-furnace dryness of Kuşadasi, from which a bus took them the half hour to Ephesus.

The scattered ruins of this ancient Greek settlement told the story of a highly evolved civilization. An amphitheater on the site once accommodated twenty-five thousand people, and more than a hundred columns supported the Temple of Artemis, one of the Seven Wonders of the World. Now the most breathtaking surviving structure sat at the end of a long plaza: two levels of the partially reconstructed Library of Celsus, oriented so a reader in AD 200 could catch the morning light.

At one point Niko separated himself from the group and took a seat on a stone bench alongside this ancient plaza. That's where my sister found him, weeping.

In the space of that moment she realized that something had surfaced in him, emotions a half century of striving and assimilation had put off. "It was as if a flap flew open and he was skinless," Kathy wrote me later. "Here were the markers of a civilization laid bare, ghostly in their sadness and wastefulness —something once there, now ruined. He was accessing feelings he never allowed me to see."

At Ephesus, Niko had encountered "oozing rubble" and "thick porridge," visions of the Darmstadt he described in that letter to his father just after the war. A memory socked away, unlocked.

We had seen this from him before—some suddenly surfaced emotion catching us unawares. It might be triggered by the particular slant of late-afternoon sunlight or the smell of linden blossom or the first few bars of the slow movement of Schubert's String Quintet in C Major. I've come to believe that each of these moments thrived in a kind of emotional negative space. The more beautiful the sensation at hand, the more starkly it threw the offsetting memory into relief. And with us he was scrupulous about sharing only the beauty.

Born during an air raid in 1944, my cousin Jon is Maria's eldest child and the family genealogist and archivist. I take the high-speed train to Munich, where he lives, to avail myself of his historical thoroughness.

Almost thirteen years older than me, Jon got to know our grandmother Elisabeth as I never did. Perhaps the most emotionally disorienting event in her life took place on a mid-July day in 1921, exactly one week after she gave birth to my father. It was then, on the twenty-second birthday of her younger sister Annemarie, that Annemarie killed herself. To do so she used the military pistol of her husband, Jesko von Puttkamer, Kurt's friend from World War I, with whom, as her letters and diaries make achingly clear, Elisabeth had fallen in love.

If there's another clan irretrievably tangled up in ours, it's the Puttkamers of eastern Pomerania. You'll recall that, in 1926, Jesko von Puttkamer's sister, another Annemarie, gave birth to Kurt's illegitimate son, my father's half brother Enoch Crome. But it's Jesko himself, pictured here, who nips in and out of the family story like some Zelig from beyond the Oder: as a fellow officer in Kurt's artillery regiment; as an in-law upon marriage to

Elisabeth's suicidal sister; and, in a final act during the late sixties, as my grandmother's companion.

Jesko came from an old Junker family with landholdings near the town of Stolp. He had been a difficult adolescent. Twice he ran away with money stolen from his parents. At fifteen he was sent to a youth home, and three years later his secondary school cited a "lack of moral maturity" in refusing to grant him a leaving certificate. Only with the help of private tutors did Jesko earn his *Abitur*, after which he spent three years at the Stern Conservatory in Berlin, where he studied voice, piano, and violin, and—fatefully, I'll learn—met the Danish conductor and composer Fritz Crome. When war broke out in August 1914, Jesko was sent to the Western Front with Kurt.

Striking and cultivated, Jesko charmed men and women alike. On his birthday in March 1915, Kurt wrote Elisabeth about "the devilish guy" in his unit who had taken note of Kurt's birth-date while leafing through personnel files: "Right after breakfast he appeared in my office to present me, as if I were some prima donna, a huge, gorgeous bouquet of orchids."

Elisabeth would come to know those charms well. The following month, during a rendezvous with Kurt in Kassel while his unit spent a week there, she met Jesko for the first time. Her diary records her tumbling emotions over the following days, from "he's a very handsome guy and frightfully snobbish" to "he's very musical" to regret that Jesko hadn't handed over to her a bouquet of yellow roses before returning to the front.

Later that year, with Jesko set to embark on leave from their unit's posting in Macedonia, Kurt urged him to stop off in Vienna to see Karl Kraus, whom Kurt was then trying to land as an author. Kurt recalled that mission years later:

> *Kraus was not the sort of person to whom one casually sent friends and acquaintances. Not until Jesko had left did I realize that my very tall friend would doubtless make Kraus, who was quite short, feel particularly dwarf-like and irritable, a not uncommon phenomenon; in any event, I awaited the outcome of my rather daring initiative with some trepidation.*
>
> *My fears were groundless. As I soon learned, Kraus gave my friend Puttkamer a warm welcome and apparently took an immediate liking to this young man whose purity of vision and intellectual gifts were accompanied by equally extraordinary good looks. On his return from Vienna, Puttkamer reported that he had been fascinated and swept away by Kraus' personality, artful conversation, and the depth and richness of his mind, which could shift with the speed of lightning from deadly satire to the most affable good humor, and from there to a display of aphoristic verbal fireworks.*

In early 1917 Jesko left the front lines after suffering what Kurt described as "a severe nervous breakdown." He nonetheless soon began courting Elisabeth's nineteen-year-old sister Annemarie, and in the fall of 1918 the two became engaged. "Everyone's destiny gets fulfilled, each is God's to decide, but it is up to us to keep ourselves from being sidetracked by pursuing someone else's," Elisabeth wrote her mother, not even half-cryptically. "I am now an old woman" — she was twenty-eight — "but I've had my share of luck and wish Annemarie only the greatest happiness with the husband-to-be she loves so much."

On February 6, 1919, Annemarie and Jesko, shown here in their engagement photograph, were married. The newlyweds settled in Bonn, where Jesko began to study mathematics at the university as he picked his way back to health. In the meantime Annemarie was dealing with her own difficulties.

My father hardly shared a word with me about the events of July 14, 1921, but they have nonetheless come down from others through the years. About Annemarie demanding to know of her husband if he truly loved her. About Jesko's apparently obtuse

or too-honest reply. (Whether that reply implicated her sister, we don't know.) The death certificate indicates that Annemarie shot herself sometime between 10:15 and 11:00 p.m. in their apartment on Buschstrasse. It does not stipulate what Maria told me—that Jesko sat at the end of their bed, watching as she pulled his pistol from beneath a pillow.

A week later—the day after her sister's burial—Elisabeth was rushed to the clinic with those postpartum complications from my father's birth.

Over many ensuing months, Elisabeth; her mother, Clara; and Jesko's mother, Margarethe, wrote one another, despairing over the tragedy and Jesko's depression and aimlessness. Margarethe von Puttkamer implored my grandmother. "Dearest Elisabeth, help poor Jesko!" she wrote. "Be to him a sister, a girlfriend, a mother, all he needs." The following summer Elisabeth and Jesko spent time together in Berg, on Bavaria's Starnberger See. Forty-three years later my grandmother would recall those days in a letter to him: "Oh, how vivid the memory of 1922 still is! The two of us in a boat, you in your zip-neck sweater, I in a violet linen dress, finally released from cruel reality, abandoning ourselves to the wind, the water, and our love."

But by the summer of 1923, Jesko had gone incommunicado. It took months for my ancestors to sort out the truth. He had apparently fallen in with a married couple, the Fockes, whose interest in him was twofold—as someone who could supply capital for some sort of enterprise and, at least on her part, as a love interest. He had liquidated his possessions, including everything from the Bonn apartment he and his late wife briefly shared, turning the proceeds over to these business partners. For six months he lived with the Fockes in Wiesbaden's Nassauerhof Hotel, until they realized he had no further money to bring to the business.

A family from Venezuela, the Guevaras, happened to be staying at the Nassauerhof too. As Jesko fell out with the Fockes, the Guevaras' daughter Theodora, twenty-nine and single, fell hard for Jesko. The two married the following May, settling in Maracaibo, where Jesko busied himself as a merchant. In 1929 they moved to the United States, where he took a job with Vacuum Oil. By 1930 they had returned to Germany, to Hamburg—but then the Jesko trail goes cold in our family's papers.

His place in my grandmother's life would not pick up again for more than thirty years. In November 1963, Elisabeth made a note in her diary: "Letter from Nino [Jesko] . . . ! Unaware of Kurt's death. No return address. *Il pleut dans mon coeur / comme il pleut sur la ville.*"

Another eighteen months passed, until, on May 31, 1965, Annemarie von Puttkamer phoned my grandmother with news that her brother would be arriving in Munich that evening.

Two days later he and Elisabeth spent six hours together. "Looks horrible, but otherwise he's the same," she wrote in her diary. "Endless conversation. I am happy."

Of their reunion, Jesko told his sister, "It was wonderful."

Jesko, it turned out, was still married. "Theo wants to hold on to you at any cost and keep you at her disposal," my grandmother wrote him that fall, when he seems to have landed back in the Americas. "Come on over the big ocean to me, she cannot do anything more than file for divorce, as we will—after all we've been through over the years—get through all this together. For now I miss you, you, my other self, every hour without you is a wasted one."

Not three weeks later she wrote him again.

You must have the strength to tell [Theodora] to her face that you no longer want to share a life with her, that you

*want to be completely free for the rest of your earthly
life.... Then she can respond as she sees fit: to keep her
calm or file for divorce.*

*I'm compelled to think back on my own situa-
tion.... Kurt told me that he "could no longer live in a
marriage" (he had not lived in such a thing for a long
time). Well, I let him go without any drama, just great
sadness—after all I had two children and at the beginning
of that year had just lost a third. I would have continued
living alone with my children, but in 1930 Hans Albrecht
burst into my life, so I divorced Kurt in January 1931. Of
course, Kurt took the blame....*

*Let's not waste any more time.... We are determined
to be together before God and humanity.*

In April 1966, Jesko left for Southampton on an Australian
steamer, then traveled onward by train to Munich. He was in failing health, but he had made his decision. "A little over a year ago
I wouldn't have believed, this close to the end of one's life, one
could experience a state of grace as has been granted me now," he
would write Maria several months later. "All the more so because
it fulfills destinies I've been aware of for fifty years, and which,
after many years of greater and ever more hopeless divergence,
converge after all."

Jesko and Elisabeth visited each other in their respective
Munich apartments. They talked about people and places known
to them both, filling in the years. When they felt up to it, they
would go to the opera or for walks in the countryside. By September 1967 they had moved to a retirement home in Diessen,
on Bavaria's Ammersee, into adjacent apartments, and for nearly
two and a half years lived side by side.

I do remember my father mentioning in passing that one of my grandmother's sisters had taken her life. But he told me nothing of how she did so or why she might have, or anything about her husband, his uncle Jesko, much less of his mother's later relationship with him. Niko left unmentioned much of the past, omissions that extended well beyond matters pertaining to the war and the Third Reich.

Not long after this photograph was taken, Elisabeth died, in February 1970, in Munich, where she was being treated for cancer. Jesko left a note by the urn at her cremation. "In this life we had to wait so long for each other," it read. "Now you won't have to wait too much longer. I'll follow you soon."

Alongside the note he placed a bouquet of yellow roses.

One morning the following June my cousin Jon went to Diessen to clear out our grandmother's apartment. He looked in on Jesko next door and, finding him in extremis, summoned a doctor. Jesko died that afternoon. Our family honored his wish to be buried alongside my grandmother in Darmstadt's Alter Friedhof.

*   *   *

The Jesko saga may have all the earmarks of an Old World tab-
loid tale, but it helps explain why my ancestors came to be who
they were. The most striking thing I learn from Jon is how many
emotional blows my father's mother absorbed during her lifetime. With one late-in-life exception, those days in Leipzig before
World War I—young, in love, buoyed by the social whirl—were
as good as life got. After Versailles came her sister's suicide, the
Weimar hyperinflation, and Kurt's funk and infidelities. Then the
stillbirth, the sudden death of her mother, and the divorce, all at
essentially the same time, as Germany was about to go mad. Cancer took Dr. Albrecht in 1944, after they'd had barely a dozen
years together, and during the final months of the war Munich
became a charnel house. This all happened before my father
turned twenty-four, and Niko witnessed much of it up close.

Elisabeth's grip on privilege, her reluctance to adapt, and her
flirtation with Christian Science all begin to make more sense.
So do my father's gallantry toward women and his aversion to
private complications.

Sixteen
Shallow Draft
Niko and Alex, 1996

A s my father pushed through his seventies, I was closing in
on forty. We continued to honor an unspoken understanding that we would look forward, not back—or so we did until a
brief stretch during the summer of 1996. A year earlier Niko had
taken that Mediterranean cruise with my sister. Now it would be
my turn to spend a week with him, this time floating down the
Danube. That's when I pulled from him the fullest accounting of
his time in the war. Only later did it occur to me that it might be
symbolic that our cruise began in Nuremberg.

As a "mighty liquid belt that held Europe's trousers up," the
Danube makes its way through ten countries between the Black
Forest and the Black Sea. It's a fluvial misdirection, the only
major river in Europe to flow west to east, along whose banks
"different peoples meet and mingle and crossbreed," writes
the Italian academic Claudio Magris, in contrast to the Rhine,
"mythical custodian of the purity of the race." Its transnationalism has made the Danube a witness to serial historical trauma,
from the Napoleonic Wars, through both world wars, to the fall
of the Iron Curtain and the violent disintegration of Yugosla-
via. But whenever the guns fell silent, the river reverted to its
role as artery of life. Boatmen trafficked in wine and salt, ore and

charcoal, lumber and lime. Centuries before, these waters carried Crusaders to the Middle East; now the cargo tended to be human once more, elderly tourists in narrow cruise ships like ours.

The Danube-Main-Rhine Canal took us to Kelheim to join Dame Donau herself. We hadn't yet left Germany when Niko pointed out a spot on the shoreline where he had camped on a trip during his boarding school days. On a hilltop a few kilometers into Austria we picked out Schloss Rannariedl, the castle we visited as a family in 1964, when Niko's cousin Lukas lived there with his wife, Herta. Soon came the hillside apricot orchards of the Wachau, and the village renowned for the Venus of Willendorf, the thirty-thousand-year-old stone pageant queen unearthed there in 1908. At the edge of the Vienna Woods we passed Kierling, site of the sanatorium where Kafka died while correcting proofs of "A Hunger Artist," a perfectionist attending to the perfectionist of his own making.

To cruise the Danube is to run a gauntlet of reminders of the Third Reich, and we took note of these too. The Alpine snowmelt flowing through the Inn doubled the river's size in Passau, where Hitler lived as a child. Passauers would prefer that visitors instead take note of its church organ, the world's largest, and overlook that not ten years earlier many residents had shunned, threatened, and ultimately hounded from town one of their own, a young woman who wanted to research the city's history under the Nazis. Linz is where the *Führer*-to-be spent his adolescence and planned to retire with Eva Braun after vouchsafing his Thousand-Year Reich to some successor. Just beyond Linz came Mauthausen, home to the concentration camp that specialized less in killing by gas or gun or starvation than by working inmates to death.

I recount this travelogue for a reason. Like the boat we had boarded, our draft was not deep, my father's and mine. It was easier to take up safe subjects in lazy, riverine fashion. Better to share trivia, like how the river gave German its longest word, the insuperable barge convoy that is *Donaudampfschifffahrtsgesellschaftskapitänsmützenabzeichen*—the badge on the cap of a captain of the Danube Steamship Company. Or ponder the paradoxes of Hungarian, in which *szia* (pronounced "see ya") means "hello," and *hallo* can mean "see ya." Or assign racy biographies to fellow passengers, such as the timorous British couple from the Midlands or the crisply dressed Frenchman with a newspaper always wedged under one arm. Or remark on the signs in the shop windows of Bratislava—unlikely collocations like BALKAN HOLIDAYS and SLOVAKIA STYLE. Or behold how the Human Flowchart preprogrammed his Hewlett-Packard calculator with the exchange rates for currencies of three of the countries we would sail through. Alone with Niko on the observation deck or back in our cabin, I didn't do anything so grand as interrogate him. Instead I would throw out a subject, and he would pull things from the past, and while writing them down I hoped the lull in conversation might induce him to say more. For the most part that's how he told me what he told me, and that's as far as my asking went.

My father dredged up his earliest childhood memory. It came from a family vacation on the North Sea island of Sylt, where someone took the picture overleaf of him on top of a washed-up naval mine casing. In whatever hotel room his family was staying, the finials of the poster bed were rounded brass, and Niko could still recall his distorted reflection in one of them. "In the background I could see through the window the blue sky beyond," he said. "And the little person inside would move. I was fascinated. A silly little thing, but it sticks. I must have been . . . about five?"

I learned that an episode from my own childhood—that snowballing adventure while "making the precinct scene"—

echoed one from my father's youth. During the early thirties a factory on the Gulf of Saint-Tropez manufactured steel cable for submarines and ships. The owner, a Monsieur Gramont, was subsidized handsomely by the French government to supply the military if war were to break out, and with hostilities still some years off, life was good. One day, out for a walk, Niko, Maria, and Helen were eating grapes plucked from vines along the roadside and heedlessly spitting out the skins and seeds. That's when one of Niko's expectorations landed on the windshield of a fancy car just then rolling by, with Monsieur Gramont at the wheel.

The Frenchman slammed on the brakes and demanded an explanation. "Just wait until this boy sees his father," Helen told him, quickly adding an offer to clean the windshield. As soon as Monsieur Gramont drove off, satisfied, the three laughed, co-conspirators as my father and I would be on a winter's night years later.

Back in the cabin one afternoon, Niko told me about a frequent childhood playmate before the Nazis came to power, his mother's goddaughter Renée-Marie Hausenstein.

"Will you marry me?" she asked him one day.

"Of course not."

"Well, later on you'll want to." In German: *Später willst du denn doch*. Renée-Marie's hard, alliterative *d*'s conveyed an accusatory certainty.

Kurt had published her father, Wilhelm Hausenstein, an art critic and cultural historian. Renée-Marie's Belgian mother, Margot, whose first husband had been killed in Flanders during World War I, was Jewish. For years the Hausensteins generously supported Munich's Circus Krone, for which Margot once nursed an elephant with a broken ankle back to health. Some fifteen years after that veterinary duty, she took Niko and Renée-Marie to the circus and brought them backstage to meet the same elephant. "It raised its foot and lifted its trunk and made a trumpeting sound," Niko told me. "They never forget."

As my father shared this story, Margot was still alive, living in Miami with Renée-Marie, who escaped to Brazil in 1941 after marrying not my father but, much more usefully, a young German engineer of Brazilian descent. In 1946 she made it to Florida; her parents lived out the war in the Bavarian village of Tutzing, sometimes under house arrest, sometimes in hiding. Niko believed the Nazis spared Margot in part because she was foreign-born and in part because of the prominence of her Gentile husband—even though Wilhelm was no friend of the regime, having been fired as literary editor of the *Frankfurter Zeitung* after refusing Goebbels's demand to purge one of his books of all references to Jews. In fact, I would later learn, Margot survived because she burned the summons to report to Munich that would have led to the fate of her brother, who was murdered in the camps. By the time she received a follow-up order she paid no price for ignoring it, because the Third Reich was disintegrating.

Margot would die at 106, the year after our Danube cruise. "Some people live forever," my father said. "And the husband of the poor Krämer woman"—the spouse of the Wolff children's chaperone during those train trips between Munich and Saint-Tropez—"jumped out a window."

In his musings, Niko didn't have to mention the dispositive modifier. Margot Hausenstein and Emil Krämer were both Jewish. We both knew what had imperiled her and doomed him.

One day late in the cruise, Niko explained why he had left Munich and his mother after the war. "You spend winter in a foxhole at the Battle of the Bulge and come home to silver to be polished," he said, the strain of justification still hanging from his words. "I didn't want to live an anachronistic lifestyle, rattling around in this beautiful house with Canalettos on the wall, where you couldn't eat with paper napkins and you spent so much time on trivial details for the sake of tradition. My mother came from a generation where those things not only mattered but held first importance.

"I could have kept studying in Munich and worked for Merck in a research lab and had a happy, easy life. But I wanted to get out from my past. It wasn't so much a matter of wanting to emigrate or become a US citizen. It was more that the country was damaged goods. At no time had I felt I was defending my fatherland. For five years of my life I'd been duped and forced to do the Nazis' bidding. At the first opportunity I was going to open the cage door and fly out."

Germany, he said, using a phrase I would hear from him again, had "too much baggage."

I'd always thought of my grandfather as the exile and my father as the emigrant. But here I realized that Niko laid claim to being a kind of exile too.

Niko spoke often of the good fortune of his "nine lives"—the birthright, he came to believe, of someone born on July 7, 1921: seven/seven/three times seven. One afternoon in our cabin he ticked off several lives expended during the war.

There was that time in Dnipropetrovsk when members of his unit sat around a table cleaning their sidearms. A good-natured Bavarian failed to check the chamber, sending a bullet into the wall directly over my father's head. (Since hearing that story I've never been able to look at the photograph here, in which Niko works on his pistol, the same way.) And there was "that time" during my father's foxhole days in the Eifel, when a whistle and boom might have been the last two sounds he heard. One day there was a whistle but no boom—only a ping, right overhead, and later he and several fellow soldiers worked it out: an Allied

shell had struck the flat surface where their gun barrel attached to its turret, but at such an angle that the shell caromed away without exploding, a stone skipping off the surface of a pond.

We were well past Bratislava before I finally asked about the camps. He was aware of them at the time, he said. His parents knew people who had been sent to Dachau. "They were places for forced labor and police detention," he told me. But about the worst—about the death camps—he knew nothing, he said, even though he had overnighted at Auschwitz that time on his way to another posting. "I had no idea what was going on there," he said. "I saw trucks with prisoners in striped suits being transported back and forth, all men. We were told they were working in the factories."

In the quarter century after the war, millions of young Germans might have posed questions like mine to members of their own families. But a deep and broad reckoning quickly became attenuated. The extent of people's collaboration with the regime, the double standards of the de-Nazification process, the urgency of turning West Germany into a counterweight to the Soviet Bloc, the desire of a defeated people to declare *Stunde Null*—all of this contributed to the country's losing itself in the *Wirtschaftswunder*, which wound up "inducing a vanquished nation to feel itself a victor." Yet for all that postwar ducking, questions insisted on answers, and young Germans paid a price for the delay in getting them. In 1967, a twenty-three-year-old student described for journalist Gitta Sereny the fraught way a generation was left to regard its elders: "We must either brand them as liars, or construct our lives upon a void."

I believed I had something more solid than a void. I had the America of my American father. He anointed our lawn with Scotts Turf Builder. He bought us frozen Cokes on the boardwalk at Rehoboth Beach. He brought home a late-model Ford Mustang, a stablemate for our Ford Fairlane wagon, and lavished care on both. He flew the flag each Memorial Day and Fourth of July, flaunting his citizenship so enthusiastically that I never believed he spoke with an accent, even as friends insisted he did. The fifties gave Niko the perfect background in which to recede, to take on the protective coloring of red, white, and blue, to get on with the anaesthetizing business of dissolving into the Lonely Crowd. By the mid-sixties he was raising three kids in a world where the Russian front had become a laugh line on *Hogan's Heroes*. I watched my father grow his shell hard and tuck his head in. I'm not sure it's a word, but he *turtled*.

A few ports of call upriver, Niko had explicitly said that to stay, to take a chemist's job with Merck in Darmstadt, would have made for "a happy, easy life." But my father had also conceded that, by remaining, his path would have been psychologically and emotionally strenuous. Standing in the way, Grass wrote, was "the massive weight of the German past. . . . There was no getting around it. As if prescribed for me, it remained impenetrable: Here was a lava flow that had barely cooled down, there a stretch of solid basalt, itself sitting on even older deposits. And layer upon layer had to be carried away, sorted, named."

German history makes elephants of everyone it touches. Even to be born clear of the *Nazizeit* only wins you a kind of half exoneration, for which there's a phrase, my cousin Charlie would explain to me: *die Gnade der späten Geburt*, "the grace of a late birth." It's cheap bravado to insist you would have acted more nobly if faced with the same moral challenges as generations before you. At the same time, to ask deep into the twenty-first century for forgiveness from European neighbors, as some Germans still do, feels like fishing for compliments. As a result,

Charlie says, "It's like being trapped in a circle." No wonder Grass got geological when taking up the subject. He was desperately seeking some terra firma from which to engage it.

It became a running joke that our cruise director, a Dutchwoman named Marlies, would appear smartly before us each morning at breakfast to say, "The weather today is changing." Day after unremittingly wet and cold day the weather never did. And so things continued until we disembarked in Budapest—trapped in a circle, turtling in our cabin, all the while being borne in that single direction historical events are condemned to flow.

From the riverside quay we took a cab to the airport. There, before boarding our flight back to Munich, we heard a familiar name summoned over the terminal's PA system. This couldn't be the same one, for ours—Kurt's army buddy, Tante Annemarie's widower, the love of my Oma Albrecht's life—had died a quarter century ago. But history has a long memory. Cue the elephant's trumpet: the man being paged was a certain Jesko von Puttkamer.

Twenty-two years later, another trip, alone this time. Only this journey feels like something sprung from a Richard Scarry book.

Two U-Bahns and an S-Bahn from Kreuzberg to Berlin Hauptbahnhof. An InterCity Express to Hamburg. A change there to a Danish State Railways train headed north over the Schleswig-Holstein plain, where grazing horses regard us with nonchalance. In Puttgarden we roll on to a ferry; after docking at the Danish port of Rødby, we continue on. An hour later I alight in Roskilde, just southwest of Copenhagen. It's a ten-minute cab ride from there to a small airfield, where I fold myself into a prop-engine air taxi for the flight to Laesø, a flat patch of land off Denmark's northeast coast.

I'm met planeside by my cousin Annemarie, whom I lay eyes on for the first time. Enoch Crome's daughter, now sixty-three, has lived here since the pace and cost of Copenhagen ground her down. I'd cold-called her a few weeks ago after discovering her mobile number online. On the phone she had taken several beats to process the shock of a call from a stranger eager to speak of personal things, but soon said she was grateful to be reached. And she suggested that kismet might be at play: since the death of her father four months earlier, at ninety-one, while she awaited permission from a probate court to clear out Enoch's apartment in a Copenhagen suburb, she happened to have been reading about the grandfather we share and she never met.

We sit down to dinner at a pub overlooking Vesterø Harbor, where Norwegian yachts bought with oil dividends bob at anchor. There she describes for me the course of that life Kurt Wolff launched long ago.

Upon learning she was carrying Kurt's child, Annemarie von Puttkamer panicked. "She was from a very conservative and religious Pomeranian family," her granddaughter tells me. "They weren't going to accept that she had an illegitimate child with a Jew." Through her brother, Jesko, Enoch's mother-to-be knew a Danish musician and composer named Fritz Crome, pictured on the previous page as a young man, who had studied and taught in Berlin. Annemarie von Puttkamer knew too that Fritz Crome's career was suffering from whispers about his homosexuality. Sometime in 1925 she wrote to him. *I have a problem*, her letter essentially said. *You have a problem. Let's solve both our problems.* They married that November, and her son Enoch Karl Gerd Crome was born the following July.

Kurt's diaries make clear that from time to time he did see his son, who went by the nickname Pflaume (Plum). But after my grandfather fled Germany in 1933, Annemarie von Puttkamer Crome raised Enoch more or less alone while scratching out a living in Munich as a novelist, biographer, and translator. For a stretch she packed him off to Pomerania, to live on the estate of her landed parents. Children at the local school ostracized Enoch for being of the Junker elite. Meanwhile his grandfather Bernhard, and grandmother Margarethe, shown here with Enoch and his mother, had him take his meals in the kitchen—in part, Enoch couldn't help but later conclude, because of his status as a *Kuckucksei*, a "cuckoo's egg" or illegitimate child.

Sometime in the late thirties, alarmed as the Nazis made participation in the Hitler Youth compulsory, Enoch's mother hurried to the Danish consulate in Munich. Although she was now divorced, the ruse that Fritz Crome was her son's father held up. She secured a Danish passport for Enoch and put him on a train for Copenhagen. Barely a teenager, he appeared at Fritz's door and introduced himself as "your son, Enoch Crome."

"I'm not your father," Fritz replied. "Kurt Wolff is your father."

That was how and when Enoch learned the truth.

Fritz Crome nonetheless found Enoch a place to stay. He had him over for a meal every week or so, gave him regular spending money, and took him to the opera from time to time. "It was unpopular to be German," Annemarie tells me. "My father had to learn Danish in a hurry." Enoch rode out the war as a Dane and after enrolling in the university met Karen Arentzen, a woman from a local dairying family—a family, their daughter says, "all about food and warmth and holiday celebrations, all the things my father never had." Enoch studied English and German, and after Karen became pregnant with their first child, she abandoned her legal studies and the two married. They named their son Hans. Annemarie came along a year and a half later.

It was a tempestuous marriage. Karen came to regard family obligations as burdens and staged several suicide attempts. One of Annemarie's earliest memories is of her six-year-old brother running to fetch a neighbor after Karen swallowed a fistful of pills. Eventually, when their mother made a threat, Hans would tauntingly hand her the phone and urge her to call the paramedics in advance.

Enoch finished his studies but never sat for final exams. Years later Annemarie asked him why. "Because then I would have had to teach," he replied, "and I didn't want to teach." Instead he went into the import trade, often handling millwork, like doors and windows, tied to housing starts and the business cycle. His daughter remembers the stress of boom and bust and the recurring fear that their home would be repossessed. The counterfactual curse hanging over the family was that Karen would have been a reliable breadwinner if only she had gone on to become a lawyer. Enoch began to find comfort with other women, affairs Karen apparently never learned of before her death in the early 2000s.

As a young adult Hans broke off contact with his parents and changed his name. For three months after his death in 2013, his body lay undiscovered in his apartment. Annemarie also wound up estranged from her parents, although she did see her father in the final year of his life.

Several years after Karen died, Enoch met a widowed American woman online. Joan Shepherd Meske had worked long ago as a railroad keypunch operator before getting married and raising a family. She and Enoch spent almost a decade together, alternating summers in Denmark with winters at her home in Lakeland, Florida, until her death from cancer in 2015.

I let Annemarie know how much I regret having just missed the chance to meet my uncle Enoch. But traces online offer a glimpse of him late in life. On Facebook, Enoch described bountiful orange trees and activity at the bird feeder in Joan's backyard. On Amazon he contributed a five-star review of a reprint of a Kurt Wolff Verlag volume of Tagore—"a very personal and biased evaluation," he confessed, for his mother had done the translation. And in July 2013 he wished Joan a happy birthday and that "many more happy years together" might be theirs. "Being part of a family the way I am here is really a new experience for me," he told Joan's daughter and son-in-law in one Facebook exchange. "Neither my German nor my Danish family life has been anything like it."

Annemarie Crome never met Joan Meske. "But," my cousin tells me, "I have no doubt that he found happiness with her."

Annemarie has no car, only a scooter to get around the island. So after breakfast the next day I walk the forty minutes from my inn by the harbor to her simple cottage on the edge of town.

Glass doors invite the outdoors in, and interior walls burst with the colors of her own paintings. She exhumes old photographs: of Enoch; of the von Puttkamer estate near Karzin; of her namesake, her father's mother, whom she calls Amo, a truncation of Annemarie and anagram of *Oma*, German for "grandmother." She pulls out pictures of Jesko and tells me that, his two marriages and many female admirers notwithstanding, it's her understanding that our childless great-uncle was bisexual. And she shows me evidence that Kurt himself must have known the man to whom the raising of the adolescent Enoch would be outsourced: a copy of the Kurt Wolff Verlag's *1925 Almanac of Art and Poetry* has been dedicated, dated, and signed, "For Fritz Crome, with heartfelt greetings, 1925, Kurt Wolff."

In return I swipe through photographs loaded on my phone, most of them images from family albums, including the one shown here of Kurt—forehead broad, head canted, eyes alluringly preoc-cupied, cigarette wedged between the fingers of a spread hand.

"Jeremy Irons," Annemarie says, not quite suppressing a gasp.

Growing up, Annemarie had heard her father refer to Kurt as "my uncle in America." But it wasn't until she was eighteen and visiting Amo in Munich that she heard the full story. Upon her return to Denmark, she confronted her father. Enoch simply said, "Fritz Crome was my father."

She now has a sense of what he meant. "My father and Kurt Wolff wrote but had little face-to-face contact," she tells me. "So my father probably felt a little overlooked. It's just a feeling I had—he never actually told me that, as he wasn't one to open up. Maybe he didn't want to accept that Kurt Wolff was his father. Fritz Crome wasn't his real father, but he somehow filled that role."

Over the years Annemarie would better understand Enoch's conflicted emotions and their ramifications. In 1980 she became pregnant at the end of a boozy evening out and wrestled with

whether or not to keep the baby. Only after the father promised to be involved in raising their child—not simply pass along birthday wishes once a year but be an active parent—did she decide to do so. But he has been all but absent from the life of their son, and she has had to watch Mikkel, now thirty-eight, confront some of the same questions that haunted Enoch. "It can lead to identity problems," she says. "*Why is my father not in my life? Was it something I did?* It strikes you deep."

I share with Annemarie a handful of letters that Kurt and Enoch exchanged. Their correspondence ramps up during the fifties, after Fritz Crome has died and Enoch begins to face more adult responsibilities. Enoch reports on the novels he's reading and offers to sit for a professional portrait and send the photo to New York. For his part, Kurt pays out a regular stipend as Enoch finishes up his schooling. He counsels him on his troubles with Karen, which have already surfaced, and urges him to find a circle of trusted male friends. He sends along books from Pantheon's list and at one point wonders whether Enoch might be interested in translating *Gift from the Sea* into Danish. With a reference to Germany's robust economy, he offers to connect him with Helen's brother-in-law, whose family runs that paper mill in Bavaria, to see whether there might be a future for him there. It seems impossible that Kurt wouldn't know Enoch's birth date, for it's the same as Niko's. But there it is: "Please let me know your birthday in your next letter."

The two apparently met up in Hamburg sometime in the early fifties. Christian recalls Enoch and his mother visiting Manhattan, where the half brothers discovered a common interest in jazz. But despite the intimate pronouns, *Dus* and *Deins*, the father-son exchanges have an awkward formality. Raising a child can't be done by letter, not in the way you can flatter an author or pitch a reviewer or order up a print run.

Even though he grew up more or less fatherless, Enoch was fatefully lucky for his mother's sham marriage and every kindness Fritz Crome showed him. As Hitler threw young bodies at two fronts, a German boy born in 1926 was doomed to be cannon fodder during the fading days of an unwinnable war—like the son of Kurt's sister Else, Eduard Grafe, who fell in battle in 1944 at nineteen. Annemarie von Puttkamer's desperate appearance at the Danish consulate in Munich that day during the late thirties probably saved my uncle Enoch's life.

When I return to Berlin I pull out Kurt's last will and testament. It's written in French and notarized in Geneva, listing as his legal residence a hotel there. In a codicil added four months before his death, Kurt left $10,000 each to Niko, Christian, and Enoch. But the fine print holds one of them at arm's length. The first two are identified as *mes deux fils*—my two sons. Enoch is simply *Enoch Crome à Copenhague*.

SEVENTEEN
PLAY ON THE BONES
OF THE DEAD

Niko and Alex, 2002

If he had wanted to assimilate fully, my father would have adopted the backslapping, other-directed ways of the postwar American salaryman. Niko had no interest in doing so. He continued to cultivate the "inner boundlessness" that Helen remarked upon long ago. Even after decades as a US citizen, he never shed a reserve that made him uncomfortable bantering about sports around backyard grills, to say nothing of swapping war stories. In the meantime sports was captivating me, teaching arithmetic and narrative and a way to express Americanism with the fluency my father never acquired. He had been a teenager when the Berlin Olympics and the Max Schmeling–Joe Louis fight galvanized Germany, but Niko shared no memory of either—only the trauma of playing field hockey at boarding school, where he broke his nose multiple times when he would rather have been building theater sets. His own father's disapproval of sports had come down through the years and even crossed the ocean; in Manhattan, Kurt frowned on Christian's choice to play intramural basketball at his Quaker secondary school, calling the game "unhealthy and dangerous."

But to play sports, even to follow or talk them, was a way for me to leave behind my ancestors' immigrant ill ease. Sports could help consummate the assimilation my grandfather gave up on and my father never entirely completed, and thereby plant the flag for all future Wolffs. My mother had passed on to me some athletic aptitude, which I took first to the driveway and then to playgrounds and gyms farther afield. Basketball offered community and a way into a world alien to the ones that had produced my parents. There was no better way to keep at bay Niko's German origins (NBA imports Detlef Schrempf and Dirk Nowitzki were still decades off), and the slaveholders and restrictive covenants in my mother's family's Southern and WASP past, than to explore this unbuttoned game tied up in the African American experience.

When I showed an interest in journalism in high school, my parents let slip their hope that I would someday find my way to *National Geographic*. But no—I wound up instead pandering to "the sportsman's heart." Niko and Mary were never as explicit as the snobs back in turn-of-the-century Bonn. But with them the raised eyebrow was an involuntary tic.

It took reading Sebastian Haffner years later for me to realize that my forefathers' wariness of sports might have come from something darker than a few broken noses. During Niko's adolescence and throughout Kurt's European exile, spectator sports in Germany came bound up in Nazism.

> *The Nazi leaders love Germany in the way an inconsiderate racehorse owner "loves" his horse. He wants it to win the race, nothing more. To this end it has been trained and ridden as hard and as inconsiderately as possible. Whether the horse shares his desire for glory and wants to be a racehorse; whether it comes to grief or is henceforth lamed for*

life; [these] are questions that do not concern him. . . . Cer-
tainly nations and the men composing them are not there
to be collective athletic teams, the fate that the Nazis have
imposed on the German people. The Nazi leaders aim at
converting Germany into a gigantic sports club which is
always winning "victories"—and thereby losing its hap-
piness, character, and national identity.

I had been pushing a notebook as a writer at *Sports Illustrated* for more than two decades when an assignment catapulted me back to my father's birthplace. Two years before the 2004 Olympics in Athens, the first to be staged in the aftermath of the September 11 attacks, I was asked to revisit the 1972 Munich games, where Black September terrorists murdered eleven Israelis in the athletes' village.

From New York came the news-peg rigging with which good editors equip their writers: we're exactly thirty years on; the Palestinian mastermind of the attack has just written a memoir; the Athens organizers seem to suffer from a security deficit, the perils of which the 1972 Olympics serve as an abiding reminder. But all I needed to hear was "Munich." Watching on TV as a fifteen-year-old, I had followed those events in real time, hanging on every update from ABC's Jim McKay—first the shock of the hostage taking, then the false hope of a successful rescue, finally the horrifying endgame, a fireball at an airfield on the outskirts of the city. The point—really the entire point—of the Munich Olympics had been for the Federal Republic of Germany to stage an event to repudiate the catastrophe foreshadowed by the 1936 games in Berlin. And then, more catastrophe.

I had watched knowing that the athletes of the world were gathered in the city where my aunt and uncle and cousins all still lived. The undulations of the Olympic Park came from bulldozed rubble—"so the young play on the bones of the dead," I remember Maria's husband, my uncle Peter, telling me. When the 1972 games delivered more death, I was prepped for the irony.

Details about the backstory to the attack had emerged over the years, and as I set out to learn all I could, a few paragraphs of an old newspaper clipping caught my eye. I reread them several times, wondering whether my rusty German was playing tricks on me. There was a man, this brief item seemed to say, a security professional, who had prepared crisis scenarios in advance of those Munich games. He had predicted the actual attack with a haunting accuracy. Yet the organizers had refused to listen to him.

A few weeks before leaving for Europe, I asked my father to translate that clipping and flag anything else he might find in reports I'd culled from German newspapers and magazines. He was eighty-one now, half-consumed by the cancer that would kill him. But Niko confirmed the account about the clairvoyant consultant, a Dr. Georg Sieber. Not since those Watergate evenings on the couch had my father's interests and mine aligned so closely. For him, here was the confluence of history and his hometown, fateful events in which sports were swallowed up rather than wallowed in. In the premise of my assignment he could surely hear what I heard—the devil's whisper of "condemned to repeat it." Upon landing in Munich in search of Georg Sieber, I felt Niko at my elbow.

Two months later I turned in a story that would fill seventeen pages in the magazine. This is how it began:

> *For a citizen of a country manacled to its past, Dr. Georg Sieber had a remarkable knack for seeing the future. In the months leading up to the 1972 Olympic Games in Munich, West German organizers asked Sieber, then a 39-year-old*

*police psychologist, to "tabletop" the event, as security
experts call the exercise of sketching out worst-case scenarios. Sieber looks a bit like the writer Tom Clancy, and
the crises he limned drew from every element of the airport novelist's genre: kidnappers and hostages, superpower
patrons and smuggled arms, hijacked jets and remote-
controlled bombs. Studying the most ruthless groups of
that era, from the Irish Republican Army and the Palestinian Liberation Organization, to the Basque separatist
group ETA and West Germany's own Baader-Meinhof
Gang, he came up with twenty-six cases, each imagined
in apocalyptic detail. Most of Sieber's scenarios focused on
the Olympic Village, the Games' symbolic global community; one that did not—a jet hired by a Swedish right
wing group crashes into an Olympic Stadium filled with
people—foreshadowed a September day in another city
many years later.*

*But on September 5, 1972, at the Munich Olympics,
history would not wait. It hastened to crib from one of
Sieber's scenarios virtually horror for horror. The psychologist had submitted to organizers Situation 21, which
comprised the following particulars: At five o'clock one
morning, a dozen armed Palestinians would scale the
perimeter fence of the Village. They would invade the
building that housed the Israeli delegation, kill a hostage
or two ("To enforce discipline," Sieber says today), then
demand the release of prisoners held in Israeli jails and a
plane to fly to some Arab capital. Even if the Palestinians
failed to liberate their comrades, Sieber predicted, they
would "turn the Games into a political demonstration"
and would be "prepared to die. . . . On no account can
they be expected to surrender."*

I had found Georg Sieber at his home in Nymphenburg, only a few blocks from the site of my father's *Heimkehr*. He now worked as a consultant to insurance companies eager to pare back their risk. But he had never fully put behind him his time with the Munich police department and the events of 1972. Over the course of several hours, he laid out his story with striking matter-of-factness and clarity of detail. It was as if he had been waiting thirty years for someone to appear on his doorstep to hear him out.

To guard against Sieber's "situations," Munich organizers would have had to scrap the kind of games they had been planning for years. The "Carefree Games" were to be a sporting jubilee, free of barbed wire or police bristling with sidearms. Where Hitler's Olympics had been festooned with swastikas and opened with a cannon salute, Munich would feature a one-worldish logo, with security personnel, blazer-clad "Olys," prepared for little more than ticket fraud and drunkenness. Organizers asked Sieber to get back to them with less-frightful scenarios—threats better suited to the games they intended to stage.

And so the Munich Olympics went off as a premature Oktoberfest. Mimes and bands gamboled through the village alongside Waldi, the dachshund mascot. After late-night runs to the *Hofbräuhaus*, virile young Olympians didn't bother using the official entrance when they could easily scale a two-meter high chain-link fence while Olys looked the other way. A police inspector in charge of security in the village cut back nighttime patrols because, as he put it, "at night nothing happens."

Nothing, except what Sieber foretold. To be sure, he turned out to have been slightly off. Black September commandos scaled the fence about fifty minutes earlier than envisioned in Situation 21. To gain entry to the Israelis' ground-floor apartment they did not, as Sieber had imagined, have to ignite a blasting compound, because they could jimmy the door open. But the rest of his details—from the demands for a prisoner exchange and an airliner; to the eventual change of venue from the village; even to the two Israelis killed in the first moments of the takeover—played out exactly. By the next morning, after that bungled rescue attempt, nine more Israelis were dead, as well as five of the terrorists and a Munich policeman.

Sieber recounted all this with neither bitterness nor any apparent sense of vindication. He betrayed only the clinical detachment characteristic of his profession. "The American psychologist Leon Festinger developed the theory of cognitive dissonance," he told me. "If you have two propositions in conflict, it's human nature to disregard one of them."

Late on the day the hostages were seized, Sieber had fielded a call from his boss. His services were no longer needed, Munich police chief Manfred Schreiber told him. "[Israeli prime minister] Golda Meir is involved," Schreiber said. "This is no longer a psychological matter but a political one."

At that, Sieber returned home, flicked on the TV, and poured himself a cup of coffee.

Ten Olympiads later, before the 2012 games, I would spend those months in London with my family. Early that summer our children—then ten and nine—cheered for Germany during the soccer Euro. They thought nothing of wearing their Bastian Schweinsteiger and Mesut Özil national team jerseys, gifts from cousins back in Bavaria. But it had been impossible for Vanessa and me to take the kids around the city, not just to the Cabinet War Rooms but to places like Saint Paul's Cathedral and the Underground, without speaking of the Blitz. And when we spoke of the Blitz, we had to speak of Nazi Germany and share with them some essentials of history and how those events touched our family. There was a time not long ago, we told them, when the German government killed millions of people simply because they were Jews. A time when Germany would have had a place for a Schweinsteiger, but an Özil would have been sent to the camps. All of which helped lead Clara to ask, "Isn't there some way Opa could have been a spy?"

Over the years I've asked questions like it. They first occurred when I was a teenager in suburban Rochester, upon seeing the old men with the camp tattoos in the locker room at the Jewish Community Center and wondering what they would think if they knew of our membership.

They now occur when I hear Vanessa play the violin, an heirloom from my father, who had himself inherited it from his stepfather, Dr. Albrecht, the man I now knew to have been a financial supporter of the SS. An instrument with glorious sound and compromised provenance, it emblemizes the breathtaking marks Germany has made on the world, beautiful and evil.

They occur as part of an exercise: Was my father's service in the Wehrmacht at all mitigated by the Nazis' having burned so many of the books his father published? Would my own moral inheritance be cleaner had not 80 percent of the Kurt Wolff Verlag catalog but all of it been declared a threat to the German race and nation?

Is there indeed such a thing as a "moral inheritance"?

If some deficit of virtue has come down to me on my father's side, did the efforts of that cousin on my mother's, Caroline Ferriday, go any distance toward closing it? How many good works was Caroline obliged to perform to square accounts with her slaveholding ancestors?

And then the exercise ends. There's a case to be made for moral balance sheets, but if they exist, every child deserves a blank one on the day of its birth. At the same time, let that blank one come with a ledger accounting the family debt. And may the significant figures of shame—clarifying, activating shame—fill the lines of that ledger, to help inform the task before us.

History tends to overwhelm individuals who try to control its course. But for the occasional black swan, a Hitler or bin Laden or Gavrilo Princip, only a critical mass of citizens can steer it. Georg Sieber came to understand this, and in his own way my father did too. Of course organizers wanted to turn the page, to banish from their Olympics anything that smacked of Nazism. But to take history seriously is to understand that you can't "get back to us with less-frightful scenarios" more in keeping with the games that modern Germany wished it could stage.

For all the truth to Santayana's nostrum that those who can't remember the past are condemned to repeat it, the organizers of the 1972 Olympics were confounded by a paradox for which eleven Israelis paid the ultimate price. To dig into the detail is to discover that the tragedy of the Munich games was not that anyone failed to remember the past. It was that Germans, trapped in a circle, recalled their past all too well.

With Vanessa and our children I've come by train and company car to Darmstadt, longtime seat of the family firm. Three hundred and fifty years after a common ancestor founded the original pharmacy across from the palace moat in the center of town, we're joining relatives to celebrate Merck's status as grande dame of the world's drug companies. Despite how my father disentangled himself long ago from a silent partner's stake in the business, management still regards blood as blood. So I'm plied with regular mailings and the latest edition of the family tree, its boughs now laden with the fruit of thirteen generations. The executive board has invited us to the M-Sphere, a geodesic pavilion built for the festivities, which will include dinner, speeches, and a performance by the Deutsche Philharmonie Merck.

During the Enlightenment, the Merck family had grown its wealth not only by selling powders and potions, but also by lending money in and around the landgraviate of Hesse-Darmstadt. Thus, when Emanuel Merck made his breakthrough with alkaloids in the 1820s, the business could tap capital to begin production on an industrial scale. My ancestors' instinctive cosmopolitanism led them to pursue markets around the world, which guaranteed huge losses in the aftermath of world wars that left German industry ruined and isolated. Yet that same global vision helped lead to renewal during the *Wirtschaftswunder*. Since the end of the war Merck has enjoyed almost uninterrupted growth, from acquisitions as well as expansion into biotech, semiconductors, and materials like pigments and liquid crystals.

Today the company grounds are as much research center as factory, with a racially diverse, multilingual workforce that has the look and feel of the student body at some campus in the California system. Merck now routinely tries to put down markers on the side of the angels. The company participates in the Access Accelerated Open Platform initiative, which targets treatable, preventable, noncommunicable diseases around the world. And it invests in cultural causes like the orchestra that takes its name as well as the annual Tagore Award in India, a literary prize that highlights Kurt's connection to the Bengali Nobel Prize winner. Much of this corporate citizenship—and recent willingness to confront National Socialism in the company's past—began under the chairmanship of Maria's son Jon, who for twelve years led the executive board and is among those assembled in the M-Sphere tonight.

"Always Curious" is one of the birthday slogans for which Angela Merkel, in her recent celebratory visit, chided her hosts for failing to render in German. But "Always Curious" has been my mantra all year long. During the war Darmstadt was as thoroughly destroyed as any German city, yet my father never told me how the Royal Air Force had made it a target on a September night in 1944—a September 11, in fact. Appraising the city nine miles away from the edge of his palace grounds, the Prince of Hesse described how "the light grew and grew until the whole of the southern sky was glowing, shot through with red and yellow." The raid killed eight thousand people, forced almost half the population into the countryside, and chased Niko's uncle Wilhelm into that garden shed. It had taken centuries to build what those planes needed less than an hour to destroy. Three months later American B-17s would make a specific target of the Merck factory, dealing the second blow of a one-two punch.

"When I think of Germany," says one of the exile characters of W. G. Sebald's imagination, "it feels as if there were some kind of insanity lodged in my head." Germany never triggered anything like that in me. The country I came to know from visits during my youth was home to gentle aunts and uncles, cousins my own age engaged in my interests, and comfort food. *Stunde Null* is a problematic concept, for in seeking to lop off what has come before, it disrupts the continuities essential to memory and accountability. But the Merck cousins I've come to know best adamantly refuse to foreshorten remembrance. They include Harald Binder, an independent scholar who dedicates some of his Merck wealth to the Center for Urban History of East Central Europe, which he founded in the Galician city of Lviv, in Ukraine. Harald's institute is as pointed as possible a repudiation of his great-grandmother, the Ahnenerbe patroness Mathilde Merck.

Of course, in a country where *Stolpersteine* are routinely vandalized, younger Germans aren't entirely free of the viruses still coursing through the political bloodstream. Here this weekend is a family shareholder recently in the news for his involvement with Deutsches Kolleg, an antisemitic, racist "think tank" that rejects the Federal Republic and believes in the restoration of a Reich purged of immigrants and returned to its Nazi-era borders. A 2017 German TV documentary placed this relative at a meeting of the group's directorate in Thuringia in July 2016. And it included footage of him joining American Klansman David Duke at two racist events during the mid-2000s—a gathering of Holocaust deniers in Teheran and Duke's own European-American Conference in New Orleans.

Other family members assure me that he is shunned, but that's cold comfort. A globally engaged company based in modern Germany came to realize that its first reaction to that documentary—a bloodless comment that Merck doesn't concern itself with the private activities of its shareholders—wouldn't fly. The family, Merck ultimately said in a statement several weeks later, "resolutely distances itself from these political views and associated ideologies."

Merck is using yet another English-language slogan to celebrate its birthday: "Imagine the next 350 years." But I'm not quite ready to do so. Several weeks later I return to Darmstadt, to the firm's corporate history department, to finish up with the first 350.

The Merck archive has traced much the same morally compromised path as twentieth-century Germany. For three years during the early sixties it was run by Friedrich Wilhelm Euler, who even before the Nazis' rise to power subscribed to theories of "racial hygiene" and conducted antisemitic genealogical research.

During tricentennial festivities in 1968, Merck made no mention of the company's relationship to the Third Reich. But by the late nineties the firm had begun to take up its past. It joined Erinner-ung, Verantwortung und Zukunft (Remembrance, Responsibility and the Future), a movement launched by German businesses in 2000, to identify and compensate those conscripted into forced labor during the war, and in advance of the 350th anniversary the company commissioned four independent scholars to produce a history with an emphasis on the Nazi era. The archive to which I've come is now staffed by seven specialists whose instinct is to honor the historical record before protecting anyone in the family. The current director, Sabine Bernschneider-Reif, works in an office housing dozens of volumes of Mathilde Merck's notori-ous diaries, and in 2015 she made them available unrestrictedly to graduate students at Darmstadt's Technical University. History is what history is. And so, at a table one floor up from large-as-life blowups of family figures including Kurt and Tante Tilla, I set out unencumbered on the paper trail, come what may.

Walter Brügmann, the fervent Nazi who served as Merck's head of personnel through the end of the war, destroyed com-promising employment records as the Americans closed in. Yet I still learn that female laborers forcibly brought from the east were paid only about 75 percent of a standard wage, which after deductions for food and lodging left them with no more than roughly forty Reichsmarks — about four dollars — a month. More cruelly, they were barred from air-raid shelters, which helps explain why so many died during the December 1944 bombing of the factory, in which all but one of the barracks for forced laborers were destroyed.

For years Merck had produced hydrogen peroxide as a dis-infectant or bleaching agent. With the war, it turns out the com-pany entered into secret deals to supply that substance to German armaments factories for use in fuel for torpedoes, rockets, and jets. "If, after 1945, the Allies had more thoroughly investigated the company's wartime activities—which conflicted with its pre-war focus—Merck's continued existence probably would have been endangered," the 350th anniversary history concludes. "The American authorities would have found arguments for classifying Merck among the major industrial 'warmongers.'"

Karl Merck, the lead family partner through the war, was a Nazi Party member who held prominent positions with the National Socialist Motor Corps, the National Socialist League of German Technicians, and the Nazified German Chemical Society. On May 1, 1933—the day he, his cousin Fritz, and my great-uncle Wilhelm all joined the party—Karl presided over a companywide celebration of a day of national labor on the factory grounds that included the singing of the "Horst Wessel Song." Returning to Darmstadt from the 1936 Nuremberg Rally, Karl used a company roll call to rhapsodize about the "tremendous honor and love that all show the *Führer*." In 1939, the company's by then Nazi-dominated Council of Trust was boasting that Merck "no longer even hires people who are one-quarter Jewish"—which is to say someone like my father, then about to begin his final year at boarding school.

But even though cousin Karl was the active partner most central to the company during the Third Reich, it's Wilhelm's story that fascinates me most—for his relationships with both Karl, whom he answered to, and the most powerful figure in Merck's modern history. To tell that story we have to go back to World War I and its consequential aftermath.

Before being called up to the army in May 1915, Wilhelm Merck had begun work toward an engineering degree at the University of Dresden. With the armistice, the company put him in charge of technical matters at the factory and in 1921 named him an active partner. But Wilhelm and three cousins—the other hands-on family members of this ninth generation included Karl, Fritz, and Louis Merck—quickly realized how ill-prepared they were to lead. The war had interrupted their studies and upended the essence of the business they were being entrusted to run. Under the Treaty of Versailles, an industrial firm like Merck suffered much more than a business like the Kurt Wolff Verlag; every German pharmaceutical company was required to hand over half its inventory to the Allies as reparations, and for several years afterward sell another 25 percent at an extortionate fixed price. During the Ruhr crisis of 1923, in which French and Belgian troops occupied Germany's industrial heartland and exacerbated the economic chaos that led to the hyperinflation that would peak that fall, Merck executives legitimately feared that foreign forces would advance on Darmstadt and seize the factory.

To meet these challenges, the firm felt compelled for the first time to bring in substantial numbers of managers from outside the family. In 1923 Merck revamped its executive board, and in January 1924, to win the favor of desperately needed lenders, made a fateful decision. After long negotiations and despite much internal dissent, the company hired and gave a largely free hand to the chief of the local Darmstädter und Nationalbank, a decorated World War I officer named Bernhard Pfotenhauer. He's in the middle of the front row in the photograph overleaf, with Wilhelm to his right. As this newcomer overhauled the board's role and streamlined management, "the family was largely reduced to the function of 'constitutional monarchs.'" Pfotenhauer's tenure would end only with the fall of the Third Reich.

To study the Pfotenhauer era at Merck is to see how an opportunist exploited a crisis to get his hooks in the company and how, steeped in an ideology that prized and empowered

autocratic behavior, he became in name and practice a *Wehr-wirtschaftsführer*, a "leader of military industry," the title given to executives at those companies most solidly behind the Nazi war effort. But family members made this deal with the devil willingly, to avoid having to float public shares that would have diluted their wealth and diminished their power. "I am really overjoyed that we managed to get this Pf[otenhauer]," Wilhelm wrote Karl and Louis after the deal was struck. "Considering that he is only thirty-eight years old and is a really tip-top employee in financial matters, I believe he will truly do a lot for us."

In fact, the initial misgivings of others would be borne out. Pfotenhauer looked down on the family partners as dilettantes unworthy of responsibility, and beginning in 1933 he courted local Nazi capos like Jakob Sprenger, the *Gauleiter* of southern Hesse-Nassau. Studying and then emulating Hitler, he became infected with what another Merck executive after the war would call the "dictator mania." US investigators concluded in late 1945 that Pfotenhauer "often overrode the active partners and owners; he pursued policies unknown to them, and generally ran the firm as he wished." As one observer put it in a 1948 affidavit: "Just as a lasso thrower knows how to tie up a man from head to foot in a few seconds, so Pfotenhauer possessed the strange power and ability to paralyze many of those around him almost instantly so that they lost all their will and became soft putty in his hands."

Eventually even Wilhelm soured on Pfotenhauer and his high-handedness. Matters came to a head in December 1941, after Pfotenhauer clashed with Wilhelm and Louis Merck during a heated meeting. Four months later Karl Merck prevailed on both dissident cousins to accept relegation to the status of silent partners. But this only forced another impasse, for Karl also insisted that Wilhelm and Louis waive the right to rejoin the company as active partners in perpetuity, something neither was willing to do.

Karl and Fritz Merck sided with Pfotenhauer, leaving Wilhelm and Louis outgunned. On May 29, 1942, Wilhelm was summoned to the Nazi Party *Gauhaus* in Frankfurt, where he found Karl and Pfotenhauer waiting for him. After the war Wilhelm said the Nazi economics official in the room that day had made clear to him the stakes—that he, Wilhelm, "knew what would happen if he didn't sign" the waiver agreement. So he signed "under protest." Louis did so the following day.

Afterward, Pfotenhauer mopped up. He fired a longtime executive who had sent Karl a lengthy memo complaining about Pfotenhauer's overreach. (After unsuccessfully taking his case to the local labor court, this employee found the Gestapo at his door.) Pfotenhauer also curtailed the power of the two remaining active family members, his putative allies Karl and Fritz.

But Pfotenhauer's fortunes were entirely bound up with those of the regime, and the Third Reich would soon be in steep decline. Pfotenhauer's daughter Ursula testified after the war that the RAF's bombing of Darmstadt in September 1944 had left him a "broken man." On March 23, 1945—using Luminal, a barbiturate he took from a warehouse on the factory grounds— Pfotenhauer poisoned his wife, two of his daughters, and four of his grandchildren before shooting himself. He was unwilling, he had told a co-worker shortly beforehand, to face the prospect of "having to clean the shoes of an American Jew from tomorrow on."

Two days later American troops occupied the Merck factory, which was soon handed over to a US-appointed trustee.

In a yellowing set of papers, I'm astonished to discover who became involved in the postwar intrigue surrounding the company. In early August 1947, upon his return to the United States from the trip that included his reunion with Niko and Maria at the Swiss border, my grandfather checked in with Merck & Co. CEO and founding Pantheon investor George W. Merck.

> *You know that I have remained on very friendly terms with my first wife—your first cousin, Elisabeth Albrecht Merck [sic]—and as my oldest son is living with his mother you will not be astonished to learn that I accepted Elisabeth's hospitality and stayed at her home in Munich. . . . On June 30 Wilhelm Merck and his cousin, Lisbet Merck Pfarr, came to see me. Mr. Günther John, the right hand of Dr. [Karl] Merlau, Trustee of E. Merck, Darmstadt, drove them in his car from Darmstadt to Munich. My talks with your*

relatives and Mr. John were quite interesting and I feel I
should report to you about them.

Kurt had learned that a coalition of Social Democrats and
Communists in Hesse were making a target of the company.
The German Mercks and the US-appointed trustee hoped that
George W., who would appear on the cover of *Time* a few years
later as the beau ideal of the responsible American CEO, might
put in a word with their US overlords. "[The political left is] trying by all means to have the firm nationalized and to bring about
a spectacular trial proving that for political or other reasons the
Mercks should no longer be allowed to own the firm," Kurt
wrote. "Everything should be done to keep the firm as a private
enterprise. . . . They do not ask for any material support, but for
ideological support only."

In that same letter Kurt also addressed the March 1942
confrontation that led to the ouster of Wilhelm and Louis and
consolidated Pfotenhauer's power. "Mr. John pointed out that it
would have been out of the question to throw out Pfotenhauer,"
he reported. "He called Pfotenhauer a kind of 'Himmler of Hessen' and a man whose position in the Nazi Party was so strong
that if the partners had tried to throw him out he would have
easily managed to throw out the entire Merck family by party
action, and nationalized the firm at once with himself dictator of
the business."

Scarcely a year later, on September 1, 1948, the trustee
unblocked Merck's assets and returned the company to family
control. The Allies' victory had mooted the 1942 *Gauhaus* agreement, paving the way for Wilhelm to rejoin Karl and Fritz as active
partners now that all had gone through the de-Nazification process and at least superficially patched up their differences. (Louis
died in 1945.)

The story I learn isn't simply that fear of the Red Menace helped short-circuit full de-Nazification and return the firm to the family after the war. It's that, back in the early twenties, Bernhard Pfotenhauer rescued Merck Darmstadt from economic disaster; that accommodations to the man my grandfather called "the Himmler of Hessen" kept the company thriving and in my ancestors' hands throughout the Third Reich; and that those compromises ensured that my father, in 1977, would have Merck shares to cash in. Down to the day I write this, I enjoy some of that wealth.

Back in the company archives a day later, I find an undated, type-written statement from Wilhelm Merck, clearly submitted for his de-Nazification hearing. To read it is to literally hear what Uncle Wilhelm had to say for himself.

> *First of all, until 1933 I was neither politically active nor a member of any political party. At that time the situation in Germany forced me to choose sides politically—many people had to. I joined the Nazi Party in the belief that this organization could lead us to a better future. After all sorts of coaxing by acquaintances I joined the SS in September 1934. I did so because of the requirement that I belong to a [party] organization to continue my activity with what was then the Motorflugsportklub, which was subsequently subsumed by the DLV [Deutscher Luftsportverband]. As regards this I must note that I had been involved in flying gliders since 1911 and really enjoyed it. . . .*
>
> *Later I understood what [the SS] was really about. That is why I again tried to leave this organization, which was impossible unless you were kicked out for some offense.*

With the 1937 merger of the DLV and the Nationalsozialist-isches Fliegerkorps (NSFK), Wilhelm seems to say, he no longer needed to remain an SS member and tried to leave. "My activity in the NSFK was merely to give young glider pilots the oppor-tunity to dedicate themselves to the sport," he says. "I did not participate in any political or ideological training courses either actively or passively."

But the NSFK and the DLV before it were not recreational sports clubs. They were stalking horses for Nazi Germany to rearm in violation of the Treaty of Versailles. And Wilhelm goes on to concede that, shortly after the war began, he learned that he in fact had not disentangled himself from the SS, for his status in the NSFK led to his promotion to the rank of an *SS-Hauptsturmführer*, or captain. "However," he says, "I never took an oath to either the party or the SS, nor was I asked to take such an oath. . . . Very soon after the [Nazis'] seizure of power, I realized the essential goal of the party, with which I had never been in agreement. . . . I tried not to stand out in any case and also avoided appearing in public. . . . I believe I can assert with a clear conscience that I have never spoken to the collective workforce in the National Socialist sense, except for anniversaries of employees or workers, or participation in the training of managers."

Yet that's not nothing. And in a 1939 speech to employees, Wilhelm vaunted "trust in our *Führer*" and Germany's "unde-featable army," adding, "We want to show at home that we want to and can fight if the *Führer* calls. Only a united people at arms, as in a vise, only determination leads to victory." The histori-ans detailed to Merck's 350th anniversary history conclude that, even as he "tried to portray himself after 1945 as a non-political aesthete," and "despite his heritage and social position," Wil-helm "was not capable of keeping his distance from National

Socialism." Invoking testimony submitted to the de-Nazification tribunal by the Merck Works Council, an organization representing labor, the historians write: "He had 'been there,' had been a poor model for the employees and had 'helped to build up the Nazi empire.'"

Wilhelm insists that he "repeatedly tried" to prevent the dismissals of Rudolf Engelmann, a "non-Aryan" engineer at Merck, and personnel director Otto Henkel, who "was forced to leave under the threat of violence" by local Nazi *Kreisleiter* Karl Schilling because of his Jewish wife, Emmy. "I very much regret that these two gentlemen, especially Dr. Henkel, who is now back at the factory as head of human resources, were booted out because of their political leanings," he writes, "but I was personally powerless to oppose it."

Two *Stolpersteine* in the sidewalks of Darmstadt speak to Wilhelm's impotence. One honors Rudolf Engelmann. The other memorializes Emmy Henkel. Both were murdered in the camps.

In his defense Wilhelm also invokes his defeat in the "palace coup," as the Pfotenhauer episode came to be known among my ancestors. "In 1942 I detached myself from the factory I loved, in which I had been boss and partner for almost twenty-five years," he writes. "My departure was also done in a way that could have easily been fatal to me and might have landed me in a concentration camp." Yet for all of Pfotenhauer's Nazi ties, this self-pity misses the point. It was the family's stake in the company that hung in the balance during that power struggle, and every Merck family member stood to forfeit shares if an unappeased Pfotenhauer were to invite the Nazis to nationalize the firm. Wilhelm lost out to Karl, Fritz, and "the Himmler of Hessen" for a number of reasons. Some ideological clash over National Socialism wasn't one of them.

In the final paragraph of his statement, Wilhelm includes one more thing: "My brother-in-law Kurt Wolff, who was a half Jew, happily stayed over at my house."

Yes, the "some of my best brothers-in-law are half-Jewish" defense.

Wilhelm, seen here chauffeuring my grandparents sometime in the early twenties, was de-Nazified as a Class IV *Mitläufer*, or collaborator, in June 1948 and ordered to pay a fine of 2,000 Reichsmarks, or $200. The tribunal cited several witnesses who testified on his behalf. One, a Dr. Hammer, said the sight of a copy of the antisemitic newspaper *Der Stürmer* one day had led Wilhelm to express to him "his disgust at the persecution of the Jews . . . so strongly and emphatically that the voicing of his opinion might have led to him being sent to a concentration camp." Another, a Herr Weigand, who taught music to one of Wilhelm's sons, testified that Wilhelm had provided financial assistance after Nazi thugs hounded Weigand from his apartment during Kristallnacht.

In Berlin we did our laundry with a detergent called Persil. After the war cynical Germans referred to exonerative certificates of de-Nazification as *Persilscheine*. Someone with Wilhelm's standing and connections would have had little difficulty getting a Persil slip. Yet for all his self-interested pleadings, the picture of my great-uncle to emerge from the tribunal is less of a monster than of an invertebrate. He wasn't as deeply implicated as his cousin Karl. But Wilhelm was fatefully representative. Dazzled by uniforms and rank, drawn to the whispering glider as much as the revving motor, he had no reservations about serving as a tool on behalf of the "gigantic sports club" of Sebastian Haffner's description. Nazism swept up the German people because of the willingness of scores of Wilhelms and millions of Wilhelm wannabes.

As proof of the farce of the whole de-Nazification process, Karl Merck—who had gone underground before the Americans reached Darmstadt, and whom prosecutors wanted to convict as an activist, or Class II Nazi—received the same verdict and punishment as Wilhelm: Class IV *Mitläufer*; fine of 2,000 Reichsmarks. He was soon reinstated as head of the company.

EIGHTEEN
THE END, COME BY ITSELF
Niko, 2003 to 2007

G rowing up in Nazi Germany, Niko could count one close
American relative—his cousin Albert (Albie) Merck,
George W.'s son in New Jersey. In 2004, then eighty-three and
living outside Boston, Albie unearthed his first exchange of letters
with my father after the war and sent copies to him in Vermont.

A year after V-E Day, Albie had written Niko in Munich
from his Harvard dorm room to share news of his impending
marriage. My father replied in his imperfect English, enclosing a
photo he had taken of his cousin in lederhosen during a hiking
trip they took together through Austria in 1938. Niko's reply had
to clear American censors before reaching Cambridge:

> *Let me tell you how happy I am, and I wish you good luck
> and almost the best for your engagement. My congratula-
> tions to such a beautiful girl as I can imagine her by the
> picture. Do you remember the days we were very young
> and happy boys walking, swimming, rowing and taking
> movies and pictures in Austria? I looked this day and found
> some couloured pictures, one of you, as a real "Bavarian"
> and another of the "Schloss Mirabell" at Salzburg. Do you*

remember it? I often wish the time may come back, but unfortunately it is impossible.

I hope that one day I can come to the States to join my father so I wouldn't be dammned to finish my life in this dammaged country where it is quite impossible to have real studies. I lost about five years during the war and now it seems I loose still more. —

I hope you have not already forgotten your cousin but I lay a picture of mine in this letter too, so you can see how I'm looking now.

Please excuse my bad English but I shall learn it better in the States.

"What a discouraging place Germany must have been," Albie wrote in a note. "But you *did* succeed in getting to the USA after all. And the rest is history."

I can imagine my father nodding. As he grew older, Niko seemed to become more conscious of the unlikely distance he had covered. There was an assertiveness to him in those final years, the cancer notwithstanding. He told his financial adviser which stocks to buy. He described to his oncologist the molecular structure of his medications. And he loved nothing more than to strip from daily life anything that might interfere with what he wanted most, the company of my mother and his grandchildren, and the few fruits of the *Glotzofon* worth organizing an evening around. Otherwise, as he'd say, "Who needs it," which became a family catchphrase, both balm and incantation. As a birthday gift one year, Kathy's husband gave his Internet-averse father-in-law the domain-name rights to WhoNeedsIt.org. Niko delighted in this who-needs-it twofer: rights he would never exercise to something he would never use.

There was a flip side to "Who needs it?" Those things he adored—my mother's company, pasta, Poirot mysteries—he would binge on. At a concert a few years before he died, hearing a quintet perform his favorite Schubert, he whispered to Vanessa, "They're taking the repeats!" If Niko suffered from lingering PTSD, Kurt had modeled a way to counteract it: helping oneself to any sensual pleasures at hand.

My nonreligious father insisted he was a spiritual man. He didn't believe a scientist at his bench could miss the divinity in what lay before him. But he had no use for the capital-C Church, which in the country of his youth had failed its biggest test. The closest thing to a statement of belief Niko ever shared with me was to boil down the history of the universe to a hypothetical year: if the Big Bang took place on January 1, life on earth began four seconds before midnight the following December 31. Human beings have our place in all this—a sacred and glorious one, to be sure—but only as arrivistes. We should be accordingly humble.

He did have a healthy sense of the larger arc traced by time, of not getting mired in the slog, either while living out a citizen's public life or a mortal's private one. Notations my mother made in her journal bear this out. "From Niko, February 2002. Democracy—you have to fight for it. . . . Expect to take one day at a time." Two years later, in May: "Niko, on a bad day: 'It's important to remember that not all days are the same.'" And in October 2006: "Nick talks of grace, which helps us accept the mystery of life, death, living. He says his many near-death experiences and rational way of thinking have helped him live with the 'not knowing'—not knowing his end. 'You don't have to work on the end. The end comes by itself.'"

Aware of the carbon that makes up our cells, he trusted nature as only an organic chemist can. One night, awake and glimpsing the moon out the window against a bell-clear sky, he delivered a report to my mother. "Nature," he whispered across the pillow. "Just going about her little rounds."

When her brother was a child, Maria once told me, he had a certain stoic tic on family trips. If you asked him how he felt, and the answer came back *Sag's lieber nicht*, "I'd rather not say," he was about to get carsick. Before her own death Maria recounted for me the phone call in which Niko brought up his failing health. She pressed him for details. "*Sag's lieber nicht*," he replied.

"That's when I knew," Maria said.

The cancer reached his gall bladder, a section of small intestine, eventually a lung. Before launching into an itemization, Niko would pull together a thin smile and announce an impending "organ recital." He went into hospice care several months before the end.

The last thing I remember telling him was, "Your life has been a miracle." He didn't reply. But the look he threw back at me confirmed that he knew this, and that it meant something to him that I knew it too.

Niko may have been correct that the end comes by itself. But it was hard not to conclude that death was ultimately a choice he made, an act to flout all the times he had been denied agency during that first third of his life. On his last morning, the visiting nurse ordered a hospital bed for the living room. Niko couldn't explicitly say so, but we all knew he had no desire to spend even one night outside the connubial bed.

The *Times* crossword from three days earlier lay half-finished on a side table. He had filled in JESU for *Bach's "____, Joy of Man's Desiring"* and ESSEX for *English county on the North Sea*. I took a moment to supply SIGNOTHETIMES for *1987 Prince song and album*. As dusk fell, sitting alongside him as he lay in that interloping slab of furniture, Christian and I watched him take his final breath.

The last word anyone heard from him—after he was asked how many pills he needed—came in German. *Drei*.

My father wore a gold ring that had belonged to his father, engraved with the colophon of the Kurt Wolff Verlag, Romulus and Remus suckling at the she-wolf of Rome. Moments after he died, my mother slipped it off his finger and gave it to me.

We returned to America to find that several boxes of books, sent weeks earlier to avoid airline surcharges, hadn't arrived. The one package to do so came with a shipping label in my handwriting, but none of the dozen volumes inside were ours. The box must have come apart in some handling facility between Berlin and Vermont, where a postal worker had reassembled it and filled it with random titles. Among the books standing in for ours were Jean-Paul Sartre's *No Exit* and Thich Nhat Hanh's *Your True Home*.

Vanessa said the postal service simply wanted to enrich my understanding of the travails of transatlantic relocation.

The year has left a series of afterimages.

A violin. My father took one to Hitler's war. What kind of world produced a young man who would do that? Surely my grandfather deserves credit for recognizing important writing and doggedly finding a readership for it. But at the risk of blaming the victim, for Kurt was clearly that, I now wonder if, in their devotion to *Bildung*, my ancestors helped blind Germans to the obligations of citizenship, which include getting out of the salon to stand up for the neighbor down the street. Didn't the *Bildungsbürgertum* propagate an illusion of security to German Jews, so many of whom refused to believe the country they loved, the land of Beethoven and Goethe and Kant, would target the very people who most appreciated that culture, who indeed helped create and elevate it?

Elisabeth Krämer's husband on Kristallnacht, lifeless on the ground beneath the window of his own home. How much nobler it would have been to practice citizenship sooner, so as not to be tested in friendship later. Not easier, but nobler. And in so doing lay the foundation for a sturdier and more just civil society.

The dome of the Reichstag, translucent and insurmountable. A year in Berlin let me see up close modern Germany's enshrinement of history in the public square; her civic vigilance and, yes, humility; and her draining of almost all militarism from a society in which men not long ago made sure to include a reservist's rank on business cards. In the space of two generations the Federal Republic has built a consensus that the Allies knew better what was right for her than Germans themselves did. For all this, I returned to the United States with great respect for today's version of Kurt and Niko's native country, and believing that Americans can learn much from it.

Another image: A house of cards on a table. Kurt loved a parable that Kafka shared in a 1923 postcard to Max Brod. To me it speaks to the failure of the Weimar Republic, even if the author didn't live to see the end of Germany's first stab at democracy. "Rage is something a child has when his house of cards collapses because a grown-up has shaken the table," Kafka wrote. "But the house of cards didn't collapse because the table was shaken, but because it was a house of cards. A real house doesn't collapse even if the table is chopped into firewood; it doesn't need a foundation from somewhere outside." Democracy came to France and the United States in the aftermaths of their own revolutions.

But Germany had its first democratic government essentially imposed, after the humiliation of a lost war, on a people who knew only how to be subjects, not citizens—which only underscores how fragile, how tied to context, democracy is.

My father, seeing his father off. It's a recurring image. How many times did Niko say goodbye to Kurt wondering if he'd ever see him again? In Munich in 1930, on Elisabeth's "worst of days." In France and Italy during the thirties, then again in Freiburg in 1947, in "horrible, agonizing train stations." At New York's Idlewild Airport in 1959, as Kurt "shuffled to the plane" for Switzerland.

I feel for my grandfather, betrayed in both countries of which he was a citizen. But I feel too for my father. He was condemned to travel the morally murkier path, even if his father was in some ways the morally murkier man.

And so it comes time to take inventory of what my father never told me that I now know.

Two ancestors, father and son, chased from the same family home during the nineteenth century in antisemitic riots, twenty-four years apart.

My father's younger sibling, a stillborn baby boy.

My father's half brother Enoch, saved by the grace of the Danish nationality of the beard his desperate mother chose.

My father himself, a "*Mischling*" with a *Nachweis*, a party to genocide simply for having eaten the rations made available to him.

His favorite uncle, in the SS; his imperious "Tante," Himmler's pen pal; his beloved magician stepfather, a financial supporter of the SS—with party connections that may have helped conjure for Niko protection from the regime.

His aunt, celebrating her twenty-second birthday with a gunshot to her head.

Merck Darmstadt during the Third Reich—using forced labor; supplying the drugs that likely addled Hitler's judgment; collaborating on secret arms projects; submitting to "the Himmler of Hessen"; standing by while the Nazis made a widower of one employee and a corpse of another.

Jesko von Puttkamer, my father's uncle and, nearly a half century later, virtual stepfather.

The home in which my grandmother grew up, and her brother then lived, destroyed in an Allied bombing raid.

The inheritance of my father's godson, my cousin Niko, who had a victim for a grandmother and a perpetrator for a grandfather.

A comrade in my father's unit, fragging their ranking officer in the dying days of the war.

A few of these things Niko was likely unaware of. And of course I could hardly ask after things about which I had no clue. But I was reluctant to ask. Why? Maybe I was afraid he would tell me a painful truth. Maybe I was afraid he *wouldn't* tell me the truth, out of wanting to protect me or not wanting me to think less of him—to think him a coward or worse—and, sensing as much, I spared him by withholding my questions.

Or maybe, like my father, taking America to be staging ground for the clean break and the fresh start, I did what so many Germans once did and kept my counsel.

It's hard to tell, just as this has been hard to tell. "Those things about which we cannot theorize," Umberto Eco has said, "we must narrate." So I have tried to do. But it's a strange place to sit, between wanting to know and not wanting to know, which may be why I've come home uncertain about so much still.

Epilogue

Though we returned to the United States at the end of July 2018, for the entirety of our time in Europe we kept our eyes fixed on a date several months after that. The midterm elections on November 6 would give Americans their first opportunity since Donald Trump's inauguration to check his presidency at the ballot box.

"There is no inevitability in history," Fritz Stern wrote. "Thinking about what might have happened, what could have happened, is a necessary element in trying to understand what did happen. . . . We deem the future in a free society, however constrained by preexisting conditions, to be open, and if this is so, then civic engagement also becomes a moral and political imperative."

I'm moved to set Stern's observation alongside what Helen wrote Maria in August 1946, shortly after she and Kurt became American citizens.

> It is a very strange feeling to have status in the world once more, to belong somewhere, and to enjoy protection, after having been an exile and an alien for so long. If one lives long enough, the wheel has time to turn, and fortune and misfortune invert themselves. It seems that just yesterday we were living in France in fear of our lives

and completely at the mercy of our hosts. And now to be a
citizen of what the oath-taking judge called "the mightiest
nation on earth," with even an atom bomb or two to back
you up—I can't quite get used to "the last shall be first."
This great, strange country, still so much in the making,
showed its best face the day I was sworn in.

But when the wheel next turns, it could do so in the devil's
own direction. That's why we put our shoulder to it. So on Election
Day morning, in that spirit—infused in me by the lives of Kurt and
Niko, lifted by the harmonizing voices of Helen and Maria and
Elisabeth—I headed off to the white clapboard town hall in our
village in Vermont. To be a citizen. To act on my stake in a country
"still so much in the making." To engage the task before us.

My vote would be consonant with a forty-seat swing to the
Democrats in the House of Representatives and the repudiation
of a president who had made the midterm campaign a referen-
dum on immigration and asylum seekers. Some 54 percent of
voters surveyed that day agreed that "immigrants strengthen our
country." This figure wasn't remotely high enough, but it out-
stripped by twenty points the number who disagreed, and came
despite nearly two years of anti-immigrant hysteria and lies from
the White House and its propagandists.

Americans have long shared a consensus that we don't
indulge in Nazi analogies to describe our own domestic circumstances. To do so diminishes the singular horror of the Third
Reich, and besides, Americans have good reason to consider our
institutions more durable than those of Weimar Germany. Of
course, Nixon and his Watergate henchmen weren't just like the
Gestapo. But my father held America to a higher standard, and
that's why he regarded the Saturday Night Massacre as a moment
of peril for his adopted country.

From across the ocean I had recognized the parallels, just as my father would have. At the beginning of our time in Berlin, the white supremacists brandishing torches in Charlottesville didn't constitute some Sturmabteilung formally reporting to the White House, and refugees legally seeking asylum at the border were only detained and deported, not sent to camps. But Trump soon began to give a wink and a nod to followers spoiling for a fight. And agents of Customs and Border Protection now warehoused would-be asylees in flight from violence, even separating children from their parents—and to make that easier, sometimes telling families that a child needed to be taken away "for a bath." To be sure, this wasn't comparable to what the Nazis began to do in 1933. But by the light of American norms, it was unprecedented and took place under cover of falsehoods, insults, stunts, and gaslighting from the president and some of his supporters that echoed darker times. Kafka died before the Nazis came to power, but he knew. "Evil," he wrote, "is whatever distracts."

Several weeks after the midterms I showed up for an appointment at the German consulate in Boston. I came to invoke Article 116 of the *Grundgesetz*, the Federal Republic's basic law. It provides for German citizenship to anyone stripped of it by the Third Reich for religious or political reasons, as well as to two generations of their descendants.

A consular official named Herr Brosse summoned me to his window, where I presented documents that detail much of what I've recounted here. They included a scholarly investigation of the Kurt Wolff file in the archives of the Emergency Rescue Committee; Kurt's letter to Varian Fry pleading for a visa; his diary entry from the day after the Reichstag burned; and his unavailing letters from Tuscany during the late thirties, petitioning the Nazi bureaucracy to renew his passport.

Herr Brosse inspected them all, but he was left unmoved. "Citizenship matters would run first through your father," he said. Because my immediate forebear never had his German citizenship taken away—Niko held a valid passport of the Federal Republic until the late fifties—Article 116 did not, he explained, apply to me.

And then through the Plexiglas I could see that something had caught Herr Brosse's eye.

He fingered my birth certificate, marked February 3, 1957.

He set it alongside my father's US naturalization certificate, dated December 16, 1957.

"You are German," he said, looking up at me.

I hadn't realized the implication of those two dates.

"And my children?" I asked.

"You have children?"

"Two."

"They were born to a German. So they are German too."

"And this in no way would affect my US citizenship or theirs?"

"If you were all born in the United States, no."

It would take more than a year for the paperwork to make its way from Boston and reach the front of the queue at the Bundesverwaltungsamt in Cologne, where some bureaucrat might in any case pick nits with Herr Brosse's interpretation. But I stepped out into the bright sunshine of Copley Plaza that morning on light feet. This development wouldn't wind back the clock to February 27, 1933, before the Reichstag fire and Kurt's flight. But because my father's particulars, not my grandfather's, could deliver me a German passport, it seemed to acknowledge the Third Reich's expropriation of his youth. And it cinched tight a tie that now felt immediate and real.

To embrace my German roots was also a way to signal that, for the moment, Germany is doing a better job of being American than America is. To hold a passport of both countries would be a symbolic way of urging the best of each to regard the other as example. As a product of both, a student of both, invested in both, I recognize that not only Germans and Americans share in the stakes of how we take up what Kurt called "the same task before us." To move beyond the brutal history of the twentieth century is work that citizens the world over are called to do.

ACKNOWLEDGMENTS
AND SOURCES

T his book is an amalgam of history, journalism, and memoir, folded around two biographical chronologies I've tried to launch toward some vanishing point of understanding. This is nonetheless not my memoir, nor an attempt to adjudicate histo-riographic disputes. It's rather a story I felt called to tell in the form of a journey I took—a journey put off for years and made urgent by the headlines. Sometimes the thread of that story sat in plain sight. Sometimes I benefited from a paradox: rather than further shrouding the past, the passage of time can bring events into sharper focus, as archives place more and more material online and posterity exposes the trivial for what it is, allowing significant moments to stand out.

For years I'd collected random things family members shared with me. I began to take notes in earnest sometime in the mid-nineties and during several concentrated years between 2017 and 2020 called on relatives in Europe and the United States to fix dates, supply details, and help find supporting material. Again and again I said grace that I come from a long line of writers and pack rats—they kept diaries, wrote reminiscences, hoarded records, and preserved letters—and that so much survived upheaval and relocation. My grandmother kept each letter her son sent home from the front, returning it to the envelope in which it came, often with photographs he had enclosed with his requests for more film. That parade of postmarks and *Feldpost* numbers maps his movements as a soldier of the Reich, and before he died my father translated and annotated every letter. I'm also grateful to the authors of dozens of books that provided context, the many memorials and research centers dedicated to the Nazi era, and the generous academics, archivists, and scholars who spoke to me. Merck KGaA, the old family business in Darmstadt, maintains a staff of historians who threw open their archives and responded unflinchingly to my queries. As much as Germans reflexively trimmed or looked away during the first decades of the postwar, it's a ritual of twenty-first-century Germany to let the chips of National Socialism fall where they may.

"It's the only immortality I know, living on in the thoughts of others." So my aunt Maria Wolff Stadelmayer told me—that, and so many things besides. Nor could I have told this story without two other women close to Kurt and Niko, my grandmother Elisabeth Merck Albrecht and step-grandmother Helen Mosel Wolff. Their voices underscore how much this narrative, despite its patrilineal spine, owes the women of our family. It's a truism borne out to me repeatedly over years of writing about sports figures, many of them alpha males reluctant to reveal their vulnerabilities: all praise to the mothers and sisters and wives who dress the skinned knees, keep the scrapbooks, vividly recall the failures, and thus better sense the full arc of a story.

My half-uncle, Kurt and Helen's son, Christian Wolff, let me rummage through boxes of family papers and patiently answered questions, revisiting his fractured childhood as best he could. My first cousin, Maria's son, Jon Baumhauer, curates the family archives with a fastidiousness and good faith that leaves the rest of us in awe. Marion Detjen, Helen Wolff's grandniece, is an academic who brings scrupulous care to all her areas of work, including literary history. Each supplied more elaboration and context than I could have hoped for.

I leaned heavily on kin beyond those three. It's easiest to tell a family story with family assistance, and in Europe support came in the form of hospitality as much as lent ears and good memories. Thanks especially to Maria's daughters, Christiane Clemm and Sibylla Schliep, and to Adelheid Baumhauer, Niko Merck, and Ute Frings-Merck, for repeatedly opening their hearts and homes. I'm also grateful to other Baumhauers (Philipp, Luise, Elisabeth, Johannes, Caroline, Matthias, and Laura), Clemms (Christoph, Emanuel, and Raphael), Mercks (Jonja and Lilly), Millers (Norbert and Gabi), and Schlieps (Gregor, Charlie, Niko, and the late Peter), as well as to Harald Binder, Annemarie Crome, Stephan Detjen, Martin Gillan, and Hanne Helfrich, for *Gemütlichkeit* and then some. It was a gift to be able to spend a year in their company. Stateside, my stalwarts included Katherine Wolff, Steve D'Amato, Hope (Holly) Wolff, Nicholas (Tico) Wolff, Dena Wilkie, and the late Ann James, as well as those who made it to Kreuzberg: Ethan Wolff-Mann, Tamsen Wolff, Charles Ireland, Tristram Wolff, Corey Byrnes, and Sadie James.

At archives on both sides of the Atlantic, I relied on the professionals who know their collections so well. In Germany, they included Nikola Herweg and Dörthe Perlenfein at the Deutsches Literaturarchiv in Marbach; Sabine Gresens at the Bundesarchiv in Berlin-Lichterfelde; Monika Haidt-Nass and Katja Schmalholz at the Stadtarchiv in Karlsruhe; Sabine Bernschneider-Rief and Peter Conradi at the Merck Corporate History Archive in Darmstadt; Lupold von Lehsten and Volkhard Huth at the Institut für Personengeschichte in Bensheim; and Claudia Heinrich at the Deutsche Dienststelle (Wehrmachtauskunftstelle) in Berlin-Reineckendorf. In the United

States, I was welcomed by Erin Farley, collections manager for Connecticut Landmarks, and site administrator Peg Shimer to the Bellamy-Ferriday House in Bethlehem; by Jessica Aldi, Ellen Doon, John Monahan, and Adrienne Sharpe to Yale University's Beinecke Rare Book and Manuscript Library; and by the collections staff to Columbia University's Rare Book and Manuscript Library.

With David Meola, professor of history and director of the Jewish and Holocaust Studies Program at the University of South Alabama, I discovered two happy coincidences—that my ancestors, the von Habers of Baden, are a focus of his academic work; and that one of his research trips to Karlsruhe fell during my year in Germany. I'm particularly grateful for his time and insights.

Fiction helped inform my feel for the times and places I've tried to evoke in these pages, so it's worth highlighting several historical novels cited in the bibliography that follows. Sybille Bedford's *Jigsaw* captures the southern France where on-the-lam Germans like Kurt and Helen holed up during the thirties. Anna Seghers's *Transit* and Julie Orringer's *The Flight Portfolio* re-create the occupied Marseille in which Varian Fry and the Vichy French sparred with each other. Lara Prescott's *The Secrets We Kept* conveys the intersection of fifties culture and Cold War geopolitics in which *Doctor Zhivago* landed. Martha Hall Kelly's *Lilac Girls* has introduced my ancestor Caroline Ferriday to countless readers. And there's my ur-text, Uwe Johnson's *Anniversaries*. "This seems to be the only appropriate way to speak and think . . . in the interplay of generations and across two continents," Hannah Arendt wrote Johnson after reading a draft of his opus. The book served as inspiration not just because of its time-shifting, venue-switching daybook structure but also because the author signed for me what I would come to regard as a kind of invitation to tackle this project—a copy of an interim edition of *Anniversaries* that Helen published in translation in 1974, almost a decade before Johnson completed the final installment of a work that would ultimately run more than seventeen hundred pages. With his invention of Marie Cresspahl, the inquisitive ten-year-old of that novel, Johnson nods both forward to the W. G. Sebald epigraph that opens this book and back at a leitmotif in the work of Günter Grass—children asking questions of their elders. In *Anniversaries* the author also sounds a cautionary note I tried to keep in mind while looking back. "The moment of recall," he wrote, "the fact of bringing it into the present, corrodes both at once: past memory and present view." (Uwe Johnson, *Anniversaries: From a Year in the Life of Gesine Cresspahl*, vol. 1, trans. Damion Searls [New York: New York Review Books, 2019], 446.)

In most cases, information of oral provenance—as well as material drawn from unpublished or privately circulated family letters, diaries, appointment books, essays, stories, speeches, monographs, genealogies, and reminiscences—goes unattributed in the text. Everything else comes with a corresponding endnote. If an endnote indicates a published English-language version of a German or French source, I used that translation from the original. Otherwise translations are mine.

The Israeli writer Etgar Keret likes to say that translators are the ninjas of the literary world: if you notice them, they're lousy at their job. The bibliography name-checks no fewer than eight winners of the Helen and Kurt Wolff Translator's Prize, established by the Goethe Institute shortly after Helen's death to recognize masters of rendering German into English. To Susan Bernofsky, Shelley Frisch, Michael Hofmann, Damion Searls, and Krishna Winston, as well as the late Anthea Bell, Margot Bettauer Dembo, and Michael Henry Heim, *herzlichen Dank* and huge thanks for all that they've done or do.

For assistance with my own translations I'm grateful for the resourcefulness, patience, and imagination of Deborah Cohen of Sprachwerk in Kreuzberg. And I thank Christina Ilgner of the School of German at Middlebury College for her tenacity in riddling out the handwriting of several of my ancestors and their correspondents.

To Bettina Matthias, director of Middlebury's School of German, as well as Middlebury Language Schools administrators Stephen Snyder and Beth Karnes Keefe, a special thanks for facilitating my matriculation as a day student for several weeks during the summer of 2017 in advance of our relocation to Berlin. Isabel Meusen, Alexis Smith, Sören Steding, and Friederike Tebben all helped scrape rust off my German.

These pages surely contain errors, and not simply because I relied on memories—those of others as well as my own. For any mistakes I take full responsibility; that there aren't more is to the credit of Amy Hughes and Hilary McClellen, who expertly copyedited and fact-checked the manuscript, respectively.

Andrew Blauner, my agent, midwifed this project from start to finish. On the front end he helped persuade the Federal Republic to grant our family a year's residence permit. On the back end he found a home for the book at Grove Atlantic, where I've been in the sure hands of Julia Berner-Tobin, Emily Burns, Salvatore Destro, Amy Hundley, Gretchen Mergenthaler, Erica Nuñez, Elisabeth Ruge, Deb Seager, Sara Vitale, the polyglot Peter Blackstock, and the Kurt Wolff of latter-day Manhattan, Morgan Entrekin. Every manuscript, my grandfather once said, "is an adventure when it arrives, one that makes my heart beat faster." After surviving palpitations occasioned by mine, Morgan and Peter supplied the notes that made for a better book.

At Merck Darmstadt—or Merck KGaA, to distinguish it from its stateside cousin—I thank Frank Stangenberg-Haverkamp and Cornelia Nitsch, who keep me connected to the family firm. Thanks also to supportive friends we made in Berlin, including Joshua Hammer and Cordula Krämer; Bill and Laurel Martin; the Berlin Brandenburg International School community; Vanessa's crew at Give Something Back to Berlin's Open Art Shelter; Christine Gerkrath, who helped settle us into the Bergmannkiez; and Jörg Hecker, Christian Schulze Aquack, Moritz Micalef, and all the hospitable *Mitarbeiter* at the AHA Factory in Kreuzberg. From the beginning, Craig Neff, Thomas Powers, and Carol Rigolot championed my efforts to get to Germany. Those beyond my family who read drafts and offered invaluable feedback include Robert Cohen, Andreas Kossert, and Amy Trubek. And I was buoyed at one time or another by the support of Rob Alberts, Bruce Anderson, Kelli Anderson, Alex Belth, David Brenner, Bill Burger, Jim Callahan, Michael Collier, Maria Considine, Nicholas Dawidoff, Richard Deitsch, Luzi Dressler, Rainer Dressler, Dick Friedman, Philip Glouchevitch, Jack Goodman, Will Goodman, Céline Gounder, Susan Greenberg, Diane Hare, Peter Hare, Carrie Herzog, Teresa Hyndman, Pico Iyer, Woody Jackson, Claude Johnson, Rachael Joo, Greg Kelly, Alden King, Jerry Kirshenbaum, Ernest Kolowrat, Lloyd Komesar, Lindsay Krasnoff, Alex Laskaris, Tim Layden, Franz Lidz, Maggie Lidz, Karl Lindholm, Eva Mantell, Andrew Maraniss, Jack McCallum, Jamie McCallum, Gabe Miller, Brett Millier, Anette Neff, the late Merrell Noden, Todd Purdum, Michael Roy, Steve Rushin, Pierre Sauvage, David Shields, Timothy Snyder, Tim Spears, Mike Unger, Edward Vasquez, Will Voigt, Grant Wahl, Barbara Weidle, Stefan Weidle, Jon Wertheim, and Doug Wilhelm.

John McPhee believes that no kind of student is more receptive to writing instruction than the college sophomore. As a sophomore at Princeton, I was lucky that a master of historical narrative, the late Robert K. Massie, filled in to teach Humanities 406, the Literature of Fact, during the spring of 1977 while John was off reporting in Alaska, and that Bob made a place in his class for this freshly declared history major. Four years earlier, as a sophomore at Brighton High School outside Rochester, New York, I had learned the importance of rigor and revision in the Critical Reading and Writing class of Elizabeth Hart. Hers has been the voice inside my writing head ever since.

My late parents, Nikolaus and Mary Wolff, were adamantly private people. They were also fiercely dedicated to the commons and raised me not just to practice good citizenship but to proselytize for it. To tell this story was to set one instinct of my parents against the other. Which one won out was entirely my call.

Frank and Clara—by making fatherhood real for me, you helped fire this story with meaning.

Finally, Vanessa. First to support this. First to read it. Always first to put us first, and first in my heart, always. *Budějovice.*

BIBLIOGRAPHY

Archives

Bundesarchiv-Lichterfelde: Federal Republic of Germany Archive, Nazi Party Records, Berlin-Lichterfelde, Germany.

Caroline Ferriday Papers: Bellamy-Ferriday House and Garden, Bethlehem, CT, owned and operated by Connecticut Landmarks.

Deutsche Dienststelle-Reinickendorf: Federal Republic of Germany, Military Records Facility (Wehrmachtauskunftstelle), Berlin-Reineckendorf, Germany.

DLA-Marbach (Deutsches Literaturarchiv-Marbach): German Literary Archive, Marbach, Germany.

H&KW Papers: Helen and Kurt Wolff Papers. Yale Collection of German Literature, Beinecke Rare Book and Manuscript Library, New Haven, CT.

KW Papers: Kurt Wolff Papers. Yale Collection of German Literature, Beinecke Rare Book and Manuscript Library, New Haven, CT.

Merck-Archiv: Merck KGaA Corporate History Department Archive, Darmstadt, Germany.

Pantheon Papers: Pantheon Books Records 1944–1968. Columbia University Rare Book and Manuscript Library, New York.

Stadtarchiv-Karlsruhe: City Archive and Historical Museum, Karlsruhe, Germany.

Books

Améry, Jean. *At the Mind's Limits: Contemplations by a Survivor on Auschwitz and Its Realities.* Bloomington: Indiana University Press, 1980.

Arendt, Hannah. *The Origins of Totalitarianism.* San Diego: Harcourt, 1973.

Asmus, Sylvia, and Brita Eckert. "Emigration und Neubeginn: Die Akte 'Kurt Wolff' im Archiv des Emergency Rescue Committee." In *Kurt Wolff: Ein Literat und Gentleman,* edited by Barbara Weidle. Bonn: Weidle, 2007.

Azar, Gudrun. *Ins Licht gerückt: Jüdische Lebenswege im Münchner Westen, eine Spurensuche in Pasing, Obermeuzing und Aubing.* Munich: Herbert Utz, 2008.

Baier, Annette C. "Ethics in Many Different Voices." In *Hannah Arendt: Twenty Years Later,* edited by Larry May and Jerome Kohn. Cambridge, MA: MIT Press, 1996.

Bedford, Sybille. *Jigsaw.* New York: New York Review Books, 2018.

Béguin, Rebecca. *Finding Delos: Kurt and Helen Wolff's Far-Flung Author Mary Renault.* Royalton, VT: Lichen Limited Editions, 2019.

Behringer, Wolfgang. "Climate and History: Hunger, Anti-Semitism, and Reform During the Tambora Crisis of 1815-1820." In *German History in Global and Transnational Perspective*, edited by David Lederer. London: Palgrave Macmillan, 2017.

Bessel, Richard. *Germany 1945: From War to Peace*. London: Pocket Books, 2010.

Bogart, Leo. *Commercial Culture: The Media System and the Public Interest*. Piscataway, NJ: Transaction, 2000.

Brooks, Christopher A., and Robert Sims. *Roland Hayes: The Legacy of an American Tenor*. Bloomington: Indiana University Press, 2016.

Burhop, Carsten, Michael Kißener, Hermann Schäfer, and Joachim Scholtyseck. *Merck 1668–2018: From a Pharmacy to a Global Corporation*. Translated by Jane Paulick, Timothy Slater, Patricia Sutcliffe, and Patricia Szobar. Munich: C. H. Beck, 2018.

Croose Parry, Renée-Marie. "Ostracism and Exile," "Life in Brazil," and "One Day in Miami." In *Odyssey of Exile: Jewish Women Flee the Nazis for Brazil*, edited by Katherine Morris. Detroit: Wayne State University Press, 1996.

Dagerman, Stig. *German Autumn*. Translated by Robin Fulton Macpherson. Minneapolis: University of Minnesota Press, 2011.

Detjen, Marion. "Zum Hintergrund des Hintergrunds." Afterword to Helen Wolff, *Hintergrund für Liebe*. Bonn: Weidle, 2020.

Dundy, Elaine. *Ferriday, Louisiana*. New York: Donald I. Fine, 1991.

Eames, Andrew. *Blue River, Black Sea: A Journey along the Danube into the Heart of the New Europe*. London: Black Swan, 2010.

Elon, Amos. *The Pity of It All: A Portrait of Jews in Germany, 1743–1933*. London: Penguin Books, 2004.

Fellinger, Raimund, ed. *"Seismograph": Kurt Wolff im Kontext*. Berlin: Insel, 2014.

Fermi, Laura. *Illustrious Immigrants: The Intellectual Migration from Europe, 1930–41*. Chicago: University of Chicago Press, 1968.

Fest, Joachim. *Hitler*. Translated by Richard and Clara Winston. San Diego: Harcourt Brace Jovanovich, 1974.

Fisher, Marc. *After the Wall: Germany, the Germans and the Burdens of History*. New York: Simon & Schuster, 1995.

Frevert, Ute. "Bourgeois Honour: Middle-Class Duellists in Germany from the Late Eighteenth to the Early Twentieth Century." In *The German Bourgeoisie: Essays on the Social History of the German Middle Class from the Late Eighteenth to the Early Twentieth Century*, edited by David Blackbourn and Richard J. Evans. Abingdon, Oxon, UK: Routledge Revivals, 2014.

Ginzburg, Natalia. *Family Lexicon*. Translated by Jenny McPhee. New York: New York Review Books, 2017.

Grass, Günter. *Crabwalk*. Translated by Krishna Winston. Orlando: Harcourt, 2002.

———. *Peeling the Onion: A Memoir*. Translated by Michael Henry Heim. Orlando: Harcourt, 2007.

Grass, Günter, and Helen Wolff. *Briefe 1959–1994*. Göttingen, Germany: Steidl, 2003.

Haffner, Sebastian. *Defying Hitler: A Memoir*. Translated by Oliver Pretzel. New York: Picador, 2000.

——. *Germany Jekyll & Hyde: A Contemporary Account of Nazi Germany*. Translated by Wilfrid David. London: Abacus, 2008.

Heilbut, Anthony. *Exiled in Paradise: German Refugee Artists and Intellectuals in America from the 1930s to the Present*. Berkeley: University of California Press, 1983.

Helm, Sarah. *Ravensbrück: Life and Death in Hitler's Concentration Camp for Women*. New York: Anchor Books, 2016.

Henseler, Theodor. *Bonner Geschichtsblätter: Das musikalische Bonn im 19. Jahrhundert*. Vol. 13. Bonn: Bonner Heimat- und Geschichtsverein und dem Stadtarchiv Bonn, 1959.

Hesse, Hermann. *Hymn to Old Age*. Translated by David Henry Wilson. London: Pushkin Press, 2011.

——. *The Seasons of the Soul: The Poetic Guidance and Spiritual Wisdom of Hermann Hesse*. Translated by Ludwig Max Fischer. Berkeley, CA: North Atlantic Books, 2011.

Hicks, Michael, and Christian Asplund. *American Composers: Christian Wolff*. Urbana: University of Illinois Press, 2012.

Hilmes, Oliver. *Berlin 1936: Sixteen Days in August*. Translated by Jefferson Chase. London: Bodley Head, 2017.

Hockenos, Paul. *Berlin Calling: A Story of Anarchy, Music, the Wall, and the Birth of the New Berlin*. New York: New Press, 2017.

Isenberg, Sheila. *A Hero of Our Own: The Story of Varian Fry*. New York: Random House, 2001.

Jähner, Harald. *Wolfszeit: Deutschland und die Deutschen, 1945–1955*. Berlin: Rowohlt Berlin, 2019.

Jarausch, Konrad H. *Broken Lives: How Ordinary Germans Experienced the 20th Century*. Princeton, NJ: Princeton University Press, 2018.

Johnson, Uwe. *Anniversaries: From a Year in the Life of Gesine Cresspahl*. Translated by Damion Searls. New York: New York Review Books, 2019.

Jungk, Peter Stephan. *Franz Werfel: A Life in Prague, Vienna, and Hollywood*. Translated by Anselm Hollo. New York: Grove Weidenfeld, 1990.

Kafka, Franz. *The Blue Octavo Notebooks*. Translated by Ernst Kaiser and Eithne Wilkins. Cambridge, MA: Exact Change, 2004.

——. *Letters to Friends, Family and Editors*. Translated by Richard and Clara Winston. New York: Schocken Books, 1977.

——. *Lost in America*. Translated by Anthony Northey. Prague: Vitalis, 2010.

Kelly, Martha Hall. *Lilac Girls*. New York: Ballantine Books, 2016.

Kershaw, Ian. *The End: Germany 1944–45*. London: Penguin Books, 2012.

Kolowrat, Ernest. *Confessions of a Hapless Hedonist*. Middletown, DE: Xlibris, 2001.

Kossert, Andreas. *Kalte Heimat: Die Geschichte der deutschen Vertriebenen nach 1945*. Munich: Pantheon, 2008.

Krockow, Christian von. *Hour of the Women*. Translated by Krishna Winston. London: Faber and Faber, 1993.

Krug, Nora. *Belonging: A German Reckons with History and Home*. New York: Scribner, 2018.

Kurt Wolff: 1887-1963. Frankfurt: Verlag Heinrich Scheffler, and Pfullingen: Verlag Günther Neske, 1963.

Kurt Wolff zum Hundertsten. With contributions by Helmut Frielinghaus, Wolfram Göbel, Heinrich Maria Ledig-Rowohlt and Michael Kellner, Thomas Rietzschel, Klaus Wagenbach. Hamburg: Michael Kellner, 1987.

Ladd, Brian. *The Ghosts of Berlin: Confronting German History in the Urban Landscape*. Chicago: University of Chicago Press, 1997.

La Farge, Henry, ed. *Lost Treasures of Europe*. New York: Pantheon Books, 1946.

Lindbergh, Anne Morrow. *Gift from the Sea*. New York: Pantheon Books, 1955.

Magris, Claudio. *Danube*. Translated by Patrick Creagh. New York: Farrar, Straus and Giroux, 1989.

Mak, Geert. *In Europe: Travels through the Twentieth Century*. Translated by Sam Garrett. New York: Vintage Books, 2008.

Marino, Andy. *A Quiet American: The Secret War of Varian Fry*. New York: St. Martin's Press, 1999.

Musil, Robert. *Tagebücher: Hauptband*. Edited by Adolf Frisé. Reinbek, Germany: Rowohlt, 1976.

Natonek, Hans. *In Search of Myself*. Translated by Barthold Fles. New York: G. P. Putnam's, 1943.

Neff, Anette. "Merck, Ursula." In *Stadtlexikon Darmstadt*. Historischer Verein für Hessen. Darmstadt: Konrad Theiss, 2006.

Neiman, Susan. *Learning from the Germans: Race and the Memory of Evil*. New York: Farrar, Straus and Giroux, 2019.

Nelson, Stanley. *Devils Walking: Klan Murders along the Mississippi in the 1960s*. Baton Rouge: Louisiana State University Press, 2016.

Neumann, Alfred. *King Haber*. Translated by Marie Busch. New York: Alfred H. King, 1930.

——. "Tagebücher." In *Exil am Mittelmeer: Deutsche Schriftsteller in Südfrankreich von 1933–1941*, edited by Ulrike Voswinckel and Frank Berninger. Munich: Allitera, 2005.

Ohler, Norman. *Blitzed: Drugs in Nazi Germany*. Translated by Shaun Whiteside. London: Penguin Books, 2017.

Orringer, Julie. *The Flight Portfolio*. New York: Knopf, 2019.

Pasternak, Boris. *Doctor Zhivago*. Translated by Max Hayward. New York: Pantheon Books, 1958.

Péguy, Charles. *Basic Verities*. Translated by Ann and Julian Green. New York: Pantheon Books, 1943.

Posner, Gerald. *Pharma: Greed, Lies, and the Poisoning of America*. New York: Avid Reader Press, 2020.

Prescott, Lara. *The Secrets They Kept*. New York: Knopf, 2019.

Reeve, Simon. *One Day in September*. New York: Arcade Publishing, 2000.

Reichman, Amos. *Jacques Schiffrin: A Publisher in Exile, from Pléiade to Pantheon*. Translated by Sandra Smith. New York: Columbia University Press, 2019.

Remarque, Erich Maria. *The Night in Lisbon*. Translated by Ralph Manheim. New York: Harcourt, Brace & World, 1964.

Rigg, Bryan Mark. *Hitler's Jewish Soldiers: The Untold Story of Nazi Racial Laws and Men of Jewish Descent in the German Military*. Lawrence: University of Kansas Press, 2002.

Rose, Wolfgang. *Diagnose "Psychopathie": Die urbane Moderne und das schwierige Kind*. Vienna: Böhlau, 2016.

Roth, Joseph. *The Hotel Years*. Translated by Michael Hofmann. New York: New Directions, 2015.

———. *What I Saw: Reports from Berlin, 1920–1933*. Translated by Michael Hofmann. New York: W. W. Norton, 2004.

Sax, Boria. *Animals in the Third Reich*. Pittsburgh: Yogh & Thorn Press, 2013.

Schiffrin, André. *The Business of Books: How International Conglomerates Took Over Publishing and Changed the Way We Read*. London: Verso, 2000.

———. *A Political Education: Coming of Age in Paris and New York*. New York: Melville House, 2007.

Sebald, W. G. *Austerlitz*. Translated by Anthea Bell. New York: Modern Library, 2011.

———. *The Emigrants*. Translated by Anthea Bell. London: Vintage Books, 2002.

———. *On the Natural History of Destruction*. Translated by Anthea Bell. New York: Modern Library, 2004.

Seghers, Anna. *Transit*. Translated by Margot Bettauer Dembo. New York: New York Review Books, 2013.

Sereny, Gitta. *The German Trauma: Experiences and Reflections, 1938–2001*. London: Penguin Books, 2001.

Snyder, Timothy. *Bloodlands: Europe between Hitler and Stalin*. New York: Basic Books, 2010.

Stach, Reiner. *Kafka: The Decisive Years*. Translated by Shelley Frisch. Princeton, NJ: Princeton University Press, 2013.

———. *Kafka: The Early Years*. Translated by Shelley Frisch. Princeton, NJ: Princeton University Press, 2017.

———. *Kafka: The Years of Insight*. Translated by Shelley Frisch. Princeton, NJ: Princeton University Press, 2015.

Steiner, John M. "The SS Yesterday and Today: A Sociopsychological View." In *Survivors, Victims, and Perpetrators: Essays on the Nazi Holocaust*, edited by Joel E. Dimsdale. Abingdon, Oxon, UK: Taylor & Francis, 1980.

Steinweis, Alan E. *Studying the Jew: Scholarly Antisemitism in Nazi Germany*. Cambridge, MA: Harvard University Press, 2008.

Stern, Fritz. *Einstein's German World*. Princeton, NJ: Princeton University Press, 2016.

———. *Five Germanys I Have Known*. New York: Farrar, Straus and Giroux, 2007.

———. *Gold and Iron: Bismarck, Bleichröder, and the Building of the German Empire*. New York: Vintage Books, 1979.

Taylor, Frederick. *Exorcising Hitler: The Occupation and Denazification of Germany*. New York: Bloomsbury Press, 2011.

Thorpe, Nick. *The Danube: A Journey Upriver from the Black Sea to the Black Forest.* New Haven, CT: Yale University Press, 2013.

U.S. Strategic Bombing Survey, Morale Division. *The Effects of Bombing on Health and Medical Care in Germany.* Washington, DC, 1945.

U.S. Strategic Bombing Survey, Area Studies Division. *A Detailed Study of the Effects of Area Bombing on Darmstadt.* Washington, DC, 1945.

Vonnegut, Kurt. *Palm Sunday.* New York: Dial Press, 1999.

Walser, Robert. *Berlin Stories.* Translated by Susan Bernofsky. New York: New York Review Books, 2012.

Weidle, Barbara, editor. *Kurt Wolff: Ein Literat und Gentleman.* Bonn: Weidle Verlag, 2007.

Wirtz, Rainer. *"Widersetzlichkeiten, Excesse, Crawalle, Tumulte und Skandale": Soziale Bewegung und gewalthafter sozialer Protest in Baden, 1815–1848.* Frankfurt: Ullstein, 1981.

Wolfe, Thomas. *You Can't Go Home Again.* New York: Scribner Classics, 2011.

Wolff, Helen. *Hintergrund für Liebe.* Bonn: Weidle, 2020.

Wolff, Kurt. *Kurt Wolff: A Portrait in Essays and Letters,* edited by Michael Ermarth, translated by Deborah Lucas Schneider. Chicago: University of Chicago Press, 1991.

———. *Kurt Wolff, Autoren-Bücher-Abenteuer: Beobachtungen und Erinnerungen eines Verlegers.* Berlin: Klaus Wagenbach, 2004.

———. *Kurt Wolff: Briefwechsel eines Verlegers, 1911–1963.* Edited by Bernhard Zeller and Ellen Otten. Frankfurt: Heinrich Scheffler, 1966.

Zuckmayer, Carl. *A Part of Myself.* Translated by Richard and Clara Winston. New York: Harcourt Brace Jovanovich, 1970.

———. *Second Wind.* Translated by Elizabeth Reynolds Hapgood. London: G. G. Harrap, 1941.

Articles, Dissertations, Monographs, and Speeches

Auden, W. H. "In Praise of the Brothers Grimm." *New York Times Book Review,* November 12, 1944.

Borchardt-Wenzel, Annette. "Das Duell—Seltsamer Ehrbegriff fordert viele Opfer." *Badische Neuesten Nachrichten,* September 3, 2016.

Brooks, Christopher A. "Roland Hayes and the Countess." Indiana University Press News Blog, February 27, 2015. iupress.typepad.com/blog/2015/02/roland-hayes-and-the-countess.html.

Bruckner, D. J. R. "The Prince of Publishers," *New York Times Book Review,* January 5, 1992.

Calder, John. "Obituary: Helen Wolff," *Independent* (London), April 20, 1994.

Chase, Jefferson. "AfD Candidate in Hot Water over Breivik Statements." DeutscheWelle.com, April 21, 2017. dw.com/en/afd-candidate-in-hot-water-over-breivik-statements/a-38537022.

Cords, Suzanne. "Curator of the Largest Holocaust Memorial Turns 70, but His Life's Work Continues." DeutscheWelle.com, October 27, 2017. dw.com/en/creator-of

-the-largest-holocaust-memorial-turns-70-but-his-life-work-continues /a-41107926.

Detjen, Marion. "Kurt and Helen Wolff." *Immigrant Entrepreneurship: German-American Business Biographies, 1720 to the Present*. Vol. 5. Edited by R. Daniel Wadhwani. German Historical Institute, 2012. ImmigrantEntrepreneurship .org/entry.php?rec=83.

Deutsche Friedensgesellschaft Vereinigte KriegsdienstgegnerInnen Darmstadt. "Von Adelung bis Zwangsarbeit: Stichworte zu Militär und Nationalsozialismus in Darmstadt." May 2000. dfg-vk-darmstadt.de/Lexikon_Auflage_1/Von_ Adelung_bis_Zwangsarbeit_Auflage1.pdf.

Eco, Umberto. "Umberto Eco: The Art of Fiction No. 197." Interview by Lila Azam Zanaganeh. *Paris Review*, Summer 2008.

Economist. "Special Report: The New Germans." April 14, 2018.

Evans, Richard J. "*Blitzed: Drugs in Nazi Germany*, a Crass and Dangerously Inaccurate Account." *Guardian* (UK), November 16, 2016.

"Expressionism Today." *Times Literary Supplement*, November 6, 1970.

"Ferriday Started as 3,600-Acre Wedding Present." *Natchez Democrat*, November 22, 2006.

Förster, Birte. "Seitenweise Aufschlussreiches." *Hoch³: Die Zeitung der Technischen Universität Darmstadt*, December 2015.

Grass, Günter. Laudation for Helen Wolff upon posthumous awarding of Friedrich Gundolf Prize. April 30, 1994. DeutscheAkademie.de/en/awards/friedrich -gundolf-preis/helen-wolff/laudatio.

Greenberg, Stanley B. "Trump Is Beginning to Lose His Grip." *New York Times*, November 17, 2018.

Haas, Willy. "Kurt Wolff: 3 März 1887–22 Oktober 1963." *Die Welt*, December 28, 1963.

Hamilton, Nigel. "Heinrich Mann and the Underdog." *Times* (London), June 24, 1972.

Havill, Kristin Peterson. "Caroline Ferriday: A Godmother to Ravensbrück Survivors." *Connecticut History*, Winter 2011–12.

Hennig, Falko. "Investieren in verlegerischen Gewinn." *Die Tageszeitung*, July 24, 2007.

Herweg, Nikola. "Helen und Kurt Wolff in Marbach." Deutsches Literaturarchiv-Marbach. *Spuren* 106, 2015.

Huggler, Justin. "Five Names to Watch as the Anti-Immigrant AfD Looks to Stir up Trouble for Angela Merkel." *Telegraph* (London), October 1, 2017.

Kazin, Alfred. "A Legend among Publishers." *New York Newsday*, October 20, 1991.

Kuenstner, Molli E., and Thomas A. O'Callaghan. "The *Führerprojekt* Goes to Washington." *Burlington Magazine* 159, May 2017.

"Kurt Wolff." *Neues Deutschland*, October 25, 1963.

Leavenworth, Jesse. "Caroline and the *Lapins*." *Northeast: Sunday Magazine of the Hartford Courant*, October 20, 2002.

Meola, David. "Mirror of Competing Claims: Antisemitism and Citizenship in *Vormärz* Germany." *Antisemitism Studies* 4, no. 1 (Spring 2020).

"Merck KGaA Plans Nazi-Era Forced Labour Compensation." ICIS.com, December 8, 1999.

Mitgang, Herbert. "Imprint." *New Yorker*, August 2, 1982.

"Mr. Kurt Wolff." *Times* (London), October 29, 1963.

Nelson, Howard. "Speaking Volumes: The Wide World of a Publisher." *Washington Post Book World*, April 4, 1971.

Nicholas, Elizabeth. "Hitler's Suicide and New Research on Nazi Drug Use." *Time* online, April 28, 2017. https://time.com/4744584/hitler-drugs-blitzed/.

Oltermann, Philip. "German Rightwing Party Apologises for Jérôme Boateng Comments." *Guardian* (UK), May 29, 2016.

Özdemir, Cem. "Cem Özdemir Compares Germany's Far-Right AfD Party to the Nazis in Hard-Hitting Speech." European Greens, February 22, 2018. European Greens.eu/news/cem-özdemir-compares-germanys-far-right-afd-party-nazis -hard-hitting-speech.

Packer, George. "The Quiet German." *New Yorker*, November 24, 2014.

Pinthus, Kurt. "Wie Literatur gemacht wurde: Zur Erinnerung an meiner Freund Kurt Wolff." *Die Zeit*, November 1, 1963.

Redlich, Fritz. "German Literary Expressionism and Its Publishers." *Harvard Library Bulletin* 17, no. 2 (April 1969).

Reemtsma, Jan Philipp. "Wozu Gedenkstätten?" *Politik und Zeitgeschichte*, June 21, 2010.

Reuters. "AfD Co-Founder Says Germans Should Be Proud of Its Second World War Soldiers." *Guardian* (UK), September 14, 2017.

Riding, Alan. "A Tale of Two Germanys." *New York Times*, December 14, 2000.

Scheffler, Heinrich. "Kurt-Wolff-Marginalien." *Börsenblatt für den Deutschen Buchhandel* 95, November 26, 1963.

Schnee, Heinrich. "Hofbankier Salomon von Haber als badischer Finanzier." *Zeitung für die Geschichte des Oberrheins* 109, no. 2 (1961).

Schuetze, Christopher F., and Michael Wolgelenter, "Fact Check: Trump's False and Misleading Claims about Germany's Crime and Immigration." *New York Times*, June 18, 2018.

Schuhladen-Krämer, Jürgen. "Haber-Skandal." Stadtlexikon Karlsruhe, 2012. https:// stadtlexikon.karlsruhe.de/index.php/De:Lexikon:ereig-0279.

———. "Hepp!-Hepp!-Unruhen 1819." Stadtlexikon Karlsruhe, 2012. https:// stadtlexikon.karlsruhe.de/index.php/De:Lexikon:ereig-0216.

———. "Moritz von Haber." Stadtlexikon Karlsruhe, 2013. https://stadtlexikon .karlsruhe.de/index.php/De:Lexikon:bio-0802.

———. "Salomon von Haber." Stadtlexikon Karlsruhe, 2013. https://stadtlexikon .karlsruhe.de/index.php/De:Lexikon:bio-1013.

Schuyler, Steven. "Kurt Wolff and Hermann Broch: Publisher and Author in Exile." PhD thesis, Harvard University, Department of Germanic Languages and Literatures, 1984.

———. "Kurt Wolff's Publishing Odyssey." *AB Bookman's Weekly*, September 6, 1999.

Schwarz, Benjamin. "Hitler's Co-Conspirators." *Atlantic*, May 2009.

"The Seismographer of Expressionism." *Times Literary Supplement*, February 2, 1970.

Simoncini, Giuseppe. "Kurt Wolff, Soggiorno a Lastra." LastraOnline.it, 2008. Lastra Online.it/p/storia.php?idpag=374&idpag=374.

Simpendorfer, Werner. "The Strange Must Cease to Be the Strange: In Memoriam Ernst Lange (1927–1974)." *Ecumenical Review* 49, no. 2 (April 1997).

Steinmeier, Frank-Walter. "75th Anniversary of the End of the 2nd World War." May 8, 2020. https://www.bundespraesident.de/SharedDocs/Reden/EN/Frank-Walter-Steinmeier/Reden/2020/05/200508-75th-anniversary-World-War-II.html.

Taub, Amanda, and Max Fisher. "Germany's Extreme Right Challenges Guilt over Nazi Past." *New York Times*, January 18, 2017.

Tevetoglu, Cem, Matin Nawabi, and Tobi Moka. "Merck in der Zwickmühle." *Soziales Darmstadt*, March 2017.

Ueding, Gert. "Mit Hirn und Herz." *Frankfurter Allgemeine Zeitung*, March 3, 1987.

"Vor der Spruchkammer/Dr. Karl Merck in Gruppe IV." *Darmstädter Echo*, June 1, 1948.

Weizsäcker, Richard von. "Speech by Federal President Richard von Weizsäcker during the Ceremony Commemorating the 40th Anniversary of the End of War in Europe and of National-Socialist Tyranny on 8 May 1985 at the Bundestag, Bonn." Bundespräsidialamt. Bundespraesident.de/SharedDocs/Downloads/DE/Reden/2015/02/150202-RvW-Rede-8-Mai-1985-englisch.pdf?__blob=publicationFile.

Weyr, Thomas. "PW Interviews: Helen Wolff." *Publishers Weekly*, February 3, 1973.

Wolff, Alexander. "When the Terror Began." *Sports Illustrated*, August 26, 2002.

Wolff, Helen. "Elective Affinities." Address to Deutsches Haus New York. May 15, 1990.

[Wolff, Maria.] "Wiedersehen und Abschied: Selbstgespräche mit dem Vater." *Die Gegenwart*, January 1948.

Film, Radio, and Television

Central Airport THF. Karim Aïnouz, dir. Lupa Film, Les Films d'Ici, Mar Films, 2018. Documentary film.

The Exiles. Richard Kaplan, dir. PBS, September 24, 1989. Documentary film.

Das schreckliche Mädchen (The Nasty Girl). Michael Verhoeven, dir. Filmverlag der Autoren, Sentana Filmproduktion, ZDF, 1990.

Saving the Rabbits of Ravensbrück. Stacey Fitzgerald, dir. From the Heart Productions, forthcoming. Documentary film. RememberRavensbruck.com/caroline-ferriday.

Voswinckel, Ulrike. "Den Starken Atem unserer Zeit spüren: Das erste Leben des Verlegers Kurt Wolff." *Land und Leute*, Bayerischer Rundfunk, April 15, 2001. Radio documentary.

Woj, Caterina, and Andrea Röpke. "Das braune Netzwerk: Wer steuert die Wütburger?" *Die Story*, Westdeutscher Rundfunk, January 11, 2017. Television report. Otto-Brenner-Preis.de/dokumentation/2017/preistraeger/3-preis.

Wolff, Kurt. Twelve radio essays broadcast over Norddeutscher, Westdeutscher, and Bayrischer Rundfunk, 1962 and 1963. Transcripts in H&KW Papers.

Your Job in Germany. Theodor Geisel and Frank Capra. U.S. Department of War, 1945. Training film. https://www.youtube.com/watch?v=1v5QCGqDYGo?

Privately Published or Unpublished Essays, Genealogies, Monographs, Reminiscences, and Stories

Baumhauer, Jon. "Our Marx Ancestors in the Rhineland." Translated by Nikolaus Wolff. Munich, 1987.

Frensdorff, Karl. "How the Frensdorffs Came to America." Wilmington, DE, 2002.

Landheim Schondorf, Class of 1940, fiftieth-reunion book. Schondorf-am-Ammersee, Germany, 1990.

"Margot Hausenstein: The Life of 100 Years," annotated timeline. H&KW Papers, box 14, folder 463.

Wolff, Helen. "My Most Unforgettable Character." New York, ca. 1942.

Wolff, Hope Nash. "Who Was Maria Marx? Three Views." Royalton, VT, 2007.

Wolff, Leonhard. "Remembering My Musical Life." Translated by Nikolaus Wolff. Bonn, 1932.

Wolff, Maria. "Dämmerung." Pfeddersheimerwegsproduction, Berlin, 2009.

Wolff, Nikolaus. "How I Came to the United States." Norwich, VT, ca. 2000.

———. "Wolff Clan: 1743–1963." With Jon Baumhauer. Norwich, VT, 2006.

Wolff, Kurt. "Reminiscing about Bonn and Music." Translated by Nikolaus Wolff. Locarno, Switzerland, 1961.

———. "Tagebücher, October 23, 1914, to June 28, 1915." Deutsches Literaturarchiv-Marbach, Germany.

IMAGE CREDITS

All photographs and images come from family collections, with the following exceptions:

NOTES

Introduction: In the Footsteps of Kurt and Niko

Kurt Wolff had been born So as not to perpetuate Nazi rhetoric, I've avoided words or phrases like "Aryan" or "half Jewish" or "*Mischling*" without the punctuative distancing of quotation marks. It's nonetheless worth stipulating that, during much of the period covered here, "Jewish" was deployed as a racial descriptive as much as a confessional one. My grandfather was baptized, just as his mother and her parents had been. But Nazi racial ideology followed bloodlines and discounted conversions to Christianity. As it happens, rabbinical law—*Halakah*—holds the same definition of who is a Jew: "According to *Halakah*, once a person is born Jewish or properly converts to Judaism, that status remains forever." Bryan Mark Rigg, *Hitler's Jewish Soldiers* (Lawrence: University of Kansas Press, 2002), 7.

"purification ritual" This phrase, from sociologist Norbert Elias, rose out of the student protests that swept Germany in 1968.

Kurt Wolff left Germany Four weeks after Hitler was sworn in as chancellor, the Reichstag, the German parliament building, went up in flames. The Nazis blamed the fire on Communist agitators and used the arson as a pretext to curtail civil liberties. The Dutch Communist charged with starting the blaze insisted, and a court later found, that he had acted alone.

Dear Dr. Kafka Kurt Wolff letter to Franz Kafka, March 20, 1913. KW Papers, box 5, folder 164.

Kurt himself vowed Kurt Wolff letter to Hiram Haydn, June 14, 1959. H&KW Papers, box 16, folder 508. In 1959, Random House editor in chief Hiram Haydn sounded Kurt out about writing something autobiographical. But beyond a series of radio essays aired by German broadcasters during the early sixties, my grandfather never followed through. His papers nonetheless include notes in which he floats possible titles for a memoir. One is "The Obsession of an Addict: A Publisher's Life from Kafka to Pasternak." The other is a bit of German wordplay: "Vom Verleger, vom Verlegen, und was damit zusammenhängt" (Of Publishing, of Relocations, and Things Pertaining Thereto). H&KW Papers, box 80, folder 2390.

"a difficult man" D. J. R. Bruckner, "The Prince of Publishers," *New York Times Book Review*, January 5, 1992.

I brought reams Between them, the Beinecke Rare Book and Manuscript Library at Yale and the German Literary Archive in Marbach house some ten thousand of Kurt's letters and many of Helen's as well. In 1966, Frankfurt's Heinrich Scheffler Verlag published a selection, *Kurt Wolff: Briefwechsel eines Verlegers, 1911–1963*, that runs more than six hundred pages. Scheffler himself, during a visit to my grandfather's Berlin pension in the weeks before the Reichstag fire, told Kurt that he would like to follow his path as a publisher. Scheffler recalled his response: "He smiled gently, looked out the window, and said, 'For that, you'll need God's protection.'" Heinrich Scheffler, "Kurt-Wolff-Marginalien," in *Börsenblatt für den Deutschen Buchhandel* 95, November 26, 1963.

"In the case of other"   *Kurt Wolff: A Portrait in Essays and Letters*, ed. Michael Ermarth, trans. Deborah Lucas Schneider (Chicago: University of Chicago Press, 1991), 149.

"It's like magic"   Ibid., 155.

Even his insults   Ibid., 6.

We *publishers are alive*   Kurt Wolff letter to Rainer Maria Rilke, December 10, 1917, in *Kurt Wolff: Briefwechsel eines Verlegers, 1911–1963*, ed. Bernhard Zeller and Ellen Otten (Frankfurt: Heinrich Scheffler, 1966), 148.

"Who is interested"   *Kurt Wolff: A Portrait*, 137.

"In good and in evil"   Brian Ladd, *The Ghosts of Berlin: Confronting German History in the Urban Landscape* (Chicago: University of Chicago Press, 1997), 6.

Chapter One: *Bildung* and Books

Hermann was such   Kurt Wolff, "Reminiscing about Bonn and Music," trans. Nikolaus Wolff (Locarno, Switzerland, 1961).

"I remember the consternation"   Wolff, "Reminiscing." "After a 40-hour-long odyssey from Ischl [in the Tyrol], Brahms appeared at the home of Professor Wolff at five a.m., only to run off again after breakfast in disbelief"; Theodor Henseler, *Bonner Geschichtsblätter: Das musikalische Bonn im 19. Jahrhundert*, vol. 13 (Bonn: Bonner Heimat- und Geschichtsverein und dem Stadtarchiv Bonn, 1959), 286.

"Should, on occasion"   Wolff, "Reminiscing."

Besieged by "snobs"   Ibid.

"whatever I wished"   Ibid.

"Refined, handsome, studious"   Kurt Pinthus, "Wie Literatur gemacht wurde: Zur Erinnerung an meiner Freund Kurt Wolff," *Die Zeit*, November 1, 1963.

With the 100,000   Falko Hennig, "Investieren in verlegerischen Gewinn," *Die Tageszeitung*, July 24, 2007.

In 1908,   According to the evaluation of Albert Köster, the venerated literature professor at the University of Leipzig, who served as Kurt's thesis adviser, my grandfather didn't entirely abandon work toward his PhD. He eventually finished his dissertation—on how contemporaneous critics reacted to the work of the young Goethe—only to have Köster reject it. As a regular in the Leipzig salon of the doctoral candidate and his wife, Professor Köster couldn't have enjoyed concluding that Kurt "has diligently collected material for this dissertation, but that is all that can be said in his and its favor. He does nothing with it. A monotonous delivery and unpolished style put the reader off. . . . Rarely has so interesting a topic been treated in such boring fashion. What the candidate presents is little more than the fruits of his reading."

"I loved books"   Kurt Wolff, 1962, conversation with Herbert G. Göpfert, cited in Thomas Rietzschel, "Der Literat als Verleger," in *Kurt Wolff zum Hundertsten* (Hamburg: Michael Kellner, 1987).

By June 1912, Reiner Stach, *Kafka: The Decisive Years*, trans. Shelley Frisch (Princeton, NJ: Princeton University Press, 2013), 73.

In that first moment *Kurt Wolff: A Portrait*, 54–55.

"I will always be" Ibid., 55.

The relationship with Ernst Rowohlt Peter Stephan Jungk, *Franz Werfel: A Life in Prague, Vienna, and Hollywood*, trans. Anselm Hollo (New York: Grove Weidenfeld, 1990), 30–31.

"I for my part" Kurt Wolff letter to Karl Kraus, December 14, 1913, in *Kurt Wolff: Briefwechsel*, 128.

"If he wants to walk you back" *Kurt Wolff: A Portrait*, 87.

Spare thy wrath In German, *Verschon uns, Gott, mit Strafen / Und laß uns ruhig schlafen, / Und unsern kranken Nachbar auch!* Translation after Schneider, *Kurt Wolff: A Portrait*, 86. Most Germans know the poem by its opening line, *Der Mond ist aufgegangen* (The moon is risen).

"He stared at me" *Kurt Wolff: A Portrait*, 86–87.

Love of literature Kurt left extensive reminiscences about the musical forebears of his father but relatively little about the wealthy and cultured ancestors of Jewish extraction on his mother's side. It took my aunt Hope (Holly) Nash Wolff, the Vermont-born daughter-in-law Kurt never met, to flesh out Maria Marx's life and family in a privately circulated genealogical essay. Inspired by historian Fritz Stern's memoir *Five Germanys I Have Known* (New York: Farrar, Straus and Giroux, 2007), she advances a theory to explain why Kurt was so reticent about his Jewish roots. She notes that Stern, another exiled son of the *Bildungsbürgertum*, refers to "the long-term silence of these people in reference to their Jewishness, coupled with their tenacity in maintaining consciousness of it," as they determinedly acculturated themselves to German life. And she remarks on "the unthinkable end, their destruction by their countrymen . . . [and] the extent to which the unthinkable is presaged by the unsayable." Citing the Jewish authors Kurt published (Brod, Hasenclever, Kafka, Werfel) and the iconoclasm embraced by most of them (avant-garde, Expressionist, or otherwise out of the mainstream), she notes that to be a German Jew is perforce to find oneself isolated—to be marked, as Stern puts it, by "both stigma and distinction." Holly and her husband, Christian, have hung in the living room of their Vermont farmhouse a portrait of Jacob Marx, Kurt's mother's grandfather and our most modern Jewish ancestor never to convert. I like to think of this as a kind of gesture of protest against how our Jewish origins have been overlooked in the family story.

With Grand Duke Louis I Heinrich Schnee, "Hofbankier Salomon von Haber als badischer Finanzier," *Zeitung für die Geschichte des Oberrheins* 109, no. 2 (1961); and Jürgen Schuhladen-Krämer, "Salomon von Haber," Stadtlexikon Karlsruhe, 2013, https://stadtlexikon.karlsruhe.de/index.php/De:Lexikon:bio-1013.

Mobs of citizens Jürgen Schuhladen-Krämer, "Hepp!-Hepp!-Unruhen 1819," Stadtlexikon Karlsruhe, 2012, https://stadtlexikon.karlsruhe.de/index.php/De:Lexikon:ereig-0216. Historians differ over whether the rioters shouted "Hep!" because shepherds used this interjection when putting a crook to their flock, or it's an acronym for the Latin phrase *Hierosolyma est perdita* (Jerusalem is destroyed).

Escorted by a detachment Ibid.

"How corrupt people"   Amos Elon, *The Pity of It All: A Portrait of Jews in Germany, 1743–1933* (London: Penguin Books, 2004), 106–7. The sister to whom Ludwig Robert wrote, Rahel Varnhagen, was a noted Berlin saloniste of the time. Hannah Arendt, her biographer, called Varnhagen "my closest friend, although she has been dead some hundred years." Cited in Annette C. Baier, "Ethics in Many Different Voices," in *Hannah Arendt: Twenty Years Later*, eds. Larry May and Jerome Kohn (Cambridge, MA: MIT Press, 1996), 336.

In place of incendiary   Ibid., 106.

In a carriage   Wolfgang Behringer, "Climate and History: Hunger, Anti-Semitism, and Reform During the Tambora Crisis of 1815–1820," in *German History in Global and Transnational Perspective*, ed. David Lederer (London: Palgrave Macmillan, 2017), 19.

Sometime in the late 1830s   The recounting of the Haber Affair here *et seq.* relies on Annette Borchardt-Wenzel, "Das Duell—Seltsamer Ehrbegriff fordert viele Opfer," *Badische Neuesten Nachrichten*, September 3, 2016; as well as Jürgen Schuhladen-Krämer, "Moritz von Haber," Stadtlexikon Karlsruhe, 2013, https://stadtlexikon .karlsruhe.de/index.php/De:Lexikon:bio-0802; and "Haber Skandal," Stadtlexikon Karlsruhe, 2012, https://stadtlexikon.karlsruhe.de/index.php/De:Lexikon:ereig-0279. But it's based foremost on conversations with David Meola, professor of history and director of the Jewish and Holocaust Studies Program at the University of South Alabama, as well as on his "Mirror of Competing Claims: Antisemitism and Citizenship in *Vormärz* Germany," *Antisemitism Studies* 4, no. 1 (Spring 2020).

Thanks to the marriages   Ute Frevert, "Bourgeois Honour: Middle-Class Duellists in Germany from the Late Eighteenth to the Early Twentieth Century," in *The German Bourgeoisie: Essays on the Social History of the German Middle Class from the Late Eighteenth to the Early Twentieth Century*, eds. David Blackbourn and Richard J. Evans (Abingdon, Oxon, UK: Routledge Revivals, 2014), 273.

Soon gossips had Moritz   What may have been an innocent act of generosity only fueled the rumors. When Cäcilie was born, Moritz donated 100,000 gulden, about $2 million today, in her name to support the poor of Karlsruhe. In 1857 Cäcilie married the Russian Grand Duke Mikhail Nikolaievich, son of Czar Nicholas I.

For Jews, matters were   Elon, *The Pity of It All*, 243.

As soon as   Of the thirty-six members of the mob put on trial, most were acquitted or jailed only briefly. Sarachaga-Uria wound up being sentenced to four weeks of house arrest, which the grand duke commuted to sixteen days. According to the diary of Karlsruhe banker and politician Eduard Kölle, an eyewitness to the attack, "The officers call to the rioters: 'Fear not! Nothing will happen to you, and leave room, so that the mob can continue going through.'" Translation by David Meola, of Eduard Kölle, "Aus meinem Leben," from Die Handschriften 67/715, in Generallandesarchiv Karlsruhe, cited in Rainer Wirtz, *"Widersetzlichkeiten, Excesse, Crawalle, Tumulte und Skandale": Soziale Bewegung und gewalthafter sozialer Protest in Baden, 1815–1848* (Frankfurt: Ullstein, 1981), 135.

All these injustices   In mid-nineteenth-century Baden, the concentration of wealth among Jews was relatively high. A typical Christian resident, already squeezed by the elites, came to regard politics as a zero-sum game. All of which made Moritz "the perfect fall guy," David Meola says. "He was a transgressive figure, a Jewish parvenu who hung out with the elites. But all Moritz wanted was personal satisfaction, to have his honor upheld and be treated as a deserving member of the upper class. He gave generously to charity. He was an investor in a widely read liberal newspaper, the *Oberdeutsche Zeitung*. His sister Leonie had converted and married a prominent Christian army officer. His family had started those three factories and, as part of the inner workings of the state, helped make for its success." Meola likens Salomon and his sons to the Americans Louis Brandeis and Henry Morgenthau, pioneering Jews who faithfully served their government at the highest levels.

The story has Affidavit by Willy Model, "Der Fall Moritz von Haber: Eine Episode aus der Geschichte von Karlsruhe," New York, 1947, Stadtarchiv-Karlsruhe, 7/N/ Model 61. Model swore out his affidavit in New York, to which he had emigrated; *King Haber* had been published in translation in the United States in 1930. The author of the novella, Alfred Neumann, was Jewish himself. He and Kurt struck up a friendship during exile in Nice through late 1940 and early 1941, as both socked away money for boat passage and made the consular rounds applying for visas. "He's a pleasant gentleman with the requisite self-confidence and an essential fearlessness," Neumann wrote in his diary after running into Kurt at Nice's Kuoni travel agency on November 4, 1940. But an entry a month later records a crack in that bravado: "Kurt Wolff comes and confesses to me fears about his and his family's life in the US. . . . I don't share his concerns and can refute them all very persuasively." From Alfred Neumann, "Tagebücher," in *Exil am Mittelmeer: Deutsche Schriftsteller in Südfrankreich von 1933–1941*, eds. Ulrike Voswinckel and Frank Berninger (Munich: Allitera, 2005), 222–64. I have no idea whether Neumann knew that his new friend Kurt counted Moritz von Haber as an ancestor. Or why Neumann would make such a black hat of Uncle Moritz, whom he describes in the novella as "a hard, ambitious man, and not too nice in the choice of his means for the attainment of his ends." Alfred Neumann, *King Haber*, trans. Marie Busch (New York: Alfred H. King, 1930), 3.

In the anti-Moritz Georg von Sarachaga-Uria, *Vermächtnis oder neue Folgen in der Göler-Haber'schen Sache*, cited in Meola, "Mirror of Competing Claims."

"So!" read one Moritz von Haber, Beilage, *Augsburger Allgemeine Zeitung*, January 11, 1844, cited in Meola, "Mirror of Competing Claims."

"As victor of the duel" Meola, "Mirror of Competing Claims."

But my father Holly Nash Wolff says my father told her of several childhood trips to Frankfurt to meet for tea with his great-aunt Mathilde, a baroness and Louis von Haber's daughter. This niece of Moritz was known formally as Mathilde Auguste, Freiin Haber von Linsberg.

She refers to Moritz would live another thirty years before dying a natural death. Despite his exile from Baden, and the failure of several of the family's banking and business interests during the financial crisis of 1847–48, he landed on his feet. In 1853 he cofounded the Bank für Handel und Industrie Darmstadt, which in 1931 would be subsumed into Dresdner Bank; in 1855, with his brother Louis, he helped launch Austria's Creditanstalt, which is today part of the Italian holding company UniCredit. Schuhladen-Krämer, "Moritz von Haber."

The contrast appears Notwithstanding the roundups and partitions of the twentieth century, Berlin has renewed itself again and again by looking far afield. By 1900, immigrants or their offspring made up some 60 percent of the city's population.

Displaced Poles, Russians, and Hungarians arrived after the First World War; after the Second, ethnic Germans expelled from the east flooded into the city, from Silesia, Pomerania, and East Prussia. Over the three decades after the fall of the Berlin Wall, waves of the world's restless or turned-out washed up on the banks of the Spree: Bosnians fleeing war in the Balkans; Palestinians drawn to the stretch of Neukölln known as "the Gaza Strip"; two hundred thousand Russians, forty thousand of them Jews, who poured into the city with reunification; and left-wing and LGBT Israelis disturbed enough by the rightward turn of the Zionist state that they found even the site of Hitler's envisioned "Germania" a place to breathe more freely.

"Berlin was, let us" Sebastian Haffner, *Germany Jekyll & Hyde: A Contemporary Account of Nazi Germany*, trans. Wilfrid David (London: Abacus, 2008), 288–89.

Chapter Two: Done with the War

And he launched *Kurt Wolff: A Portrait*, 192. Sitting in a Leipzig bar one evening in 1913, mulling over what to call their new journal, Kurt, Hasenclever, Werfel, and another editor, Kurt Pinthus, were at a loss—until someone proposed jabbing a pencil randomly at the proofs of Werfel's latest work, which lay on the table. The pencil landed on a line that began *O jüngste Tag*—O Judgment Day. Gert Ueding, "Mit Hirn und Herz," *Frankfurter Allgemeine Zeitung*, March 3, 1987.

"Tall. Slim." Robert Musil, *Tagebücher: Hauptband*, ed. Adolf Frisé (Reinbek, Germany: Rowohlt, 1976), 293.

"The house often functioned" Willy Haas, "Kurt Wolff: 3 März 1887–22 Oktober 1963," *Die Welt*, December 28, 1963.

Kurt had no interest *Kurt Wolff: A Portrait*, 10.

"I only want to publish books" Undated note in family papers, translation after Marion Detjen, "Kurt and Helen Wolff," in *Immigrant Entrepreneurship: German-American Business Biographies, 1720 to the Present*, vol. 5, ed. R. Daniel Wadhwani, German Historical Institute, 2012, ImmigrantEntrepreneurship.org/entry.php?rec=83.

his fiancée, Felice Bauer Just after the fall of the Wall, a café called Briefe an Felice opened in the Berlin district of Prenzlauer Berg, at the address on Immanuelkirchstrasse to which Kafka wrote the famous letters to the fiancée he never married. Paul Hockenos, *Berlin Calling: A Story of Anarchy, Music, the Wall, and the Birth of the New Berlin* (New York: New Press, 2017), 285.

"He is a very beautiful man" Stach, *Kafka: The Decisive Years*, 334.

"In the beginning" Kurt Wolff acceptance speech upon receiving the medal of honor of the German Booksellers Association, May 15, 1960, cited in *Kurt Wolff: A Portrait*, 197.

Though my grandfather "We must remain as open to the present as to the past," Kurt liked to say. Alfred Kazin, "A Legend among Publishers," *New York Newsday*, October 20, 1991.

And it was an exhilarating Elon, *The Pity of It All*, 273.

Eleven of the thirteen Reiner Stach, *Kafka: The Years of Insight*, trans. Shelley Frisch (Princeton, NJ: Princeton University Press, 2015), 36.

"I flatter myself"   Kurt Wolff, "Tagebücher, October 23, 1914, to June 28, 1915," DLA-Marbach.

"The dead lie in"   Ibid.

who had passed   Ibid.

a loud and consistent critic   Elon, *The Pity of It All*, 305.

"great annihilative nothingness"   Cited in Geert Mak, *In Europe: Travels through the Twentieth Century*, trans. Sam Garrett (New York: Vintage Books, 2008), 125.

The Kurt Wolff Verlag   Stach, *Kafka: The Years of Insight*, 37.

I drive into the darkness   Kurt Wolff, "Tagebücher," DLA-Marbach.

"The British simply assume"   Ibid.

"I do not know if the weather"   Ibid.

I don't want to go   Ibid.

When I think   Ibid.

We climbed up   Ibid.

"that sloshed back"   Mak, *In Europe*, 75.

Dust, columns of troops   Kurt Wolff, "Tagebücher," DLA-Marbach.

How long the war   Ibid.

My grandfather's redeployment   Stach, *Kafka: The Years of Insight*, 37.

"I extend my"   Franz Kafka letter to Kurt Wolff, October 11, 1916, in Franz Kafka, *Letters to Friends, Family and Editors*, trans. Richard and Clara Winston (New York: Schocken Books, 1977), 127.

"I am entranced"   Cited in Helmut Frielinghaus, "Vorbilder," in *Kurt Wolff zum Hundertsten*.

The publication of *Der Untertan*   Inspiration for the novel came to Mann after he witnessed an incident in 1906, when the kaiser happened to pass by the Berlin café in which the author sat: "Almost to a man, the patrons of the café flung themselves outside to cheer His Majesty; and as they returned they noticed a rather shabbily dressed man sitting in the corner, unperturbed by the event. The manager was immediately summoned, and the unfortunate individual forcibly ejected; he was, the patrons considered, unfit to sit in the same café as men who had just saluted His Imperial Highness. The incident may sound trifling; but for Heinrich Mann it reflected a spirit rampant and disquieting: a spirit of fanatic obedience, servitude, followed by sickening brutality." Nigel Hamilton, "Heinrich Mann and the Underdog," *Times* (London), June 24, 1972.

In fact, Kurt knew   Stach, *Kafka: The Years of Insight*, 133–34.

"Your criticism of"   Franz Kafka letter to Kurt Wolff, October 11, 1916, in Kafka, *Letters to Friends*, 127.

In its 1918 catalog   Klaus Wagenbach, "Kurt Wolff," in *Kurt Wolff zum Hundertsten*.

"[The Germans] will"   Elon, *The Pity of It All*, 354.

With supply chains disrupted   Stach, *Kafka: The Years of Insight*, 313.

"More than ever"   Kurt Wolff letter to Walter Hasenclever, November 9, 1920, in *Kurt Wolff: Briefwechsel*, 265.

Nine months later   Stach, *Kafka: The Years of Insight*, 532.

"If the Kurt Wolff Verlag" *Kurt Wolff: A Portrait*, 46. Kurt was more tactful in the rejection letter he sent Joyce. He cited postwar production challenges that made it "at the moment almost impossible to do justice to the requirements of our regular authors." KW Papers, box 5, folder 162.

As the worst *Kurt Wolff: A Portrait*, 35.

"condemns Berlin forever" Ladd, *The Ghosts of Berlin*, 123–24.

Yet a protean cityscape Mak, *In Europe*, 36.

During the Reichstag's restoration George Packer, "The Quiet German," *New Yorker*, November 24, 2014.

Visible to the south To place a solemn memorial in the heart of a major tourist destination cuts two ways. In 2017, seeing young visitors to Berlin taking selfies and playing hide-and-seek in the labyrinth of stelae that make up the site, the Israeli artist Shahak Shapira was moved to juxtapose posts culled from social media with images from concentration camps. He called his exhibition *Yolocaust*; see Yolocaust.de.

"the only people" Amanda Taub and Max Fisher, "Germany's Extreme Right Challenges Guilt over Nazi Past," *New York Times*, January 18, 2017.

"You cannot delegate" "A Tale of Two Germanys," Alan Riding, *New York Times*, December 14, 2000.

In late 1944 The roughly nine hundred thousand members of the Waffen-SS, the armed wing of the SS, took an oath of personal loyalty to Hitler. About one-third of the membership consisted of conscripts like Grass and foreign volunteers.

"cultures of memory" Timothy Snyder, *Bloodlands: Europe between Hitler and Stalin* (New York: Basic Books, 2010), 408.

one particular person The *Stolpersteine* themselves come engraved with only basic information, but researchers have fleshed out the lives of many memorialized victims on the project's Berlin website, Stolpersteine-Berlin.de.

And I really don't For her 2019 book *Learning from the Germans*, the Berlin-based political philosopher Susan Neiman traveled to Jackson, Mississippi, to speak with James Meredith, the African American who integrated the University of Mississippi in 1962, and his wife, Judy. Meredith listened intently as Neiman described to him the *Stolpersteine*. "Like the Hollywood stars?" he asked. "Right in the sidewalk?" Judy Meredith couldn't believe it: "Get out of here," she said. Susan Neiman, *Learning from the Germans: Race and the Memory of Evil* (New York: Farrar, Straus and Giroux, 2019), 172.

"I grew up" *Economist*, "Special Report: The New Germans," April 14, 2018.

Her refugee policy In his May 8, 1985, speech marking forty years since the end of the war, German president Richard von Weizsäcker encouraged Germans to "use the memory of our own history as a guideline for our behavior now." Indeed, at the height of the 2015 refugee crisis, Weizsäcker seemed to be whispering this to Merkel from the grave: "If we remember how people persecuted on grounds of race, religion and politics and threatened with certain death often stood before the closed borders with other countries, we shall not close the door today on those who are genuinely persecuted and seek protection with us." "Speech by Federal President Richard von Weizsäcker during the Ceremony Commemorating the 40th Anniversary of the End of War in Europe and of National-Socialist Tyranny on 8 May 1985 at the Bundestag, Bonn," Bundespräsidialamt, Bundespraesident .de/SharedDocs/Downloads/DE/Reden/2015/02/150202-RvW-Rede-8-Mai-1985 -englisch.pdf?__blob=publicationFile.

"If the French"   Reuters, "AfD Co-Founder Says Germans Should Be Proud of Its Second World War Soldiers," *Guardian* (UK), September 14, 2017.

Another, a judge   Jefferson Chase, "AfD Candidate in Hot Water over Breivik Statements," DeutscheWelle.com, April 21, 2017, dw.com/en/afd-candidate-in -hot-water-over-breivik-statements/a-38537022; Justin Huggler, "Five Names to Watch as the Anti-Immigrant AfD Looks to Stir up Trouble for Angela Merkel," *Telegraph* (London), October 1, 2017.

But to have Boateng   Philip Oltermann, "German Rightwing Party Apologises for Jérôme Boateng comments," *Guardian* (UK), May 29, 2016.

Some 80 percent   *Economist*, "Special Report: The New Germans," April 14, 2018.

Historian Konrad Jarausch   Konrad H. Jarausch, *Broken Lives: How Ordinary Germans Experienced the 20th Century* (Princeton, NJ: Princeton University Press, 2018), 2–3.

"an irony of history"   Timothy Garton-Ash, cited in Jarausch, *Broken Lives*, 380.

Chapter Three: Technical Boy and the Deposed Sovereign

"With his long"   *Kurt Wolff: A Portrait*, 119.

enforce the rules   The motto of Fletcherism's inventor and namesake, Horace Fletcher, was "Nature will castigate those who don't masticate."

stuffed bear Zoschl   When my father went off to war, his mother sat Zoschl up on a corner shelf in the parlor of her home. There the bear remained until sometime in the fifties, when from its perch it caught the eye of Hannes Rosenow, an artist paying a visit. "This is an object that has been loved to death," Rosenow declared. "I must paint it." His portrait of Zoschl was exhibited at Munich's Haus der Kunst in 1962.

My grandparents spent   Felice Casorati (1883–1963) was a member of the Return to Order movement in European painting following World War I. In her memoir *Family Lexicon*, trans. Jenny McPhee (New York: New York Review Books, 2017), 51, Natalia Ginzburg describes the vogue in Casorati's realist, Renaissance-influenced work between the wars among the bourgeoisie of Turin, where her family and the artist both lived.

The sale grossed   Jos. Baer & Co., *Ergebnisse der Versteigerung Kurt Wolff*, Frankfurt, October 5–6, 1926. H&KW Papers, box 80, folder 2384.

Those concerns might   The Kurt Wolff Verlag published only ten titles that year—a novel by Joseph Roth and nine books on art or food.

The two exchanged scores   Wolfram Göbel, "Ernst Rowohlt und Kurt Wolff," in *Kurt Wolff zum Hundertsten*. Göbel, a literary historian, suggests that Clara Merck filled a maternal role for a young man who had lost his mother as an adolescent. For her part, Clara adored her son-in-law, who launched his first publishing venture in part with Merck family money.

Nonetheless, if you   For an exploration of who the Nazis considered a Jew, and the roughly 150,000 German men of Jewish descent who, like my father, served in the Wehrmacht, see Rigg, *Hitler's Jewish Soldiers*, especially p. 21: "Conversion to

Christianity at any stage more recent than a great-grandparent did not remove the stain of Jewish blood." Kurt's maternal grandparents were both baptized; only one of their parents, Kurt's great-grandmother Henriette von Haber Marx, was. Peter Gaupp, a Wehrmacht soldier with one Jewish parent, described to Bryan Mark Rigg his relief upon reading the Nuremberg Laws in 1935: "That was the first time you knew where you stood legally. . . . Before it was all guesswork. You could meet a Nazi in some office and he could exterminate you or you could meet a Nazi who was very human and he could help you." Rigg, *Hitler's Jewish Soldiers*, 98.

I cannot, I will not   Kurt Wolff letter to Franz Werfel, June 23, 1930, in *Kurt Wolff: Briefwechsel*, 351–52. In the early thirties Kurt sold what was left of his publishing business to the husband of his ex-wife's sister Caroline, Peter Reinhold, who had served for a year as finance minister of the Weimar Republic—finance minister of the Weimar Republic being rather like captain of the *Titanic*.

"Why did I stop?"   *Kurt Wolff: A Portrait*, xxiii.

He had made   Kurt was an enthusiast for the new, but he had his limits, and Dada exceeded them: "Even before I became aware that what was performed and deformed in the name of Dada was utter drivel, the pedantry, tedium and sheer dreariness of [the Dadaists'] correspondence had cured me of the delusion that they might be the source of any creative fun." *Kurt Wolff: A Portrait*, 16.

But after five years   Leo Bogart, *Commercial Culture: The Media System and the Public Interest* (Piscataway, NJ: Transaction, 2000), 56. None of Kafka's works went back to press during the author's lifetime. Howard Nelson, "Speaking Volumes: The Wide World of a Publisher," *Washington Post Book World*, April 4, 1971.

"That so many"   "The Seismographer of Expressionism," *Times Literary Supplement*, February 2, 1970.

But the Nazis   The 1929 stock market crash dashed Kurt's last hope—kindled by talks with a wealthy American investor—for an infusion of cash that could save his publishing business.

"like a deposed sovereign"   *Kurt Wolff: A Portrait*, 193. The phrase is from Lambert Schneider's laudation when Kurt was awarded the medal of honor of the German Booksellers Association in 1960.

"The Kurt Wolff Verlag"   Franz Werfel letter to Kurt Wolff, March 25, 1930, in *Kurt Wolff: Briefwechsel*, 350. As he aged, Kurt became steadily more reluctant to wear the mantle of "publisher of Expressionism." Several years before he died he lamented that the tag had become "my detested, indeed accursed claim to fame"; *Kurt Wolff: A Portrait*, 18–19. Fritz Redlich advances possible reasons he rejected the honorific: recognition that, in his youthful enthusiasm, Kurt published some work he realized hadn't worn well; or that Expressionism included leftists and anarchists out of step with his middle-of-the-road politics; Fritz Redlich, "German Literary Expressionism and Its Publishers," *Harvard Library Bulletin* 17, no. 2 (April 1969). My uncle Christian puts the most stock in a third theory of Redlich's: that Kurt simply disliked labels. "He felt 'Expressionism' was too exclusive," Christian told me. "Movements don't write things. People do."

Louis eventually abandoned   Helen found that vow easier to keep after the early thirties, when Louis Mosel joined the Nazi Party and settled in Berlin. There he fell on hard times but soon clawed back some power and status by taking an unpaid position with the Reichsbund der deutschen Kapital- und Kleinrentner, a National

Socialist–sympathetic lobby for pensioners who had lost their savings during the Weimar hyperinflation. Throughout, Helen refused to have anything to do with him. In Kurt and Helen's exile and émigré circles in New York, knowledge of her father's Nazi connections could have complicated their lives.

Helen had to content Marion Detjen, "Zum Hintergrund des Hintergrunds," afterword to Helen Wolff, *Hintergrund für Liebe* (Bonn: Weidle, 2020), 147. Helen's prewar travels and stopovers in the south of France with a much older, restless philanderer would inform her novel *Hintergrund für Liebe* (Background for Love), which captures the exhilarating uncertainty of their first years together. "Whoever swims, swims," Helen has one of her characters say. "And if they sink, they sink. But while you're swimming it's best not to think about sinking" (63). In April 1933, Rowohlt Verlag had verbally promised Helen that it would publish the novel, only to back out after the book burnings that took place the following month. Ullstein Verlag also lost interest, ostensibly because of the story's setting in France; Detjen, "Zum Hintergrund des Hintergrunds," 209. The novel finally appeared in print in Germany twenty-six years after Helen's death.

"It's better to spend one week" Detjen, "Zum Hintergrund des Hintergrunds," 157.

"already gloomy and sickening" Kurt Wolff letter to Walter Hasenclever, November 26, 1931, cited in Steven Schuyler, "Kurt Wolff and Hermann Broch: Publisher and Author in Exile," PhD thesis, Harvard University, Department of Germanic Languages and Literatures, 1984.

"I rest, swim" Kurt Wolff letter to Franz Werfel, June 23, 1930, in *Kurt Wolff: Briefwechsel*, 353.

In letters he was Detjen, "Zum Hintergrund des Hintergrunds," 152.

To be so far Ibid., 138.

In March 1931 Ibid., 164.

"The saplings are called" Cited in Mak, *In Europe*, 208.

"We are now" Detjen, "Zum Hintergrund des Hintergrunds," 201.

"lapse into barbarism" Ibid., 204.

"These are madmen" Helen describes this moment in *The Exiles*, a 1989 documentary film directed by Richard Kaplan.

"The news is sad" *Kurt Wolff: A Portrait*, 156–57.

"Deciding whether to" Cited in Fritz Stern, *Gold and Iron: Bismarck, Bleichröder, and the Building of the German Empire* (New York: Vintage Books, 1979), 542.

"The ideal subject" Hannah Arendt, *The Origins of Totalitarianism* (San Diego: Harcourt, 1973), 474.

the entire content Sebastian Haffner, *Defying Hitler: A Memoir*, trans. Oliver Pretzel (New York: Picador, 2000), 68–69.

Only a certain cultured class Ibid., 70. It's uncanny how closely Haffner's analysis, from the late thirties, accords with how Helen had described the German people in that letter to her brother the day before the Reichstag fire: "Life leaves them bored, thus they throw it away."

"In animals [it] is called" Ibid., 135.

Albert Einstein also remarked Fritz Stern, *Einstein's German World* (Princeton, NJ: Princeton University Press, 2016), 129.

"the worst enemy"   Ibid., 91. Joseph Roth, one of the authors of the Kurt Wolff Verlag, recorded something similar in "Germany in Winter," a December 1923 feuilleton essay that likened the effects of the hyperinflation to the symptoms of a fevered, raving patient. "The sick man will talk all kinds of nonsense, ridiculous, trivial, unworthy of himself and his condition. He is missing the regulating consciousness. That's just what is missing in Germany: the regulating consciousness." Joseph Roth, *The Hotel Years*, trans. Michael Hofmann (New York: New Directions, 2015), 33.

After Günter Demnig   Suzanne Cords, "Curator of the Largest Holocaust Memorial Turns 70, but His Life's Work Continues," DeutscheWelle.com, October 27, 2017, dw.com/en/creator-of-the-largest-holocaust-memorial-turns-70-but-his -life-work-continues/a-41107926.

When Günter Demnig   Neiman, *Learning from the Germans*, 277.

"Detached from the question"   Jan Philipp Reemtsma, "Wozu Gedenkstätten?," *Politik und Zeitgeschichte*, June 21, 2010. Translation after Neiman, *Learning from the Germans*, 283.

"You cannot choose"   Neiman, *Learning from the Germans*, 325.

Chapter Four: Mediterranean Refuge

"The conjunction of"   Sybille Bedford, *Jigsaw* (New York: New York Review Books, 2018), 76–77.

We cannot remain here   Kurt Wolff letter to Hermann Hesse, December 19, 1934, in *Kurt Wolff: A Portrait*, 158. To help raise the cash to buy the property in Tuscany, Kurt yet again put books from his library up for auction, this time at the Galerie Alexandre III in Cannes. Schuyler, "Kurt Wolff and Hermann Broch."

If an emergency   Kurt and Helen fled Italy on a tip, likely paid for with goodwill built up during their time in Lastra a Signa. A local oral history project, conducted during the mid-2000s and incorporating late-in-life recollections of two residents who grew up near Il Moro during the thirties, includes this: "The positive memory the Wolffs left in the community is also derived from this story about a three-year-old girl with bronchopneumonia, a then-fatal illness, recounted by the child's eldest sister. 'Helen and Kurt Wolff came to visit her. They too had a small child. . . . They recommended a warm compress of flaxseed flour and olive oil overnight, refreshed from time to time. . . . The next day when the doctor came to visit her, he found my sister improved. He was amazed and said, "She's much better today, what have you done to her?" My sister recovered.'" Giuseppe Simoncini, "Kurt Wolff, Soggiorno a Lastra," LastraOnline.it, 2008, LastraOnline.it/p/storia. php?idpag=374&idpag=374. Author's translation.

Willy Haas, one of the   Haas, "Kurt Wolff : 3 März 1887–22 Oktober 1963."

A flurry of letters   Various civil servants and church clerks were responsive to Kurt's requests, forwarding to him birth, death, or marriage certificates on file. For instance, in December 1936, the Protestant *Gemeindeamt* in Bonn sent to Italy proof that Kurt's grandparents on Maria Marx's side, August Karl and Bertha Isabella Marx, were married in a Protestant ceremony in 1856. But the document goes into inconvenient detail about August's forebears, citing excerpts from the death records of the "*israelitische Gemeinde*" in Mannheim. On his unsent application for a "certificate of Aryan ancestry," Kurt makes no mention of ancestors beyond his maternal grandparents—surely because his great-grandfather Jacob Marx never converted.

"because," Kurt wrote Hasenclever   Detjen, "Zum Hintergrund des Hintergrunds," 206.

"He who possesses art"   Cited in Stern, *Five Germanys*, 17.

Bertha's own parents   Marriage between cousins was common among German Jews during the nineteenth century. It strengthened family bonds and consolidated wealth—prudent safeguards in a world with so much closed off to them.

As it happens   Rigg, *Hitler's Jewish Soldiers*, 7.

And the persistence   Felix Mendelssohn-Bartholdy converted and famously celebrated the Protestant Reformation in his music, but the Nazis re-Judaized him so successfully that the composer is widely regarded as Jewish today.

He came to   In his poem *Germany: A Winter's Tale*, Heine agonized over the push and pull of his homeland, lamenting the ways it fell short of the democratic standards then prevailing in Paris, to which he had fled. Heine's epic was nonetheless a love note to the German language, the tongue he grew up with—"our most sacred possession," he called it, "a fatherland even for him who is denied one by malice and folly"; Elon, *The Pity of It All*, 118. There may be no more melancholy commentary on the fate of the acculturated German Jew—lover of Goethe, admirer of Kant, subscriber to all things classical and enlightened—than Heine's. As the poet himself put it, this unrequited longing made the German Jew like other Germans he lived among, only more so; Stern, *Five Germanys*, 21.

To be "the arriviste"   Stern, *Five Germanys*, 296. During the nineteenth century, German Jews engaged in what Amos Elon calls "reckless magnanimity"—"a desperate but vain attempt to civilize German patriotism: to base citizenship not on blood but on law, to separate church and state, and to establish what would today be called an open, multicultural society." Elon, *The Pity of It All*, 9.

By the middle   Fritz Haber won the Nobel Prize in Chemistry for developing a process for fixing nitrogen from air. He converted to Christianity to advance his career but still had to wait twelve years to be named a full professor. As a military veteran he could have remained in charge of the Kaiser Wilhelm Institute for Physical Chemistry after the Nazis' rise to power in 1933, but he would have had to fire all the Jews who worked under him. He chose to resign and died the following year. See Stern, "Together and Apart: Fritz Haber and Albert Einstein," in *Einstein's German World*, 59–164. Haber, who worked on some of the chemical weapons deployed during World War I, also helped develop Zyklon-B, which the Nazis would use in the gas chambers. Haber was Fritz Stern's godfather, and Haber's eldest son, Hermann, was Stern's uncle. Stern nonetheless addresses the irony head-on: "The horror of Haber's involvement with the gas that later murdered millions, including friends and distant relatives, beggars description." Stern, *Einstein's German World*, 135. From her genealogical research, my aunt Holly believes that Fritz Haber is a descendant of Isaac Haber, my great-great-great-great-great-grandfather and the father of Salomon von Haber. Like Fritz Haber's family, Isaac and Salomon came from Breslau.

One, who became   That ancestor, Mordechai ben Samuel ha Levi, went by the civilian name Marx Levi. In addition to being grandfather of both Karl Marx and my great-great-great-great-grandfather Jacob Meyer Marx, Marx Levi was my own grandfather to the sixth degree. I have to go back to Salomon von Haber, and to Jacob Meyer Marx's son Jacob Marx, who died in 1830, to find ancestors who identified as Jewish.

During the eighteenth century In a confidential communication, Pope Benedict XIV once called Moses Wolff "the only person with a head on his shoulders at the castle of Bonn." In 1768, Dr. Wolff was summoned to the Vatican to treat Benedict's successor, Clement XIII, for an eye ailment.

Chapter Five: Surrender on Demand

On a tip By leaving Italy on short notice, as they would flee Paris and then Nice over the next several years, Kurt and Helen left behind not only their greatest asset, Il Moro, for which they had three years earlier mobilized "all our reserves," but many of their possessions too. During a 2000 trip to Florence, Vanessa and I took a bus out to Lastra a Signa, found Il Moro, and rang the bell. The man who came to the door, Luciano Innocenti, now lived in the subdivided villa with three generations of his family, and over the following months my father struck up a correspondence with him and his daughter Laura. A year later we returned with my parents, and during that visit Niko pointed out several pieces of furniture he remembered from the thirties as having belonged to his father.

To judge by Kurt's diary Helen's mother, Josephine, died in Lastra a Signa in June 1937. She is buried in Florence at the foot of the Ponte Vecchio, on the grounds of the church of Santo Stefano.

"We cannot and do not" Detjen, "Kurt and Helen Wolff," in *Immigrant Entrepreneurship*. The friend, Elisabeth Mayer, had been Maria's piano teacher and became the mother-in-law of Wolfgang Sauerländer, who would work with Kurt and Helen as an editor at Pantheon.

Joining them there Luise Marx Wolff, Niko's unsinkable Oma Lullu, died in Nice of natural causes in June 1947. In September 1943, after Italy made a separate peace with the Allies, the Nazis invaded France's Italian-occupied zone, including Nice, and seized five thousand Jews over the following five months. Oma Lullu was nonetheless spared, despite her Jewish ancestry. Similarly, until his death in Germany in 1943, Hermann Grafe, the fully Gentile husband of Kurt's sister Else, shared his wife's fear that Else would be rounded up as a "first-degree *Mischling*." She never was and died in Rastatt in 1967.

On September 29 Kurt is making note of the meeting at which Britain, France, and Italy agreed to let Germany annex the Sudetenland. Billed at the time as a way to avoid war, the Munich Agreement only emboldened Hitler and became known as a notorious act of appeasement. "When [British prime minister Neville] Chamberlain left, we knew," my father once told me. "There was no way there wouldn't be war."

On Kristallnacht On November 9, 1938, ordinary Germans joined Brownshirts of Hitler's Sturmabteilung (or SA) to attack Jews and ransack Jewish homes and businesses in the nationwide pogrom known as Kristallnacht, the Night of Broken Glass.

Habent sua fata libelli   Cited in Schuyler, "Kurt Wolff and Hermann Broch."

From two friends   Herbert Mitgang, "Imprint," *New Yorker*, August 2, 1982.

"When she saw me"   Helen Wolff, "My Most Unforgettable Character," unpublished reminiscence, ca. 1942.

Against a solid wall   Ibid.

The Countess Colloredo-Mansfeld   Christopher A. Brooks and Robert Sims, *Roland Hayes: The Legacy of an American Tenor* (Bloomington: Indiana University Press, 2016), 107.

During long stretches apart   Ibid., 135.

After processing his anger   Christopher A. Brooks, coauthor of the Roland Hayes biography, expands on the tenor's relationship with Colloredo-Mansfeld in "Roland Hayes and the Countess," a blog post on the publisher's website, Indiana University Press News Blog, February 27, 2015, iupress.typepad.com/blog/2015/02/roland-hayes-and-the-countess.html.

It positioned her   Ernest Kolowrat, *Confessions of a Hapless Hedonist* (Middletown, DE: Xlibris, 2001), 170. Kolowrat, the countess's nephew, nested into his memoir a vivid portrait of the aunt he called Issten, after her habit of asking, "*Was ist denn?*" (What is it, then?)

"If I ever figure things out"   Helen Wolff, "My Most Unforgettable Character." The countess would die near her château in 1982 at the age of ninety-one. Her sons had continued to pay her an allowance to honor their father's wish that they "take care of Mammi because she'll never do it on her own"; Kolowrat, *Confessions*, 181. But she eventually had to sell off household effects, then paintings and antiques, and finally plots of surrounding land; Ibid., 173. Vast reserves of local goodwill forestalled her eviction, as creditors understood that they could no more extract what was owed them than they could rewrite the history of Saint-Lary and her beneficent place in it. Two of the countess's grandchildren—Maya's twin sons Igor and Grichka Bogdanoff—arrived at her funeral by helicopter from Paris; Brooks and Sims, *Roland Hayes*, 319. The Bogdanoff brothers would go on to become pseudoscience TV stars and cult figures on YouTube.

"I sat waiting"   Mitgang, "Imprint."

But as much as   In July 1942, in what became known as *la grande rafle*, collaborationist *gendarmes* seized thirteen thousand Jews, most of them foreign nationals or stateless, from their homes in Paris and delivered them to the Vélodrome d'Hiver, the same staging area to which Helen had been brought before being sent to Gurs. From there they were put on trains to the death camps.

"We had to go"   Mitgang, "Imprint."

They still had to spring   My uncle remembers wandering around La Rochelle one day and, seeing several Wehrmacht soldiers in the street, chatting them up in German. "They were a bit astonished," recalls Christian, then six years old, who only much later realized how he might have placed himself and his parents in jeopardy.

Shortly after ten p.m.   Mitgang, "Imprint."

Always he battled   Bingham's repeated acts of conscience ruined his career in the State Department. Sheila Isenberg, *A Hero of Our Own: The Story of Varian Fry* (New York: Random House, 2001), 193n.

"Like the first bird"   Hans Natonek, *In Search of Myself*, trans. Barthold Fles (New York: G. P. Putnam's, 1943), 180.

That evening Fry met   Andy Marino, *A Quiet American: The Secret War of Varian Fry* (New York: St. Martin's Press, 1999), 164ff. In Port-Bou, as Fry and his clients boisterously celebrated over a meal, "a man walked over to the table and whispered in Fry's ear. He asked in English if he could have a word with Fry outside. There he explained that he recognized Heinrich Mann, and that the chances were that the Spaniard sitting in a corner of the restaurant would too—and he was the local chief of Franco's secret police. 'He's not a very pleasant chap, really,' said the British consul to Fry. The party broke up immediately, and everyone made their way upstairs to bed." Marino, *A Quiet American*, 176.

They needed a French   To apply for an exit visa was to announce oneself to the Gestapo. Refugees could assume that the Vichy authorities shared with the Nazis the name of every applicant in a kind of "bureaucratic man-trap." Marino, *A Quiet American*, 109.

"a romantic, dirty, hard-edged"   Marino, *A Quiet American*, 104.

My publishing house   Sylvia Asmus and Brita Eckert, "Emigration und Neubeginn: Die Akte 'Kurt Wolff' im Archiv des Emergency Rescue Committee," in *Kurt Wolff: Ein Literat und Gentleman*, 139.

taped to a leg   Isenberg, *A Hero of Our Own*, 4.

The other affidavit   "The specter of the affidavit—documentary proof, required by the United States government, that the émigré would not require financial assistance—possessed a special horror for intellectuals," writes Anthony Heilbut. "Who could appreciate better than they the pointlessness of a piece of paper establishing one's potential worth as a citizen? Yet such affidavits, confirming the least essential attribute (solvency) and vulgarizing the most important (character), became the supreme focus of existence." Anthony Heilbut, *Exiled in Paradise: German Refugee Artists and Intellectuals in America from the 1930s to the Present* (Berkeley: University of California Press, 1983), 32.

On September 20   Asmus and Eckert, "Emigration und Neubeginn," in *Kurt Wolff: Ein Literat und Gentleman*, 140–41.

"The idea was"   Mitgang, "Imprint."

Fry responded   Asmus and Eckert, "Emigration und Neubeginn," in *Kurt Wolff: Ein Literat und Gentleman*, 142.

The flood waters   Erich Maria Remarque, *The Night in Lisbon*, trans. Ralph Manheim (New York: Harcourt, Brace & World, 1964), 3.

Decades later one   After Helen died in 1994, Eco's translator William Weaver faxed an English-language typescript of this characterization, apparently included in a tribute published in Italy, to Harcourt Brace in New York.

"people being disgorged"   Anna Seghers, *Transit*, trans. Margot Bettauer Dembo (New York: New York Review Books, 2013), 147.

It's impossible to seize   Benjamin Schwarz, "Hitler's Co-Conspirators," *Atlantic*, May 2009.

When Goebbels spoke   Ibid.

In Munich, five thousand   Neiman, *Learning from the Germans*, 24.

"The ignorance I claim"   Günter Grass, *Peeling the Onion: A Memoir*, trans. Michael Henry Heim (Orlando: Harcourt, 2007), 111.

Chapter Six: Into a Dark Room

his stepfather, Hans Albrecht   Niko's stepfather would die of cancer in 1944. My father took a leave to travel from the front to Munich for the funeral. In a letter, Maria described him "crying like a child in spite of his military attire."

Hitler called it   Snyder, *Bloodlands*, 166.

He once confessed   Joachim Fest, *Hitler*, trans. Richard and Clara Winston (San Diego: Harcourt Brace Jovanovich, 1974), 647.

"inner boundlessness"   Helen's use of the German *heimliche Unendlichkeit* is a reference to a passage from Nietzsche's *Beyond Good and Evil*, in which the philosopher refers to the pure core of an individual, unconstrained by ties to religion, society, or nation.

For Ukraine specifically   Frederick Taylor, *Exorcising Hitler: The Occupation and Denazification of Germany* (New York: Bloomsbury Press, 2011), 150–53.

Ukraine would no longer   Snyder, *Bloodlands*, 416.

Were all victims of   Ibid., viii.

"the beginning of a calamity"   Ibid., 155.

"Right after the invasion"   Ibid., xi.

"If German soldiers"   Ibid., 170. "Any remnants of traditional soldierly ideals had to be abandoned in favor of a destructive ethic that made sense of the army's predicament," Snyder writes. "To be sure, German soldiers had to be fed; but they were eating to gain strength to fight a war that had already been lost. To be sure, calories had to be extracted from the countryside to feed them; but this brought about essentially pointless starvation. As the army high command and the officers in the field implemented illegal and murderous policies, they found no justification except for the sort that Hitler provided: that human beings were containers of calories that should be emptied, and that Slavs, Jews, and Asians, the peoples of the Soviet Union, were less than human and thus more than expendable." Ibid., 178.

On October 13, 1941   Gitta Sereny, *The German Trauma: Experiences and Reflections, 1938–2001* (London: Penguin Books, 2001), 280.

His letters home   Snyder, *Bloodlands*, 204–5.

Family letters   A professor of history at Bard College Berlin, Marion Detjen is Helen Wolff's grandniece—the granddaughter of Helen's sister Elisabeth (Liesl) Mosel Steinbeis.

"From now on"   Jarausch, *Broken Lives*, 82.

"I want no intellectual"   Cited in Sereny, *The German Trauma*, 288.

Chapter Seven: A Debt for Rescue

"The first days"   Author's rendering after Franz Kafka, *Lost in America*, trans. Anthony Northey (Prague: Vitalis, 2010), 42.

no American guest asked   Pantheon Books's first book, a folio of woodcuts called *Danse Macabre*, would answer that unasked question. In it Frans Masereel, a collaborator of the old Kurt Wolff Verlag, depicted the fall of Paris and the flight of the French and Belgian forces of which he had been a part.

"I do not"   Helen Wolff, quoted on camera in *The Exiles*, dir. Kaplan.

seized by the US   Carsten Burhop, Michael Kißener, Hermann Schäfer, and Joachim Scholtyseck, *Merck 1668–2018: From a Pharmacy to a Global Corporation*, trans. Jane Paulick, Timothy Slater, Patricia Sutcliffe, and Patricia Szobar (Munich: C. H. Beck, 2018), 230–31. The United States entered World War I in April 1917; the expropriation of Merck Darmstadt's American subsidiary took place a year later. The two entities would never again be part of the same company.

didn't know where   Helen Wolff, quoted on camera in *The Exiles*, dir. Kaplan.

They haunted concerts   Detjen, "Kurt and Helen Wolff," in *Immigrant Entrepreneurship*.

George Merck   Despite being flung across two continents, Merck family members would maintain close ties, even after the United States seized Merck Darmstadt's New Jersey–based subsidiary in 1918. One colorful example is provided by Adam (Harry) Happel, the illegitimate son of Elise (Lischen) Happel, nursemaid to Elisabeth Merck's father, my great-grandfather Carl Emanuel Merck. Harry Happel grew up in Darmstadt as Carl Emanuel's foster brother before emigrating to the United States in the late 1870s. He spent eighteen years as a fisherman sailing out of Gloucester, Massachusetts, and several more as a homesteader in Oklahoma before lighting out for Alaska in 1898 in search of gold. From his home in Cordova he stayed in touch with George W. Merck, CEO of the by-now independent, US-based Merck & Co., once even inviting representatives of the firm out to the territory so he could show them raw materials there for the extracting. It's unclear whether Merck & Co. ever followed up. In 1946, upon Harry Happel's death of a cerebral hemorrhage at eighty-four, one of his friends in Alaska sent word to George, who shared the news with Kurt, who relayed the obituary to Darmstadt. It's all in the Merck-Archiv, A-148.

"If I wish"   *Kurt Wolff: A Portrait*, xxvi.

Eager for the   In a June 2018 presentation at Berlin's Centre Marc Bloch, Marion Detjen highlighted this photograph in an exploration of the "autobiographical strategies" émigrés like Kurt and Helen employed to advantageously reinvent themselves in their new milieu. Christian now winces at his Fauntleroy tunic and shakes his head at the Potemkin dog beside him. "We were always cat people," he says.

"You know yourself"   Thomas Mann letter to Kurt Wolff, January 11, 1946, in *Kurt Wolff: A Portrait*, 163.

Russian-Jewish refugee Jacques Schiffrin   Schiffrin, who had established the prestigious Bibliothèque de la Pléiade series and continued to edit it under the auspices of the French publisher Gallimard, was forced to flee Paris after Gallimard complied with a Vichy order to dismiss all Jewish employees.

and German with another   Detjen, "Kurt and Helen Wolff," in *Immigrant Entrepreneurship*.

Their order clerk   Schuyler, "Kurt Wolff and Hermann Broch."

"Grotesque as it may sound"   Helen Wolff letter to Maria Wolff Baumhauer, March 28, 1946, cited in Schuyler, "Kurt Wolff and Hermann Broch." Kurt's poor English was the by-product of a *Gymnasium* education, which prized the study of classical languages over modern ones.

One day the staff   Laura Fermi, *Illustrious Immigrants: The Intellectual Migration from Europe, 1930–41* (Chicago: University of Chicago Press, 1968), 280.

"One has to learn"   Detjen, "Kurt and Helen Wolff," in Immigrant Entrepreneurship.

"This wasn't a gift"   Helen Wolff, quoted on camera in *The Exiles*, dir. Kaplan.

The nippings   Schuyler, "Kurt Wolff and Hermann Broch."

"to present to the American public"   Ibid., 25.

A range of factors   Detjen, "Kurt and Helen Wolff," in *Immigrant Entrepreneurship*.

with Europe still   Helen Wolff, "Elective Affinities," address to Deutsches Haus New York, May 15, 1990.

A year later   "Don't pollute your home with Grimm this Christmas," wrote Sterling North in the books supplement of the *Chicago Sun*. "The news commentators on the radio will bring reports of enough German *Schrecklichkeit*." Cited in Schuyler, "Kurt Wolff and Hermann Broch." See also André Schiffrin, *The Business of Books: How International Conglomerates Took Over Publishing and Changed the Way We Read* (London: Verso, 2000), 21.

To Pantheon's good fortune   W. H. Auden, "In Praise of the Brothers Grimm," *New York Times Book Review*, November 12, 1944. The mother-in-law of Pantheon editor Wolfgang Sauerländer had been Auden's German tutor before the war. Schuyler, "Kurt Wolff and Hermann Broch."

"I like this country"   Helen Wolff letter to Bertha Colloredo-Mansfeld, March 29, 1942. H&KW Papers, 2019 genm 0032, box 3. Helen wrote the countess in French; the Péguy is rendered by the author after Ann and Julian Green's translation of *Basic Verities* (New York: Pantheon Books, 1943), 150–52.

"To be sure"   Franz Kafka letter to Kurt Wolff, July 27, 1917, in Kafka, *Letters to Friends*, 134–35.

"As far as your plans"   Stach, *Kafka: The Years of Insight*, 181.

"While people feared"   Ibid., 183. "So long as Expressionism lasted [Kurt Wolff] was its publisher and to a great extent its paymaster—and if anyone wants to find out how miserable the pay often was . . . Kafka in 1918 had royalties of 25 marks; in 1923, at the height of the hyperinflation, he took the equivalent in books"; "Expressionism Today," *Times Literary Supplement*, November 6, 1970. It would nonetheless be unfair to accuse Kurt of abandoning or not doing right by Kafka. In November 1921, to induce him to submit a novel-length manuscript or two, Kurt wrote, "We both know that it is usually the best and most estimable works that take time to find their response, and it does not happen instantaneously; we remain confident that the German reading public will one day be capable of giving these books the reception they deserve"; Stach, *Kafka: The Years of Insight*, 412–13. Within several years of Kafka's death in June 1924, Kurt published *America* and *The Castle*. "He was the perfect publisher for Kafka," the *Times Literary Supplement* concluded, "whom it is painful to imagine in less sensitive hands"; "The Seismographer of Expressionism," *Times Literary Supplement*, February 2, 1970.

"You really have"   Franz Kafka letter to Josef Körner, December 16, 1918, cited in Stach, *Kafka: The Years of Insight*, 183.

Chapter Eight: An End with Horror

Exploiting beachheads   Ian Kershaw, *The End: Germany 1944–45* (London: Penguin Books, 2012), 253.

Niko and another   Niko's friend Schubi would be captured near Hamburg by the British, who released him after the end of the war. But his papers weren't valid for the French occupation zone, where the family's winery was located. "I managed to find an English officer who was keen on wine and drove me to Grünhaus in a British car," he wrote for the fiftieth-reunion book of the Schondorf class of 1940. "I will never forget the feeling when I came home and found everything intact."

By early 1945   Kershaw, *The End*, 188.

"Anyone not prepared"   Cited in Ibid., 207.

"What we're going to do"   The more I learn about Nazi racial policies, the more plausible it seems that my father was witness that day to an act against a regime that might have eventually made him a target. He may have carried a "certificate of Aryan ancestry," but "*Mischling* policy remained in a state of permanent improvisation" (Rigg, *Hitler's Jewish Soliders*, 199), and the Nazis steadily culled "*Mischlinge*" from the Wehrmacht over the course of the war. "Had the war continued, or had Germany won, most half-Jews would have been exterminated. Quarter-Jews would have suffered further discrimination and probably selective extermination." Rigg, *Hitler's Jewish Soliders*, 272.

The Allies would   Taylor, *Exorcising Hitler*, 95.

But rations amounting   Günter Grass, *Peeling the Onion*, 163.

"What weighs on our hearts"   Niko had been clear of the Russian front since the fall of 1943, but news of his redeployment seems not to have reached New York.

If he hadn't fortified   Norman Ohler, *Blitzed: Drugs in Nazi Germany*, trans. Shaun Whiteside (London: Penguin Books, 2017), 128.

The other, an opioid   Elizabeth Nicholas, "Hitler's Suicide and New Research on Nazi Drug Use," *Time* online, April 28, 2017, https://time.com/4744584/hitler-drugs-blitzed/.

By the early twentieth century   Ohler, *Blitzed*, 11.

"Little Sister Euka"   Klaus Mann, *Tagebücher*, entry for January 16, 1932, cited in Burhop, et al., *Merck 1668–2018*, 238–39.

Or as a connoisseur   Ohler, *Blitzed*, 172.

Under the influence   Ibid., 167–72.

By October   Ibid., 334.

Merck drugs figured   Ibid., 195–202.

By the time   The author of *Blitzed* only deduces that the raid on the Merck factory cut off Hitler's opioid supply. But an assessment by the U.S. Strategic Bombing Survey confirms it: "The most serious loss was in the alkaloid department, which was very seriously damaged. It was here that Eukodal, a morphine substitute used by the Wehrmacht, was produced. Production ceased after the raid." U.S. Strategic Bombing Survey, Morale Division, *The Effects of Bombing on Health and Medical Care in Germany*, Washington, DC, 1945, 332, in Merck-Archiv, F15-7.

In fact, Hitler's bunker   Ohler, *Blitzed*, 230.

By January, Morell   Ibid., 267.

Two months later   Ibid., 275.

To hear Ohler tell it   While such historians as Anthony Beevor and Ian Kershaw endorse Ohler's work, Richard J. Evans faults him for implying that "Hitler was a drug addict who was in the end not responsible for his actions." And Evans cites several historians who, having also seen Dr. Morell's notebooks, do not conclude that they prove opioid abuse. Earlier historical readings had attributed Hitler's deterioration to Parkinson's disease. Richard J. Evans, "*Blitzed: Drugs in Nazi Germany*, a Crass and Dangerously Inaccurate Account," *Guardian* (UK), November 16, 2016.

Chapter Nine: Blood and Shame

Half of the country's Kershaw, *The End*, 379.

But that didn't diminish Richard Bessel, *Germany 1945: From War to Peace* (London: Pocket Books, 2010), 6.

a "scandalous deficiency" W. G. Sebald, *On the Natural History of Destruction*, trans. Anthea Bell (New York: Modern Library, 2004), 70.

During the war Victor Gollancz, cited in Stig Dagerman, *German Autumn*, trans. Robin Fulton Macpherson (Minneapolis: University of Minnesota Press, 2011), 11.

"Deserved suffering is" Dagerman, *German Autumn*, 17.

"It is impossible" Cited by Mark Kurlansky in foreword to Dagerman, *German Autumn*, xii.

Your letter of February 17 Kurt Wolff letter to Maria Wolff Baumhauer, March 18, 1946, in *Kurt Wolff: Ein Literat und Gentleman*, ed. Barbara Weidle (Bonn: Weidle, 2007), 261-63.

Oh, Maria, you should Kurt wrote this sentence in English.

"All I hope for" Helen would share this comment in a letter she sent years later to Christian's draft board in support of his application for conscientious objector status. Helen Wolff letter to Selective Service Local Board No. 4, November 23, 1958. H&KW Papers, 2019 genm 0032 box 1B.

"some cold and hunger" Taylor, *Exorcising Hitler*, 172.

In Munich in early 1946 Ibid., 194. The level V ration card for "nonproductive adults" came to be known as "the death card."

To supplement these rations CARE is an acronym for Cooperative for American Remittances to Europe. The food in CARE packages was originally to have served as rations for American troops during the invasion of Japan planned for late 1945. The provisions were freed up for humanitarian use in postwar Europe after the atomic bombs dropped on Hiroshima and Nagasaki hastened the end of the war in the Pacific.

A training film "Don't clasp that hand!" Geisel's script warned. "It's not the kind of hand you can clasp in friendship" until the German people are "cured of their disease. The super-race disease. The world-conquest disease." See *Your Job in Germany* posted by US National Archives, February 1, 2007, https://www.youtube.com/watch?v=1v5QCGqDYGo?

We're currently living My father's irritation was so widely shared that Ernst von Salomon's *The Questionnaire*, a novel that sends up the impositions of the Allied occupation from a right-wing perspective, became a best seller in West Germany during the fifties. Neiman, *Learning from the Germans*, 33.

Unless he had been Niko's own de-Nazification questionnaire consists almost entirely of *neins* and *keins*—nos and nones. He was a member of three compulsory Nazi organizations: at boarding school, the Hitler Youth; after graduation, the Labor Service; and while at the Institute of Technology in Munich, on study leave during late 1943 and early 1944, the German Student Organization.

Until her suicide   The doctor's report attributes Ernesta's suicide to "a sudden strong mental depression or an extreme emotional compulsion." A cousin supplies a story passed down among members of the family: One day, after persuading her chauffeur to let her take his place at the wheel, Ernesta struck and killed a pedestrian. When the police showed up the chauffeur took responsibility, but he soon began extorting payments from her. Unable to bear the guilt and the blackmail, Ernesta eventually shot herself. Another cousin tells a different story—that she took her life in despondency after heavy losses at the gaming tables in San Remo.

And it turned out   If Kurt hadn't become an American citizen, Niko would likely never have made it to the United States to study. The Federal Republic of Germany wasn't founded until May 1949, and passports weren't routinely available to German citizens until two years after that.

And she deployed   Nora Krug, *Belonging: A German Reckons with History and Home* (New York: Scribner, 2018), 28. In July 1953, while attending a reunion of his boarding school class, my father wrote back to Manhattan to my mother, whom he had begun dating: "I learned a lot about present-day Germany, and I can only say that I'm happy, very happy, that I have torn down my tent and settled in the United States forever. Only on occasion do I want to come back and say hello to my friends, my trees and woods, and my mountains; because those latter things are very dear to me and free from political and human fault."

You want to swap   In German, *Du willst die Heimat mit der Fremde tauschen, / Dich lockt die Neue Welt, / Der roten Ahornwälder krafterfülltes Rauschen . . . . / Europa stirbt, die müden Menschen sehnen sich nach dem Todesschlaf, / Nur Ruhe suchen sie und Kühlung für die Wunden, / Da Sie der Kriegsgott traf.*

Maria worked through   Maria's account appeared in the January 1948 edition of the German literary magazine *Die Gegenwart*.

He spent four weeks   Molli E. Kuenstner and Thomas A. O'Callaghan, "The *Führerprojekt* Goes to Washington," *Burlington Magazine* 159, May 2017, 375–85. Kurt learned of the existence of the Nazis' survey from an old friend, Walter Severin, a Berlin book dealer whose son was one of the three hundred photographers commissioned by the propaganda ministry for the project. Impressing on Washington the cultural value of the images, as well as his own credentials as a German-American with a network of contacts in occupied Germany, Kurt secured an oral agreement that the Library of Congress would reimburse him for his time and expenses. Using CARE packages, food, clothing, and sometimes film and other materials that German photographers urgently needed, he was able to barter for most of the 3,572 images he ultimately secured. The in-kind payments Kurt made were particularly prized in Berlin after June 1948, when the Soviets imposed their blockade. Yet in the end, back stateside, it took two years for Kurt to collect from the US government, and then just $5,000, only slightly more than half of what he had spent. "When Kurt Wolff began making inquiries about the *Führerprojekt*, he realized what the photographers had known, that the images were of exceptionally high quality and captured works of art that in many cases were no longer extant," write Kuenstner and O'Callaghan. "Wolff's endeavor was not only of cultural significance, but he carried out a diplomatic and humanitarian operation that bridged the divide between the United States and Germany. . . . This prominent publisher willingly risked his reputation and solvency to recover the collection and bring it to North America."

"the focal point"   Bessel, *Germany 1945*, 249.

"Get us out"   Kurt and Helen were actually in the midst of trying to arrange for Maria to move to New York to help out at Pantheon. She never did emigrate; in 1955 she remarried, making a life in Munich and Hamburg with her second husband, Peter Stadelmayer, until her death at a clinic in Bavaria in 1996. For more than seven years, beginning in late 1964, Maria and Peter did live in Manhattan, on Fifth Avenue in the Goethe House, where Peter served as its director.

The German doctor   Martha Hall Kelly, *Lilac Girls* (New York: Ballantine Books, 2016), 477.

Though barely twelve   Jesse Leavenworth, "Caroline and the *Lapins*," *Northeast: Sunday Magazine of the Hartford Courant*, October 20, 2002; and Kristin Peterson Havill, "Caroline Ferriday: A Godmother to Ravensbrück Survivors," *Connecticut History*, Winter 2011–12.

Just off the *Appellplatz*   Sarah Helm, *Ravensbrück: Life and Death in Hitler's Concentration Camp for Women* (New York: Anchor Books, 2016), 221–35. The physician who led the Ravensbrück medical team, Dr. Karl Gebhardt, had treated Reinhard Heydrich after Czech partisans blew up Heydrich's car in Prague in May 1942. Heydrich—the Nazi who chaired the Wannsee Conference and spoke that morning of "our new prospects in the east"—survived the blast, only to die eight days later of a gas gangrene infection caused by shrapnel lodged in his spleen. After Nazi higher-ups faulted Gebhardt for neglecting to treat Heydrich with sulfa drugs, the doctor ordered up the Ravensbrück experiments—presumably to save his own skin by proving that sulfonamides would have made no difference.

With a urine-based   Ibid., 247–52.

Not until April 1945   Ibid., 593–610.

And a camp   Leavenworth, "Caroline and the *Lapins*"; Havill, "Caroline Ferriday."

Upon learning that   Kelly, *Lilac Girls*, 482.

One of their sons   Elaine Dundy, *Ferriday, Louisiana* (New York: Donald I. Fine, 1991), 51–56.

According to a census   "Ferriday Started as 3,600-Acre Wedding Present," *Natchez Democrat*, November 22, 2006. As historian Timothy Snyder has pointed out, the more precise the figure—not "some 150 slaves" but precisely 149—the more meaning it carries.

In taking inventory   Caroline Ferriday Papers.

"the Louisiana town"   Ferriday is the seat of Concordia Parish, which during the civil rights movement was home to the secretive Silver Dollar Group, the most violent cell ever to splinter off from the Ku Klux Klan. See Stanley Nelson, *Devils Walking: Klan Murders along the Mississippi in the 1960s* (Baton Rouge: Louisiana State University Press, 2016). The black priest at Ferriday's Saint Charles Catholic Church, Father August Thompson, spoke at Caroline's funeral in rural Connecticut in 1990. So did an emissary of the Free French in the United States, who conveyed the condolences of Resistance figure and former Ravensbrück inmate Geneviève de Gaulle, niece of Charles de Gaulle, the French president who had bestowed on Caroline the Légion d'Honneur in 1961 for her work on behalf of families of the Resistance.

We could start Stanisława Śledziejowska-Osiczko, quoted in the trailer for the forthcoming documentary film *Saving the Rabbits of Ravensbrück*, dir. Stacey Fitzgerald, From the Heart Productions, RememberRavensbruck.com. One of the longest surviving Rabbits, Śledziejowska-Osiczko died in 2017.

As Susan Neiman Neiman, *Learning from the Germans*, 39.

To spend time Ibid., 9. Neiman, a Jew born in the segregated American South, goes on to point out that "we are historical beings, unable to describe ourselves without describing ourselves in space and time. And unlike other animals, we cannot grow up without considerable input from our parents, with whom we need to come to terms if we are ever to truly separate from them."

Chapter Ten: Chain Migration

Because of armed Bessel, *Germany 1945*, 8.

"There is still something" Epigraph to *Kurt Wolff zum Hundertsten*.

Gaining altitude After turns in Hollywood and at New York City's New School, the émigré playwright Carl Zuckmayer settled in Vermont, where he spent the war years farming. He captured the state's appeal to the exile, a quality Kurt and Niko both came to know: "The pathless woods lured me; their solitude promised me protection, asylum, consolation." Carl Zuckmayer, *A Part of Myself*, trans. Richard and Clara Winston (New York: Harcourt Brace Jovanovich, 1970), 356.

Its previous occupant Broch's fate was bound up in the upper floors of buildings: he died of a heart attack in a boardinghouse in New Haven, Connecticut, in 1951, after lugging a foot locker up three flights of stairs. Heilbut, *Exiled in Paradise*, 282. Pantheon sold barely a thousand copies of *The Death of Virgil*, in part because a rave scheduled for the *New York Times Book Review* never appeared, as a result of a newspaper strike. Thomas Weyr, "PW Interviews: Helen Wolff," *Publishers Weekly*, February 3, 1973.

Chapter Eleven: Late Evening

An encouraging early sign Schuyler, "Kurt Wolff and Hermann Broch."

"He never would" Harcourt, Brace & World published volume one of *The Great Philosophers* by Karl Jaspers as a Helen and Kurt Wolff Book in 1962. Helen finished editing the fourth and final volume shortly before her death in 1994.

He eventually liquidated Schuyler, "Kurt Wolff and Hermann Broch."

Kurt judged the fortunes Ibid.

"I remember Kurt's" Mitgang, "Imprint."

The other was the agreement Detjen, "Kurt and Helen Wolff," in *Immigrant Entrepreneurship*. The first volumes in the Bollingen Series were English translations of the works of C. G. Jung, with whom Mary Mellon had undergone analysis.

The agreement called Schuyler, "Kurt Wolff and Hermann Broch."

Forty years later Helen Wolff letter to Steven Schuyler, April 21, 1984. H&KW Papers, box 39, folder 1219.

"The accountant representing" Helen Wolff, "Elective Affinities."

I am thinking of you Detjen, "Kurt and Helen Wolff," in *Immigrant Entrepreneurship.*

Before the hammer Pasternak was almost unfathomably optimistic. In May 1958, after learning that the Soviet government would forbid him to accept the Nobel Prize, he wrote Kurt, "It is precisely these insurmountable barriers imposed by fate that give our life impetus and depth and gravity and make it quite extraordinary—joyful, magical, and real." *Kurt Wolff: A Portrait,* 179.

"How quickly do we give in" *Kurt Wolff: A Portrait,* 181–82.

"Both are great writers" Ibid., 180.

Several years earlier Detjen, "Kurt and Helen Wolff," in *Immigrant Entrepreneurship.*

"This is the first" Helen Wolff letter to Herbert Mitgang, April 3, 1970. H&KW Papers, 2019 genm 0032, box 2.

Some misunderstanding may Kurt Wolff letter to John Lewis, November 29, 1958. H&KW Papers, 2019 genm 0032, box 4.

"You are not a publisher" Kurt Wolff letter to Kyrill Schabert, November 27, 1958. H&KW Papers, box 39, folder 1186.

And Schabert himself Detjen, "Kurt and Helen Wolff," in *Immigrant Entrepreneurship.*

But the triumph Even after the success of *Gift from the Sea*, Pantheon remained a modest business. An August 1958 memo from Kyrill Schabert to Kurt on the eve of the publication of *Doctor Zhivago* reports that the firm's cash on hand has "bounced back" to $75,300. Pantheon Papers, II/25.

But Schabert and Detjen, "Kurt and Helen Wolff," in *Immigrant Entrepreneurship.*

"They exerted great" Heilbut, *Exiled in Paradise*, xi.

"I'm in the late evening" The green spiral-bound notebook can be found in the H&KW Papers, box 53, folder 1624a.

The enthusiast-on-the-page Pushkin Press has collected Hesse's writing on the subject in *Hymn to Old Age*, trans. David Henry Wilson and published in 2011.

Kurt left America Helen Wolff letter to Herbert Mitgang, April 3, 1970. H&KW Papers, 2019 genm 0032, box 2. Helen goes on: "The bitter memories, of silence and of outright betrayal, make me feel that Kurt really wouldn't care to have anything about himself appear in a place that repudiated him." Helen would nonetheless collaborate on, and be pleased with, *Kurt Wolff: A Portrait in Essays and Letters*, which the University of Chicago Press published in 1991. And the world of American letters has hardly repudiated his American-born grandchildren, who include four published or forthcoming authors.

Yet, as Marion Detjen Detjen, "Kurt and Helen Wolff," in *Immigrant Entrepreneurship.*

The East German daily "Kurt Wolff," *Neues Deutschland*, October 25, 1963. Soon after Kurt and Helen's departure, Random House acquired Pantheon and installed as its president André Schiffrin, Jacques's son. The house remained a distinguished one under his stewardship but put more emphasis on political and social topics than the Wolffs' favored themes of art, literature, and philosophy.

Kurt saw no choice During a three-week trip Kurt took through the United States in 1924, the *New York Tribune* interviewed him about his firm's imminent publication of a translation of Sinclair Lewis's *Babbitt*. "I have seen no Babbitts in New York," Kurt told the reporter. "Columbus was a great man to have discovered this country of Walt Whitmans." The story ran under the headline AMERICANS NOT BABBITTS, SAYS GERMAN EDITOR/KURT WOOLF [*sic*], MUNICH PUBLISHER, REGARDS NOVEL AS MOST SIGNIFICANT OF BOOKS, BUT CALLS IMPRESSION FALSE. Alas, the New York Babbitts would get him in the end. *New York Tribune*, March 13, 1924. H&KW Papers, box 79, folder 2361.

On April 15, 1945   Taylor, *Exorcising Hitler*, 249–50. The National Socialist German Workers Party files, known as the NSDAP-Kartei, were finally handed over to the German government in 1994. The Americans hadn't done so earlier in light of how many ex-Nazis held positions in the government of a critical Cold War ally.

Or perhaps because   The lyrics to the "Horst Wessel Song" were written by Berlin SA member Horst Wessel, who was shot and seriously wounded by two Communists in 1930. Upon Wessel's death a month later from blood poisoning, propaganda minister Joseph Goebbels moved quickly to make the song the Nazi Party anthem.

"You will understand"   Bundesarchiv-Lichterfelde, NS/12, 11377.

And in 1933   To curry favor without fully implicating themselves, businessmen or professionals might make a contribution to become an FMSS. This led to the joke that FMSS stood for *Feiner Mann Sichert Sich*—more or less, Upstanding Man Hedges His Bets. John M. Steiner, "The SS Yesterday and Today: A Sociopsychological View," in *Survivors, Victims, and Perpetrators: Essays on the Nazi Holocaust*, ed. Joel E. Dimsdale (Abingdon, Oxon, UK: Taylor & Francis, 1980), 420.

"His political attitude"   Bundesarchiv-Lichterfelde, R/9361/II, 5058.

Without at least   In 1937, after my step-grandfather delivered the Hesses' son Wolf, Ilse Hess sent Hans Albrecht a cigarette case as a thank-you gift. Thirty-five years later Maria returned the case to her, suggesting that she pass it on to her now-adult son. My grandmother, who during the war had volunteered with Ilse Hess at Dr. Albrecht's lazaretto on Rotkreuzplatz, testified before a de-Nazification tribunal that Ilse Hess had been opposed to the regime.

A folder for   Bundesarchiv-Lichterfelde, NS/21, 1953.

Yet the fattest folder   Bundesarchiv-Lichterfelde, R/9361//III, 131140.

And they put   Wilhelm himself relied on the mercies of Elfriede Wischmann, a.k.a. Schescha, the family nanny and maid who, amidst the postwar shortages, would make runs up to Frankfurt to buy morphine on the black market to satisfy the habit he traced to wounds suffered during World War I. Wilhelm died in 1952.

Three years later   Gudrun Azar, *Ins Licht gerückt: jüdische Lebenswege im Münchner Westen, eine Spurensuche in Pasing, Obermeuzing und Aubing* (Munich: Herbert Utz, 2008), 122.

Käthe's ex-husband died   Anette Neff, "Merck, Ursula," *Stadtlexikon Darmstadt*, Historischer Verein für Hessen (Darmstadt: Konrad Theiss, 2006), 628. Upon being forced to leave Schondorf in 1943, Ernst Lange survived the war and went on to become a distinguished Protestant theologian before taking his life at age forty-seven. Decades after his death he was hailed as "an ecumenical visionary in Bonhoeffer's footsteps." Werner Simpendorfer, "The Strange Must Cease to Be the Strange: In Memoriam Ernst Lange (1927–1974)," *Ecumenical Review* 49, no. 2 (April 1997).

After her graduation   Johannes Lange himself performed research into "racial hygiene" and served as a judge on a Nazi-era Erbgesundheitsgericht, one of the "hereditary health courts" that determined who the state could forcibly sterilize. Wolfgang Rose, *Diagnose "Psychopathie": Die urbane Moderne und das schwierige Kind* (Vienna: Böhlau, 2016), 260n.

Chapter Twelve: Second Exile

I am completely happy   Kurt Wolff letter to Curt von Faber du Faur, May 11, 1958, in *Kurt Wolff: Briefwechsel*, 482–83.

Man bröckelt ab   Schuyler, "Kurt Wolff and Hermann Broch."

"the great miracle"   Kurt Wolff letter to Curt von Faber du Faur, March 18, 1962, in *Kurt Wolff: Briefwechsel*, 484.

younger than Niko   William Jovanovich was in fact a year older than my father.

William Jovanovich had   Detjen, "Kurt and Helen Wolff," in *Immigrant Entrepreneurship*.

After being beholden   Ibid.

"Kurt's is, I believe"   Helen told me this story herself but also related it in a letter to Günter Grass, July 21, 1974. Günter Grass and Helen Wolff, *Briefe 1959–1994* (Göttingen, Germany: Steidl, 2003), 210.

The Esplanade permitted   Helen Wolff letter to Katharine Rosin, December 19, 1959. H&KW Papers, 2019 genm 0032, box 3.

"I've often wondered why"   Wolfram Göbel, "Ernst Rowohlt und Kurt Wolff," in *Kurt Wolff zum Hundertsten*.

"It's great that"   Barbara Weidle, "Gespräch mit Christian Wolff," in *Kurt Wolff: Ein Literat und Gentleman*, 177.

When Kurt would travel   Schuyler, "Kurt Wolff and Hermann Broch."

In 1960, after accepting   *Kurt Wolff: A Portrait*, 197.

Members of Gruppe 47   Wagenbach, "Kurt Wolff," in *Kurt Wolff zum Hundertsten*. Gruppe 47 took its name from how its members envisioned themselves—to adapt Kafka, as a collective ax for the frozen sea of Germany's epic winter of 1947, the one that turned out to be my father's last in the land of his birth.

Years later the *Independent*   John Calder, "Obituary: Helen Wolff," *Independent* (London), April 20, 1994.

The end bore   Schuyler, "Kurt Wolff and Hermann Broch."

"He had one special quality"   "Mr. Kurt Wolff," *Times* (London), October 29, 1963.

The German catastrophe   Stern, *Five Germanys*, 250.

Technically true   Nikola Herweg, "Helen und Kurt Wolff in Marbach," Deutsches Literaturarchiv-Marbach, *Spuren* 106, 2015.

"It's lovely and comforting"   "Von Herzen Ihnen Beiden: Briefe von Hannah Arendt an Kurt und Helen Wolff," in *Kurt Wolff: Ein Literat und Gentleman*, 268. In New York, Kurt and Helen had both forged relationships with the exile philosopher and political theorist—Kurt first, helping Arendt with the details of drafting contracts after she began work as an editor at Schocken Books; then Helen, who, after the

Nazis invaded France, had traced almost the identical path of incarceration and flight as Arendt, from Paris's Vél d'Hiv, to the camp in Gurs, to a post-armistice limbo before escaping through Lisbon with Varian Fry's help. Although Arendt's sanctuary in Vichy France, a peasant's barn near Montauban, was more spartan than Helen's château in Saint-Lary, "she and [her husband] Heinrich [Blücher] had been able to procure bicycles, and far from giving in to anxiety, they explored the beautiful countryside," Helen wrote following Arendt's death. "Hannah, in her high-spirited way, made of this anguishing experience a kind of gift of time, a vacation in which one slept in the hay, a hiatus within a life of work and duties." Undated and apparently unpublished reminiscence, H&KW Papers, box 73, folder 2056.

"He was able to discover" Herweg, "Helen und Kurt Wolff in Marbach."

"put the emphasis" Ibid.

Christian beginning to make Christian was started on the piano, not the cello—but quickly discovered his interest and aptitude lay not in performance but composition. His piano teacher, Grete Sultan, knew that the dancer who lived in the apartment above her, Merce Cunningham, counted as a friend the composer John Cage, and an introduction was made. Christian began working with Cage shortly after turning sixteen; by the time he left high school, he had become a member of "the New York School" of avant-garde composers that included Cage, Earle Brown, and Morton Feldman, who years later would recall the teenage prodigy as "Orpheus in tennis shoes." Cage was reluctant to charge the still-struggling Wolffs for those lessons, so in barter Christian would bring copies of Pantheon's latest, including the Bollingen edition of the *I Ching* that would help inspire Cage to develop the compositional chance procedures for which he became renowned. Kurt and Helen also hosted gatherings at which Cage mingled with such Pantheon collaborators as Alan Watts and Joseph Campbell, who influenced him too. See Michael Hicks and Christian Asplund, *American Composers: Christian Wolff* (Urbana: University of Illinois Press, 2012), 17–18.

For another thirty years After Harcourt, Brace & World shareholders voted to substitute William Jovanovich's surname into the posterior position of the company name, Günter Grass's reaction was, "I guess the World wasn't big enough for him."

Every beginning offers Hermann Hesse, "Stages," in *The Seasons of the Soul: The Poetic Guidance and Spiritual Wisdom of Hermann Hesse*, trans. Ludwig Max Fischer (Berkeley, CA: North Atlantic Books, 2011), 113. The German is *In jedem Anfang wohnt ein Zauber inne / Der uns beschützt und der uns hilft, zu leben.*

Chapter Thirteen: *Schweinenest*

"Home is the land" Cited in Sebald, *On the Natural History of Destruction*, 160. Jean Améry lived the rootlessness of which he wrote. Born in Vienna as Hanns Chaim Mayer, he was raised Catholic by his mother following his Jewish father's death in World War I. Upon Germany's annexation of Austria in 1938, he and his Jewish wife fled to France and then Belgium, only for him to be captured and tortured by the Gestapo and deported to Auschwitz. After the war he settled in Belgium, where he wrote under a Gallic-sounding anagram of his surname and, refusing to be published in Germany or Austria, contributed to newspapers in German-speaking Switzerland. Améry's 1964 treatise on how to responsibly process the crimes of the Nazis, *Jenseits von Schuld und Sühne* (Beyond Guilt and

Atonement), was published in English as *At the Mind's Limits* (Bloomington: Indiana University Press, 1980).

"ignorant and rootless" Kurt Vonnegut, *Palm Sunday* (New York: Dial Press, 1999), 20.

Pained, my father My friend Luzi and I took the train out to Dachau anyway. As lasting as any memory of that visit—as vivid today as the sight of the crematorium and the striped uniforms—was the woman on the S-Bahn platform who handed out flyers urging visitors not to hold young Dachauers like herself responsible for what had taken place in their town several decades earlier. That encounter introduced me to the early stirrings of the Federal Republic's *Erinnerungskultur*.

lines of verse Three lines from Paul Verlaine's "Chanson d'automne," broadcast on the eve of the invasion, directed the French Resistance to begin coordinated sabotage: *Blessent mon coeur / D'une langueur / Monotone* (Wounds my heart with a monotonous languor).

"We must find" "Speech by Federal President Richard von Weizsäcker," May 8, 1985. While Germany's chancellors wield executive power, its presidents tend to be philosopher kings. On May 8, 2020, the seventy-fifth anniversary of the Nazis' defeat, president Frank-Walter Steinmeier delivered remarks that picked up where Weizsäcker had left off. "Germany's past is a fractured past—with responsibility for the murdering of millions and the suffering of millions," he said. "That breaks our hearts to this day. And that is why I say that this country can only be loved with a broken heart." Speech by President Frank-Walter Steinmeier, "75th Anniversary of the End of the 2nd World War," May 8, 2020. https://www.bundespraesident. de/SharedDocs/Reden/EN/Frank-Walter-Steinmeier/Reden/2020/05/200508-75th -anniversary-World-War-II.html.

"It is not a case" Ibid.

"From our own history" Ibid.

But to Alexander Gauland Taub and Fisher, "Germany's Extreme Right Challenges Guilt over Nazi Past."

Are the German people The Federal Republic provided a kind of answer to this question in 2000, when the Bundestag passed a law easing the path to citizenship for children born to residents without German blood.

The percentage of Germans Taylor, *Exorcising Hitler*, 382.

As the Green Party Cem Özdemir, "Cem Özdemir Compares Germany's Far-Right AfD Party to the Nazis in Hard-Hitting Speech," European Greens, February 22, 2018, EuropeanGreens.eu/news/cem-özdemir-compares-germanys-far-right -afd-party-nazis-hard-hitting-speech.

But as she worked Neiman, *Learning from the Germans*, 20.

Chapter Fourteen: Turtle Bay

"Suddenly there is" Günter Grass, laudation for Helen Wolff upon posthumous awarding of the Friedrich Gundolf Prize, April 30, 1994, DeutscheAkademie.de /en/awards/friedrich-gundolf-preis/helen-wolff/laudatio.

The Germans had constructed Thomas Wolfe, *You Can't Go Home Again* (New York: Scribner Classics, 2011), 531.

"We have to be" Oliver Hilmes, *Berlin 1936: Sixteen Days in August*, trans. Jefferson Chase (London: Bodley Head, 2017), 16–17.

When refugees first spotted *Central Airport THF*, dir. Karim Aïnouz, Lupa Film, Les Films d'Ici, Mar Films, 2018, documentary film.

Chapter Fifteen: Mr. *Bitte Nicht Ansprechen*

"We must take one step" Carl Zuckmayer, *Second Wind*, trans. Elizabeth Reynolds Hapgood (London: G. G. Harrap, 1941), 236.

town of Stolp Now Słupsk, Poland.

"Right after breakfast" Kurt Wolff, "Tagebücher," DLA-Marbach.

Kraus was not *Kurt Wolff: A Portrait*, 91.

Il pleut dans mon My grandmother is quoting Verlaine: "It rains in my heart / As it rains on the town."

Chapter Sixteen: Shallow Draft

"mighty liquid belt" Andrew Eames, *Blue River, Black Sea: A Journey along the Danube into the Heart of the New Europe* (London: Black Swan, 2010), 15.

"different peoples meet" Claudio Magris, *Danube*, trans. Patrick Creagh (New York: Farrar, Straus and Giroux, 1989), 29.

Passau, where Hitler The Nazi regime marbled its madness with myth and lore. The wolf is the symbol of Passau, where Hitler moved as a three-year-old, and he spent his life vaunting the qualities of that animal—loyalty, ferocity, courage, cruelty, and fealty to hierarchy. *Wolf* was Hitler's code name, and the *Führer* liked to say that Adolf was a portmanteau of the Old High German word *adal*, meaning noble, and *Wolf*. In 1934 the German government even placed the wolf under protection—a purely symbolic act, for the animal had been extinct in Germany since the mid-nineteenth century. But by doing so the Nazis invoked "a promise of the discipline sometimes associated with 'civilization' without its accompanying decadence. Of nature without anarchy." Boria Sax, *Animals in the Third Reich* (Pittsburgh: Yogh & Thorn Press, 2013), 68.

Passauers would prefer Marc Fisher, *After the Wall: Germany, the Germans and the Burdens of History* (New York: Simon & Schuster, 1995), 24–28. As a teenager during the mid-eighties, Passau native Anna Rosmus won a nationwide essay prize for a piece she wrote about "Freedom in Europe." Townspeople cheered and feted her, so she decided to enter another contest, this time choosing as her topic, "My Hometown during the Third Reich." Suddenly neighbors and friends shunned her. The city refused to grant her access to archives in the public library, including back issues of the local newspaper. But every act of official recalcitrance made her more determined. During a four-year legal battle, Rosmus received death threats, her husband divorced her, and a neo-Nazi attack in a Munich restaurant left her unconscious. Finally she was able to conduct her research and write up her findings, among them that a Passau clergyman had denounced a Jewish merchant, which led to the man's deportation and death; and that the editor of the local Catholic newspaper, who since the war had cultivated a reputation as a resister, had in fact praised Hitler and the Nazis in print. In 1994, exhausted by the threats and harassment, Rosmus moved to the United States with her daughters. Her story is told in the 1990 film *The Nasty Girl*, dir. Michael Verhoeven.

In 1946 she made After Renée-Marie tracked Kurt down in New York, he swore out one of the two affidavits of support that allowed her to emigrate from Brazil to the United States. Renée-Marie Croose Parry, "Life in Brazil," in *Odyssey of Exile: Jewish Women Flee the Nazis for Brazil*, ed. Katherine Morris (Detroit: Wayne State University Press, 1996), 225.

By the time she received In 1950 the Hausensteins moved to Paris, where Wilhelm served as the new Federal Republic of Germany's first ambassador to France. After his death in 1957, Margot founded the Teilhard de Chardin Association, which she ran until 1975, when she moved with Renée-Marie and her daughter's second husband, Kenneth, first to London and ten years later to Florida. "Margot Hausenstein: The Life of 100 Years," privately published annotated timeline. H&KW Papers, box 14, folder 463.

"inducing a vanquished" Sereny, *The German Trauma*, 60.

In 1967 Ibid., 65.

"the massive weight" Grass, *Peeling the Onion*, 415–16.

Gnade der späten Geburt Chancellor Helmut Kohl coined this phrase in 1984—amidst the furor touched off by US president Ronald Reagan's visit to the graves of Waffen-SS soldiers in Bitburg—to distance himself from Germany's Nazi past. But in the years since, others have repurposed "the grace of a late birth," often to ironic ends. By the end of his political career, Kohl and his center-right Christian Democratic Union had actually embraced *Vergangenheitsaufarbeitung*. Neiman, *Learning from the Germans*, 270, 290, 370.

Cue the elephant's trumpet For generations, "Jesko" or "Jesco" has been a popular given name for first-born males in the sprawling von Puttkamer clan. The man we heard being paged in the Budapest airport was definitely not the diplomat Jesco von Puttkamer, who served as the Federal Republic's ambassador to Israel during the Black September terrorist attack at the 1972 Munich Olympics, for he had died nine years earlier.

her landed parents Jesko and Annemarie von Puttkamer had another sibling, Emmy von Krockow, whose daughter Lubissa engaged in derring-do that surpasses anything outlined in these pages. In April 1945, as the Red Army closed in on their Pomeranian estate, Lubissa's stepfather stood before the family in full uniform, carrying pistols. He announced that they would all now take their lives in accordance with the Prussian military code of honor. More than eight months pregnant, Lubissa felt her baby kick in dissent. She ordered her stepfather to get out of his bemedaled monkey suit, throw it with the weapons into a pond on the property, and get on with the urgent business of survival. Over the following weeks this niece of Jesko and Annemarie somehow gave birth, dodged Soviet soldiers bent on rape and pillage, fed both herself and her infant daughter, escaped to the west, stole back into Pomerania to spring that same balky stepfather from a Soviet camp, and ultimately reached the western Allies' zone, where she embarked on a new life. Lubissa's brother, the late historian Christian von Krockow, told the entire saga in *Hour of the Women*, trans. Krishna Winston (London: Faber and Faber, 1993).

near Karzin Now Karsina, Poland.

In a codicil added According to Kurt's will, he had provided Maria with her share of his estate during his lifetime.

Chapter Seventeen: Play on the Bones of the Dead

His own father's disapproval Weidle, "Gespräch mit Christian Wolff," 172–73.

The Nazi leaders Haffner, *Germany Jekyll & Hyde*, 48.

For a citizen Alexander Wolff, "When the Terror Began," *Sports Illustrated*, August 26, 2002.

At that, Sieber Ibid. After finishing the interview with Sieber, I swung by to visit my cousin Jon, a Nymphenburger and trained psychologist himself, and explained why I was in the neighborhood. "I know Georg Sieber," Jon told me. "He's a clever man. For years he served as president of the Bavarian Psychologists Association." It turned out Jon had succeeded him in that position.

All of which Our daughter was a Vermont summer-camp cabinmate of Mafalda von Stauffenberg, a great-granddaughter of Berthold von Stauffenberg, one of the participants in the Valkyrie plot to kill Hitler. In 2014, while hiking a trail with other visiting parents over midseason weekend, I chatted with Mafalda's father, Philippe, about Germany's World Cup soccer victory a few days earlier but never broached our common German ancestry. It occurred to me later—in light of Clara having asked, "Isn't there some way Opa could have been a spy?"—that this man's own Opa had indeed been a kind of spy, and paid for it with his life.

They occurred when As a result of her own *Vergangenheitsaufarbeitung*, a German cousin has come to regard the compromises of Dr. Albrecht, the supervisor of that Munich lazaretto, by the light of the Hippocratic Oath: "He was sworn to protect those in a vulnerable position. The least he could do was make sure he wouldn't be in a vulnerable position himself."

During the Enlightenment Burhop et al., *Merck 1668–2018*, 60–69.

Thus, when Emanuel Merck Ibid., 101–8.

"Always Curious" Merkel is a world-class chider. During a 2018 visit to the White House, she gave President Donald Trump a 1705 map of Germany's Rhineland-Palatinate, the region that includes Kallstadt, from which Trump's ancestors emigrated to the United States. The message in her gift could not have been clearer: don't forget that you are a descendant of immigrants.

Appraising the city Cited in Sebald, *On the Natural History of Destruction*, 23.

Three months later The RAF's September 11 attack on Darmstadt was an "area raid," according to a report by the U.S. Strategic Bombing Survey: "The city of Darmstadt was levelled in fifty-one minutes by 234 Lancasters and Halifaxes which dropped approximately 979 tons of HEs [high explosives] and IBs [incendiary bombs] on the center of the town. This was an area raid of the classic saturation type, which had so effectively razed Cologne and Hamburg. The target had been well-lighted by star flares released by low-flying Mosquitos, and the fleet of four-engined bombers, flying at high altitude, met no opposition from either anti-aircraft or enemy fighters. The mechanics of the raid, between the 'target sighted' and the 'bombs away,' were almost perfunctory, and as a consequence Darmstadt was virtually destroyed." By contrast, the bombing by the US Eighth Air Force on December 12, 1944, which targeted the Merck factory and cut off Hitler's supply of Eukodal, was a "precision raid," in which "446 B-17s, almost twice as many planes as the RAF had used in its September area attack, dropped 1,011 tons of GPs (general purpose bombs) and 310 tons of IBs on the city's chief industrial area, northwest of the center of the town. E. Merck was the chief target. . . . Sixty employees were killed. . . . Not only did the plant incur RM 40,000,000 [roughly $16 million] of material damage but it lost about 98 percent of its production for two months." The report also states that the city was of little strategic importance to the Third Reich, even as information would emerge after World War II that Merck was more involved in the Nazi war effort than previously believed. U.S. Strategic Bombing Survey, Area Studies Division, *A Detailed Study of the Effects of Area Bombing on Darmstadt*, Washington, DC, 1945, 1–29, in Merck-Archiv, F15-7.

"When I think of Germany"   W. G. Sebald, *The Emigrants*, trans. Anthea Bell (London: Vintage Books, 2002), 181.

German TV documentary   Caterina Woj and Andrea Röpke, "Das braune Netzwerk: Wer steuert die Wütburger?" *Die Story*, Westdeutscher Rundfunk, January 11, 2017.

The family, Merck   Cem Tevetoglu, Matin Nawabi, and Tobi Moka, "Merck in der Zwickmühle," *Soziales Darmstadt*, March 2017.

For three years   Friedrich Wilhelm Euler joined the Nazi Party in 1932 and soon took a post with the interior ministry, for which he performed eugenic surveys and compiled data used in drafting the Nuremberg Laws. As recently as 1975, Euler—also known as Wilfried, a portmanteau of his given names—was still editing the family journal, the *Merck'sche Familien-Zeitschrift*. Alan E. Steinweis, *Studying the Jew: Scholarly Antisemitism in Nazi Germany* (Cambridge, MA: Harvard University Press, 2008), 107; and Burhop et al., *Merck 1668–2018*, 22–23.

During tricentennial festivities   Burhop et al., *Merck 1668–2018*, 26.

It joined Erinnerung   "Merck KGaA Plans Nazi-Era Forced Labour Compensation," ICIS.com, December 8, 1999. Merck identified 257 forced laborers, mostly young women from Russia, Poland, and Ukraine, who had been assigned to its Darmstadt plant during the war. The company's offer amounted to a little more than $5,000 per person, with surviving family ineligible to collect if the exploited worker had died.

The current director   Birte Förster, "Seitenweise Aufschlussreiches," *Hoch: Die Zeitung der Technischen Universität Darmstadt*, December 2015. To open a window on nearly a century of German social and political events covered in Mathilde Merck's diaries, Professor Förster's students sorted entries by topic and logged keywords. They divvied up themes among themselves—Tante Tilla's marriage, her travels, her daughter's adolescence, as well as her Nazi views—and tweeted out their findings.

And so, at a table   Several months after my visit to the Merck-Archiv, Munich's Verlag C. H. Beck published *Merck 1668–2018: From a Pharmacy to a Global Corporation*, a study by four independent historians: Carsten Burhop, Michael Kißener, Hermann Schäfer, and Joachim Scholtyseck. Where archival holdings track what is contained in its pages, I cite the English-language edition of that volume. I cite Merck-Archiv file numbers for material with no corresponding mention in the 350th anniversary history.

Walter Brügmann   Burhop et al., *Merck 1668–2018*, 308.

Yet I still learn   Ibid., 312.

With the war   Ibid., 324–32.

"If, after 1945"   Ibid., 495.

On May 1, 1933   Ibid., 270.

Returning to Darmstadt   Ibid., 273.

In 1939   Ibid., 304–5.

With the armistice   Ibid., 227.

Under the Treaty   Ibid., 247.

During the Ruhr crisis   Ibid., 229.

To meet these challenges   Ibid., 228.

As this newcomer   Ibid., 253.

"I am really overjoyed"   Ibid., 254.

Studying and then emulating   Ibid., 313–23.

As one observer   Ibid., 256–57.

leaving Wilhelm and Louis   Ibid., 313–23. In a June 1, 1942, file memo, Pfotenhauer himself documented what the Nazi Party was prepared to do if Wilhelm and Louis refused to relent: "A commissioner [to take over the company] will be appointed without delay by the Reich Ministry of Economics at the suggestion of the *Gauleiter*."

Pfotenhauer also curtailed   Ibid., 322. A contemporaneous newspaper account of the verdict in Karl Merck's de-Nazification hearing suggests that, without the ongoing presence of Karl and Fritz in the company's directorate, "Pfotenhauer would have merged the factory with the IG [Farben] concern, and it would likewise be on the decommissioning list today." After the war the Allies broke up IG Farben, the most notorious industrial conglomerate in the Third Reich. The firm used slave labor at its Auschwitz plant and manufactured the gas used in the death camps. "Vor der Spruchkammer/Dr. Karl Merck in Gruppe IV," *Darmstädter Echo*, June 1, 1948.

Pfotenhauer's daughter Ursula   Ibid., 337.

He was unwilling   Ibid. One of Pfotenhauer's daughters, Margot, survived her poisoning. Ursula was not in Darmstadt at the time.

Two days later   Ibid.

You know that   Draft of Kurt Wolff letter to George W. Merck, August 4, 1947, Merck-Archiv, A-148. The company history *Merck 1668–2018* sources this letter not to Kurt but to Rudolf Gruber, vice president of US-based Merck & Co. But the draft in the Merck-Archiv is on Pantheon Books letterhead and includes those telltale references to Kurt's visit with my father and grandmother in Munich.

responsible American CEO   "We try never to forget that medicine is for the people," George W. Merck would say in a 1950 speech at the Medical College of Virginia. "It is not for the profits. The profits follow, and if we have remembered that, they have never failed to appear. The better we have remembered it, the larger they have been." For the most part, that spirit persisted at the American Merck & Co. through the rest of the century. In his 2020 book *Pharma*, which is broadly critical of the US drug industry, Merck included, Gerald Posner nonetheless highlights the firm's decision to supply Mectizan, an antidote to parasitic diseases in the developing world, free of charge. "It marked the only instance in modern pharma history in which a leading firm gave away a drug they discovered and patented in order to eradicate a disease," he writes. "By the time the scientists who discovered Mectizan won the Nobel in Medicine in 2015, Merck had distributed over a billion doses in thirty-three countries." Gerald Posner, *Pharma: Greed, Lies, and the Poisoning of America* (New York: Avid Reader Press, 2020), 388.

"[The political left is] trying" Draft of Kurt Wolff letter to George W. Merck, August 4, 1947, Merck-Archiv, A-148.

"Mr. John pointed out" Ibid.

The Allies' victory Burhop et al., *Merck 1668–2018*, 348–49 and 357.

First of all Merck-Archiv, A-1052.

With the 1937 merger The Nazis established the Deutscher Luftsportverband (DLV), or German Air Sports Association, and the Nationalsozialistisches Fliegerkorps (NSFK), or National Socialist Flyers' Corps, as forerunners of the Luftwaffe to train military pilots.

in a 1939 speech Burhop, et al., *Merck 1668–2018*, 278.

Invoking testimony submitted Ibid., 268.

Two *Stolpersteine* The two men Wilhelm mentions were parties to what were thought in some instances to be "privileged" mixed marriages—apparently like that of Wilhelm Hausenstein and his wife, Margot, for at least part of the Nazi era. Nazi *Kreisleiter* Schilling nonetheless ordered that Engelmann, an engineer at Merck for eighteen years, be arrested in 1943, despite the Nazis' considering his wife to be "Aryan." He was sent first to a labor camp in 1944 and then to Theresienstadt a year later, before being murdered. A *Stolperstein* at Rhönring 14 in Darmstadt marks his life and death. Henkel, a non-Jew, was fired in October 1941 on Schilling's orders. The company paid him a pension, but his Jewish wife, Emmy, was deported to Auschwitz, where she was murdered in 1943. A *Stolperstein* at Jahnstrasse 116 bears witness. Burhop, et al., *Merck 1668–2018*, 305. An inventory of *Stolpersteine* within the city of Darmstadt can be found at dfg-vk-darmstadt.de.

Another, a Herr Weigand "Spruchkammer Darmstadt-Stadt, Begründung in Sachen Merck, Wilhelm," June 30, 1948, Merck-Archiv, A-1052.

He was soon reinstated Burhop, et al., *Merck 1668–2018*, 349.

Chapter Eighteen: The End, Come by Itself

But he had no use With the establishment of the Third Reich, a preexisting movement within German Protestantism forged ahead with its vision of a "German church" that embraced Nazi attitudes toward nationalism, "racial" differences, and Jews. In response, dissidents like Dietrich Bonhoeffer and Martin Niemöller devoted themselves to a "Confessing church" that kept God and Scripture separate from any earthly political leader or movement. Meanwhile many Catholic figures accommodated themselves to the regime, even as the Nazis outlawed the Catholic Centre Party. After Hitler struck a deal with the Vatican in 1933, Joseph Roth alluded to "a time when His Holiness, the infallible Pope of Christendom, is concluding a peace agreement, a Concordat, with the enemies of Christ, when the Protestants are establishing a 'German church' and censoring the Bible." Joseph Roth, *What I Saw: Reports from Berlin, 1920–1933*, trans. Michael Hofmann (New York: W. W. Norton, 2004), 209.

"Rage is something" Franz Kafka postcard to Max Brod, September 6, 1923, in Kafka, *Letters to Friends*, 379.

But I was reluctant In his memoir, Günter Grass considers his own interrogatory reticence: "Was it because I was no longer a child that I dared not ask? Is it only children who, as in fairy tales, ask the right questions?" Grass, *Peeling the Onion*, 10.

"Those things about" Umberto Eco, "Umberto Eco: The Art of Fiction No. 197," interview by Lila Azam Zanaganeh, *Paris Review*, Summer 2008.

Epilogue

"There is no inevitability" Stern, *Five Germanys*, 10.

It is a very strange Detjen, "Kurt and Helen Wolff," in *Immigrant Entrepreneurship*.

Some 54 percent Greenberg Research poll, cited in Stanley B. Greenberg, "Trump Is Beginning to Lose His Grip," *New York Times*, November 17, 2018.

under cover of falsehoods One of many examples: A presidential tweet claimed that the German crime rate had shot up because of Merkel's decision to welcome refugees. Yet we would walk around the city and through deserted pedestrian tunnels in U-Bahn stations late at night feeling perfectly safe—because in fact, crime in Germany was at its lowest level in twenty-five years. Christopher F. Schuetze and Michael Wolgelenter, "Fact Check: Trump's False and Misleading Claims about Germany's Crime and Immigration," *New York Times*, June 18, 2018.

"Evil," he wrote Franz Kafka, *The Blue Octavo Notebooks*, trans. Ernst Kaiser and Eithne Wilkins (Cambridge, MA: Exact Change, 2004), 24. Max Brod salvaged this quote from one of the notebooks Kafka filled with fragments and aphorisms between 1917 and 1919.

As a product of both Kurt's use of "the same task before us" in his letter to Maria echoes Abraham Lincoln's "the great task remaining before us" in the Gettysburg Address—rhetorical rope that lashes together the German and American branches of my family's story.

INDEX